GENDER TROUBLE

GENDER TROUBLE

*Feminism and the
Subversion of Identity*

JUDITH BUTLER

Routledge
New York and London

Published in 1999 by
Routledge
29 West 35th Street
New York, NY 10001

Published in Great Britain by
Routledge
11 New Fetter Lane
London EC4P 4EE

Gender Trouble was originally published in the Routledge book series Thinking Gender, edited by Linda J. Nicholson.

Printed in the United States of America on acid-free paper.

Library of Congress Cataloging-in-Publication Data

Butler, Judith P.
    Gender trouble : feminism and the subversion of identity / Judith Butler.
        p.   cm.
    Includes bibliographical references and index.
    Originally published: New York : Routledge, 1990.
    ISBN 0-415-92499-5 (pbk.)
    1. Feminist theory.   2. Sex role.   3. Sex differences (Psychology).
4. Identity (Psychology).   5. Femininity.   I. Title.
HQ1154.B898   1999
305.3—dc21   99-29349
                                                                  CIP

Contents

Contents

vi

Preface (1999)

Ten years ago I completed the manuscript of *Gender Trouble* and sent it to Routledge for publication. I did not know that the text would have as wide an audience as it has had, nor did I know that it would constitute a provocative "intervention" in feminist theory or be cited as one of the founding texts of queer theory. The life of the text has exceeded my intentions, and that is surely in part the result of the changing context of its reception. As I wrote it, I understood myself to be in an embattled and oppositional relation to certain forms of feminism, even as I understood the text to be part of feminism itself. I was writing in the tradition of immanent critique that seeks to provoke critical examination of the basic vocabulary of the movement of thought to which it belongs. There was and remains warrant for such a mode of criticism and to distinguish between self-criticism that promises a more democratic and inclusive life for the movement and criticism that seeks to undermine it altogether. Of course, it is always possible to misread the former as the latter, but I would hope that that will not be done in the case of *Gender Trouble*.

In 1989 I was most concerned to criticize a pervasive heterosexual assumption in feminist literary theory. I sought to counter those views that made presumptions about the limits and propriety of gender and restricted the meaning of gender to received notions of masculinity and femininity. It was and remains my view that any feminist theory that restricts the meaning of gender in the presuppositions of its own practice sets up exclusionary gender norms within feminism, often with homophobic consequences. It seemed to me, and continues to seem, that feminism ought to be careful not to idealize certain expressions of gender that, in turn, produce new forms of hierarchy and exclusion. In particular, I opposed those regimes of truth that stipulated that certain kinds of gendered expressions were found to be false or derivative, and others, true and original. The point was not to prescribe a new gendered way of life that might then serve as a model for readers of the text. Rather, the aim of the text was to open up the field of possibility for gender without dictating which kinds of possibilities ought to be realized. One might wonder what use "opening up possibilities" finally is, but no one who has understood what it is to live in the social world as what is "impossible," illegible, unrealizable, unreal, and illegitimate is likely to pose that question.

Gender Trouble sought to uncover the ways in which the very thinking of what is possible in gendered life is foreclosed by certain habitual and violent presumptions. The text also sought to undermine any and all efforts to wield a discourse of truth to delegitimate minority gendered and sexual practices. This doesn't mean that all minority practices are to be condoned or celebrated, but it does mean that we ought to be able to think them before we come to any kinds of conclusions about them. What worried me most were the ways that the panic in the face of such practices rendered them unthinkable. Is the breakdown of gender binaries, for instance, so monstrous, so frightening, that it must be held to be definitionally impossible and heuristically precluded from any effort to think gender?

Some of these kinds of presumptions were found in what was called "French Feminism" at the time, and they enjoyed great popularity among literary scholars and some social theorists. Even as I opposed what I took to be the heterosexism at the core of sexual difference fundamentalism, I also drew from French poststructuralism to make my points. My work in *Gender Trouble* turned out to be one of cultural translation. Poststructuralist theory was brought to bear on U.S. theories of gender and the political predicaments of feminism. If in some of its guises, poststructuralism appears as a formalism, aloof from questions of social context and political aim, that has not been the case with its more recent American appropriations. Indeed, my point was not to "apply" poststructuralism to feminism, but to subject those theories to a specifically feminist reformulation. Whereas some defenders of poststructuralist formalism express dismay at the avowedly "thematic" orientation it receives in works such as *Gender Trouble*, the critiques of poststructuralism within the cultural Left have expressed strong skepticism toward the claim that anything politically progressive can come of its premises. In both accounts, however, poststructuralism is considered something unified, pure, and monolithic. In recent years, however, that theory, or set of theories, has migrated into gender and sexuality studies, postcolonial and race studies. It has lost the formalism of its earlier instance and acquired a new and transplanted life in the domain of cultural theory. There are continuing debates about whether my own work or the work of Homi Bhabha, Gayatri Chakravorty Spivak, or Slavoj Žižek belongs to cultural studies or critical theory, but perhaps such questions simply show that the strong distinction between the two enterprises has broken down. There will be theorists who claim that all of the above belong to cultural studies, and there will be cultural studies practitioners who define themselves against all manner of theory (although not, significantly, Stuart Hall, one of the founders of cultural studies in Britain). But both sides of the debate sometimes miss the point that the face of theory has changed precisely through its cultural appropriations. There is a new venue for theory, necessarily impure, where it emerges in and as the very event of cultural translation. This is not the displacement of theory by historicism, nor a simple historicization of theory that exposes the contingent limits of its more generalizable claims. It is, rather, the emergence of theory at the site where cultural horizons meet, where the demand for translation is acute and its promise of success, uncertain.

Gender Trouble is rooted in "French Theory," which is itself a curious American construction. Only in the United States are so many disparate theories joined together as if they formed some kind of unity. Although the book has been translated into several languages and has had an especially strong impact on discussions of gender and politics in Germany, it will emerge in France, if it finally does, much later than in other countries. I mention this to underscore that the apparent Francocentrism of the text is at a significant distance from France and from the life of theory in France. *Gender Trouble* tends to read together, in a syncretic vein, various French intellectuals (Lévi-Strauss, Foucault, Lacan, Kristeva, Wittig) who had few alliances with one another and whose readers in France rarely, if ever, read one another. Indeed, the intellectual promiscuity of the text marks it precisely as American and makes it foreign to a French context. So does its emphasis on the Anglo-American sociological and anthropological tradition of "gender" studies, which is distinct from the discourse of "sexual difference" derived from structuralist inquiry. If the text runs the risk of Eurocentrism in the U.S., it has threatened an "Americanization" of theory in France for those few French publishers who have considered it.[1]

Of course, "French Theory" is not the only language of this text. It emerges from a long engagement with feminist theory, with the debates on the socially constructed character of gender, with psychoanalysis and feminism, with Gayle Rubin's extraordinary work on gender, sexuality, and kinship, Esther Newton's groundbreaking work on drag, Monique Wittig's brilliant theoretical and fictional writings, and with gay and lesbian perspectives in the humanities. Whereas many feminists in the 1980s assumed that lesbianism meets feminism in lesbian-feminism, *Gender Trouble* sought to refuse the notion that lesbian practice instantiates feminist theory, and set up a more troubled relation between the two terms. Lesbianism in this text does not represent a return to what is most important about being a woman; it does not consecrate femininity or signal a gynocentric world. Lesbianism is not the erotic consummation of a set of political beliefs (sexuality and belief are related in a much more complex fashion, and very often at odds with one another). Instead, the text asks, how do non-normative sexual practices call into question the stability of gender as a category of analysis? How do certain sexual practices compel the question: what is a woman, what is a man? If gender is no longer to be understood as consolidated through normative sexuality, then is there a crisis of gender that is specific to queer contexts?

The idea that sexual practice has the power to destabilize gender emerged from my reading of Gayle Rubin's "The Traffic in Women" and sought to establish that normative sexuality fortifies normative gender. Briefly, one is a woman, according to this framework, to the extent that one functions as one within the dominant heterosexual frame and to call the frame into question is perhaps to lose something of one's sense of place in gender. I take it that this is the first formulation of "gender trouble" in this text. I sought to understand some of the terror and anxiety that some people suffer in "becoming gay," the fear of losing one's place in gender or of not knowing who one will be if one sleeps with someone of the ostensibly "same" gender. This constitutes a certain crisis in ontology experienced at the level of both sexuality and language. This issue has become more acute as we consider various new forms of gendering that have emerged in light of transgenderism and transsexuality, lesbian and gay parenting, new butch and femme identities. When and why, for instance, do some butch lesbians who become parents become "dads" and others become "moms"?

What about the notion, suggested by Kate Bornstein, that a transsexual cannot be described by the noun of "woman" or "man," but must be approached through active verbs that attest to the constant transformation which "is" the new identity or, indeed, the "in-betweenness" that puts the being of gendered identity into question? Although some lesbians argue that butches have nothing to do with "being a man," others insist that their butchness is or was only a route to a desired status as a man. These paradoxes have surely proliferated in recent years, offering evidence of a kind of gender trouble that the text itself did not anticipate.[2]

But what is the link between gender and sexuality that I sought to underscore? Certainly, I do not mean to claim that forms of sexual practice produce certain genders, but only that under conditions of normative heterosexuality, policing gender is sometimes used as a way of securing heterosexuality. Catharine MacKinnon offers a formulation of this problem that resonates with my own at the same time that there are, I believe, crucial and important differences between us. She writes:

> Stopped as an attribute of a person, sex inequality takes the form of gender; moving as a relation between people, it takes the form of sexuality. Gender emerges as the congealed form of the sexualization of inequality between men and women.[3]

In this view, sexual hierarchy produces and consolidates gender. It is not heterosexual normativity that produces and consolidates gender, but the gender hierarchy that is said to underwrite heterosexual relations. If gender hierarchy produces and consolidates gender, and if gender hierarchy presupposes an operative notion of gender, then gender is what causes gender, and the formulation culminates in tautology. It may be that MacKinnon wants merely to outline the self-reproducing mechanism of gender hierarchy, but this is not what she has said.

Is "gender hierarchy" sufficient to explain the conditions for the production of gender? To what extent does gender hierarchy serve a more or less compulsory heterosexuality, and how often are gender norms policed precisely in the service of shoring up heterosexual hegemony?

Katherine Franke, a contemporary legal theorist, makes innovative use of both feminist and queer perspectives to note that by assuming the primacy of gender hierarchy to the production of gender, MacKinnon also accepts a presumptively heterosexual model for thinking about sexuality. Franke offers an alternative model of gender

discrimination to MacKinnon's, effectively arguing that sexual harassment is the paradigmatic allegory for the production of gender. Not all
discrimination can be understood as harassment. The act of harassment
may be one in which a person is "made" into a certain gender. But there
are others ways of enforcing gender as well. Thus, for Franke, it is
important to make a provisional distinction between gender and sexual discrimination. Gay people, for instance, may be discriminated
against in positions of employment because they fail to "appear" in
accordance with accepted gendered norms. And the sexual harassment
of gay people may well take place not in the service of shoring up gender hierarchy, but in promoting gender normativity.

Whereas MacKinnon offers a powerful critique of sexual harassment, she institutes a regulation of another kind: to have a gender
means to have entered already into a heterosexual relationship of subordination. At an analytic level, she makes an equation that resonates with
some dominant forms of homophobic argument. One such view prescribes and condones the sexual ordering of gender, maintaining that
men who are men will be straight, women who are women will be
straight. There is another set of views, Franke's included, which offers a
critique precisely of this form of gender regulation. There is thus a difference between sexist and feminist views on the relation between gender and sexuality: the sexist claims that a woman only exhibits her
womanness in the act of heterosexual coitus in which her subordination
becomes her pleasure (an essence emanates and is confirmed in the sexualized subordination of women); a feminist view argues that gender
should be overthrown, eliminated, or rendered fatally ambiguous precisely because it is always a sign of subordination for women. The latter
accepts the power of the former's orthodox description, accepts that
the former's description already operates as powerful ideology, but
seeks to oppose it.

I belabor this point because some queer theorists have drawn
an analytic distinction between gender and sexuality, refusing a causal
or structural link between them. This makes good sense from one

perspective: if what is meant by this distinction is that heterosexual normativity ought *not* to order gender, and that such ordering ought to be opposed, I am firmly in favor of this view.[4] If, however, what is meant by this is that (descriptively speaking), there is no sexual regulation of gender, then I think an important, but not exclusive, dimension of how homophobia works is going unrecognized by those who are clearly most eager to combat it. It is important for me to concede, however, that the performance of gender subversion can indicate nothing about sexuality or sexual practice. Gender can be rendered ambiguous without disturbing or reorienting normative sexuality at all. Sometimes gender ambiguity can operate precisely to contain or deflect non-normative sexual practice and thereby work to keep normative sexuality intact.[5] Thus, no correlation can be drawn, for instance, between drag or transgender and sexual practice, and the distribution of hetero-, bi-, and homo-inclinations cannot be predictably mapped onto the travels of gender bending or changing.

Much of my work in recent years has been devoted to clarifying and revising the theory of performativity that is outlined in *Gender Trouble*.[6] It is difficult to say precisely what performativity is not only because my own views on what "performativity" might mean have changed over time, most often in response to excellent criticisms,[7] but because so many others have taken it up and given it their own formulations. I originally took my clue on how to read the performativity of gender from Jacques Derrida's reading of Kafka's "Before the Law." There the one who waits for the law, sits before the door of the law, attributes a certain force to the law for which one waits. The anticipation of an authoritative disclosure of meaning is the means by which that authority is attributed and installed: the anticipation conjures its object. I wondered whether we do not labor under a similar expectation concerning gender, that it operates as an interior essence that might be disclosed, an expectation that ends up producing the very phenomenon that it anticipates. In the first instance, then, the performativity of gender revolves around this metalepsis, the way in which the anticipation of a gendered essence produces that which it posits as outside itself. Secondly, performativity is not a singular act, but a repetition and a ritual, which achieves its effects through its naturalization in the context of a body, understood, in part, as a culturally sustained temporal duration.[8]

Several important questions have been posed to this doctrine, and one seems especially noteworthy to mention here. The view that gender is performative sought to show that what we take to be an internal essence of gender is manufactured through a sustained set of acts, posited through the gendered stylization of the body. In this way, it showed that what we take to be an "internal" feature of ourselves is one that we anticipate and produce through certain bodily acts, at an extreme, an hallucinatory effect of naturalized gestures. Does this mean that everything that is understood as "internal" about the psyche is therefore evacuated, and that internality is a false metaphor? Although *Gender Trouble* clearly drew upon the metaphor of an internal psyche in its early discussion of gender melancholy, that emphasis was not brought forward into the thinking of performativity itself.[9] Both *The Psychic Life of Power* and several of my recent articles on psychoanalytic topics have sought to come to terms with this problem, what many have seen as a problematic break between the early and later chapters of this book. Although I would deny that all of the internal world of the psyche is but an effect of a stylized set of acts, I continue to think that it is a significant theoretical mistake to take the "internality" of the psychic world for granted. Certain features of the world, including people we know and lose, do become "internal" features of the self, but they are transformed through that interiorization, and that inner world, as the Kleinians call it, is constituted precisely as a consequence of the interiorizations that a psyche performs. This suggests that there may well be a psychic theory of performativity at work that calls for greater exploration.

Although this text does not answer the question of whether the materiality of the body is fully constructed, that has been the focus of much of my subsequent work, which I hope will prove clarifying for the reader.[10] The question of whether or not the theory of performativity can be transposed onto matters of race has been explored by several scholars.[11] I would note here not only that racial presumptions invariably underwrite the discourse on gender in ways that need to be made explicit, but that race and gender ought not to be treated as simple analogies. I would therefore suggest that the question to ask is not whether the theory of performativity is transposable onto race, but what happens to the theory when it tries to come to grips with race. Many of these debates have centered on the status of "construction," whether race is constructed in the same way as gender. My view is that no single account of construction will do, and that these categories always work as background for one another, and they often find their most powerful articulation through one another. Thus, the sexualization of racial gender norms calls to be read through multiple lenses at once, and the analysis surely illuminates the limits of gender as an exclusive category of analysis.[12]

Although I've enumerated some of the academic traditions and debates that have animated this book, it is not my purpose to offer a full apologia in these brief pages. There is one aspect of the conditions of its production that is not always understood about the text: it was produced not merely from the academy, but from convergent social movements of which I have been a part, and within the context of a lesbian and gay community on the east coast of the United States in which I lived for fourteen years prior to the writing of this book. Despite the dislocation of the subject that the text performs, there is a person here: I went to many meetings, bars, and marches and saw many kinds of genders, understood myself to be at the crossroads of some of them, and encountered sexuality at several of its cultural edges. I knew many people who were trying to find their way in the midst of a significant movement for sexual recognition and freedom, and felt the exhilaration and frustration that goes along with being a part of that movement both in its hopefulness and internal dissension. At the same time that I was ensconced in the academy, I was also living a life outside those walls, and though *Gender Trouble* is an academic book, it began, for me, with a crossing-over, sitting on Rehoboth Beach, wondering whether I could link the different sides of my life. That I can write in an autobiographical mode does not, I think, relocate this subject that I am, but perhaps it gives the reader a sense of solace that there is someone here (I will suspend for the moment the problem that this someone is given in language).

It has been one of the most gratifying experiences for me that the text continues to move outside the academy to this day. At the same time that the book was taken up by Queer Nation, and some of its reflections on the theatricality of queer self-presentation resonated with the tactics of Act Up, it was among the materials that also helped to prompt members of the American Psychoanalytic Association and the American Psychological Association to reassess some of their current doxa on homosexuality. The questions of performative gender were appropriated in different ways in the visual arts, at Whitney exhibitions, and at the Otis School for the Arts in Los Angeles, among others. Some of its formulations on the subject of "women" and the relation between sexuality and gender also made its way into feminist jurisprudence and antidiscrimination legal scholarship in the work of Vicki Schultz, Katherine Franke, and Mary Jo Frug.

In turn, I have been compelled to revise some of my positions in *Gender Trouble* by virtue of my own political engagements. In the book, I tend to conceive of the claim of "universality" in exclusive negative and exclusionary terms. However, I came to see the term has important strategic use precisely as a non-substantial and open-ended category as I worked with an extraordinary group of activists first as a board member and then as board chair of the International Gay and Lesbian Human Rights Commission (1994–7), an organization that represents sexual minorities on a broad range of human rights issues. There I came to understand how the assertion of universality can be proleptic and performative, conjuring a reality that does not yet exist, and holding out the possibility for a convergence of cultural horizons that have not yet met. Thus, I arrived at a second view of universality in which it is defined as a future-oriented labor of cultural translation.[13] More recently, I have been compelled to relate my work to political theory and, once again, to the concept of universality in a co-authored book that I am writing with Ernesto Laclau and Slavoj Žižek on the theory of hegemony and its implications for a theoretically activist Left (to be published by Verso in 2000).

Another practical dimension of my thinking has taken place in relationship to psychoanalysis as both a scholarly and clinical enterprise. I am currently working with a group of progressive psychoanalytic therapists on a new journal, *Studies in Gender and Sexuality*, that seeks to bring clinical and scholarly work into productive dialogue on questions of sexuality, gender, and culture.

Both critics and friends of *Gender Trouble* have drawn attention to the difficulty of its style. It is no doubt strange, and maddening to some, to find a book that is not easily consumed to be "popular" according to academic standards. The surprise over this is perhaps attributable to the way we underestimate the reading public, its capacity and desire for reading complicated and challenging texts, when the complication is not gratuitous, when the challenge is in the service of calling taken-for-granted truths into question, when the taken for grantedness of those truths is, indeed, oppressive.

I think that style is a complicated terrain, and not one that we unilaterally choose or control with the purposes we consciously intend. Fredric Jameson made this clear in his early book on Sartre. Certainly, one can practice styles, but the styles that become available to you are not entirely a matter of choice. Moreover, neither grammar nor style are politically neutral. Learning the rules that govern intelligible speech is an inculcation into normalized language, where the price of not conforming is the loss of intelligibility itself. As Drucilla Cornell, in the tradition of Adorno, reminds me: there is nothing radical about common sense. It would be a mistake to think that received grammar is the best vehicle for expressing radical views, given the constraints that grammar imposes upon thought, indeed, upon the thinkable itself. But formulations that twist grammar or that implicitly call into question the subject-verb requirements of propositional sense are clearly irritating for some. They produce more work for their readers, and sometimes their readers are offended by such demands. Are those who are offended making a legitimate request for "plain speaking" or does their complaint emerge from a consumer expectation of intellectual life? Is there, perhaps, a value to be derived from such experiences of linguistic difficulty? If gender itself is naturalized through grammatical norms, as Monique Wittig has argued, then the alteration of gender at the most fundamental epistemic level will be conducted, in part, through contesting the grammar in which gender is given.

The demand for lucidity forgets the ruses that motor the ostensibly "clear" view. Avital Ronell recalls the moment in which Nixon looked into the eyes of the nation and said, "let me make one thing perfectly clear" and then proceeded to lie. What travels under the sign of "clarity," and what would be the price of failing to deploy a certain critical suspicion when the arrival of lucidity is announced? Who devises the protocols of "clarity" and whose interests do they serve? What is foreclosed by the insistence on parochial standards of transparency as requisite for all communication? What does "transparency" keep obscure?

I grew up understanding something of the violence of gender norms: an uncle incarcerated for his anatomically anomalous body, deprived of family and friends, living out his days in an "institute" in the Kansas prairies; gay cousins forced to leave their homes because of their sexuality, real and imagined; my own tempestuous coming out at the age of 16; and a subsequent adult landscape of lost jobs, lovers, and homes. All of this subjected me to strong and scarring condemnation but, luckily, did not prevent me from pursuing pleasure and insisting on a legitimating recognition for my sexual life. It was difficult to bring this violence into view precisely because gender was so taken for granted at the same time that it was violently policed. It was assumed either to be a natural manifestation of sex or a cultural constant that no human agency could hope to revise. I also came to understand something of the violence of the foreclosed life, the one that does not get named as "living," the one whose incarceration implies a suspension of life, or a sustained death sentence. The dogged effort to "denaturalize" gender in this text emerges, I think, from a strong desire both to counter the normative violence implied by ideal morphologies of sex and to uproot the pervasive assumptions about natural or presumptive heterosexuality that are informed by ordinary and academic discourses on sexuality. The writing of this denaturalization was not done simply out of a desire to play with language or prescribe theatrical antics in the place of "real" politics, as some critics have conjectured (as if theatre and politics are always distinct). It was done from a desire to live, to make life possible, and to rethink the possible as such. What would the world have to be like for my uncle to live in the company of family, friends, or extended kinship of some other kind? How must we rethink the ideal morphological constraints upon the human such that those who fail to approximate the norm are not condemned to a death within life?[14]

Some readers have asked whether *Gender Trouble* seeks to expand the realm of gender possibilities for a reason. They ask, for what purpose are such new configurations of gender devised, and how ought we to judge among them? The question often involves a prior premise, namely, that the text does not address the normative or prescriptive dimension of feminist thought. "Normative" clearly has at least two meanings in this critical encounter, since the word is one I use often, mainly to describe the mundane violence performed by certain kinds of gender ideals. I usually use "normative" in a way that is synonymous with "pertaining to the norms that govern gender." But the term "normative" also pertains to ethical justification, how it is established, and what concrete consequences proceed therefrom. One critical question posed of *Gender Trouble* has been: how do we proceed to make judgments on how gender is to be lived on the basis of the theoretical descriptions offered here? It is not possible to oppose the "normative" forms of gender without at the same time subscribing to a certain normative view of how the gendered world ought to be. I want to suggest, however, that the positive normative vision of this text, such as it is, does not and cannot take the form of a prescription: "subvert gender in the way that I say, and life will be good."

Those who make such prescriptions or who are willing to decide between subversive and unsubversive expressions of gender, base their judgments on a description. Gender appears in this or that form, and then a normative judgment is made about those appearances and on the basis of what appears. But what conditions the domain of appearance for gender itself? We may be tempted to make the following distinction: a *descriptive* account of gender includes considerations of what makes gender intelligible, an inquiry into its conditions of possibility, whereas a *normative* account seeks to answer the question of which expressions of gender are acceptable, and which are not, supplying persuasive reasons to distinguish between such expressions in this way. The question, however, of what qualifies as "gender" is itself already a question that attests to a pervasively normative operation of power, a fugitive operation of "what will be the case" under the rubric of "what is the case." Thus, the very description of the field of gender is no sense prior to, or separable from, the question of its normative operation.

I am not interested in delivering judgments on what distinguishes the subversive from the unsubversive. Not only do I believe that such judgments cannot be made out of context, but that they cannot be made in ways that endure through time ("contexts" are themselves posited unities that undergo temporal change and expose their essential disunity). Just as metaphors lose their metaphoricity as they congeal through time into concepts, so subversive performances always run the risk of becoming deadening cliches through their repetition and, most importantly, through their repetition within commodity culture where "subversion" carries market value. The effort to name the criterion for subversiveness will always fail, and ought to. So what is at stake in using the term at all?

What continues to concern me most is the following kinds of questions: what will and will not constitute an intelligible life, and how do presumptions about normative gender and sexuality determine in advance what will qualify as the "human" and the "livable"? In other words, how do normative gender presumptions work to delimit the very field of description that we have for the human? What is the means by which we come to see this delimiting power, and what are the means by which we transform it?

The discussion of drag that *Gender Trouble* offers to explain the constructed and performative dimension of gender is not precisely *an example* of subversion. It would be a mistake to take it as the paradigm of subversive action or, indeed, as a model for political agency. The point is rather different. If one thinks that one sees a man dressed as a woman or a woman dressed as a man, then one takes the first term of each of those perceptions as the "reality" of gender: the gender that is introduced through the simile lacks "reality," and is taken to constitute an illusory appearance. In such perceptions in which an ostensible reality is coupled with an unreality, we think we know what the reality is, and take the secondary appearance of gender to be mere artifice, play, falsehood, and illusion. But what is the sense of "gender reality" that founds this perception in this way? Perhaps we think we know what the anatomy of the person is (sometimes we do not, and we certainly have not appreciated the variation that exists at the level of anatomical description). Or we derive that knowledge from the clothes that the person wears, or how the clothes are worn. This is naturalized knowledge, even though it is based on a series of cultural inferences, some of which are highly erroneous. Indeed, if we shift the example from drag to transsexuality, then it is no longer possible to derive a judgment about stable anatomy from the clothes that cover and articulate the body. That body may be preoperative, transitional, or postoperative; even "seeing" the body may not answer the question: for *what are the categories through which one sees?* The moment in which one's staid and usual cultural perceptions fail, when one cannot with surety read the body that one sees, is precisely the moment when one is no longer sure whether the body encountered is that of a man or a woman. The vacillation between the categories itself constitutes the experience of the body in question.

When such categories come into question, the *reality* of gender is also put into crisis: it becomes unclear how to distinguish the real from the unreal. And this is the occasion in which we come to understand that what we take to be "real," what we invoke as the naturalized knowledge of gender is, in fact, a changeable and revisable reality. Call it subversive or call it something else. Although this insight does not in itself constitute a political revolution, no political revolution is possible without a radical shift in one's notion of the possible and the real. And sometimes this shift comes as a result of certain kinds of practices that precede their explicit theorization, and which prompt a rethinking of our basic categories: what is gender, how is it produced and reproduced, what are its possibilities? At this point, the sedimented and reified field of gender "reality" is understood as one that might be made differently and, indeed, less violently.

The point of this text is not to celebrate drag as the expression of a true and model gender (even as it is important to resist the belittling of drag that sometimes takes place), but to show that the naturalized knowledge of gender operates as a preemptive and violent circumscription of reality. To the extent the gender norms (ideal dimorphism, heterosexual complementarity of bodies, ideals and rule of proper and improper masculinity and femininity, many of which are underwritten by racial codes of purity and taboos against miscegenation) establish what will and will not be intelligibly human, what will and will not be considered to be "real," they establish the ontological field in which bodies may be given legitimate expression. If there is a positive normative task in *Gender Trouble*, it is to insist upon the extension of this legitimacy to bodies that have been regarded as false, unreal, and unintelligible. Drag is an example that is meant to establish that "reality" is not as fixed as we generally assume it to be. The purpose of the example is to expose the tenuousness of gender "reality" in order to counter the violence performed by gender norms.

In this text as elsewhere I have tried to understand what political agency might be, given that it cannot be isolated from the dynamics of power from which it is wrought. The iterability of performativity is a theory of agency, one that cannot disavow power as the condition of its own possibility. This text does not sufficiently explain performativity in terms of its social, psychic, corporeal, and temporal dimensions. In some ways, the continuing work of that clarification, in response to numerous excellent criticisms, guides most of my subsequent publications.

Other concerns have emerged over this text in the last decade, and I have sought to answer them through various publications. On the status of the materiality of the body, I have offered a reconsideration and revision of my views in *Bodies that Matter*. On the question of the necessity of the category of "women" for feminist analysis, I have revised and expanded my views in "Contingent Foundations" to be found in the volume I coedited with Joan W. Scott, *Feminists Theorize the Political* (Routledge, 1993) and in the collectively authored *Feminist Contentions* (Routledge, 1995).

I do not believe that poststructuralism entails the death of autobiographical writing, but it does draw attention to the difficulty of the "I" to express itself through the language that is available to it. For this "I" that you read is in part a consequence of the grammar that governs the availability of persons in language. I am not outside the language that structures me, but neither am I determined by the language that makes this "I" possible. This is the bind of self-expression, as I understand it. What it means is that you never receive me apart from the grammar that establishes my availability to you. If I treat that grammar as pellucid, then I fail to call attention precisely to that sphere of language that establishes and disestablishes intelligibility, and that would be precisely to thwart my own project as I have described it to you here. I am not trying to be difficult, but only to draw attention to a difficulty without which no "I" can appear.

This difficulty takes on a specific dimension when approached from a psychoanalytic perspective. In my efforts to understand the opacity of the "I" in language, I have turned increasingly to psychoanalysis since the publication of *Gender Trouble*. The usual effort to polarize the theory of the psyche from the theory of power seems to me to be counter-productive, for part of what is so oppressive about social forms of gender is the psychic difficulties they produce. I sought to consider the ways in which Foucault and psychoanalysis might be thought together in *The Psychic Life of Power* (Stanford, 1997). I have also made use of psycho-analysis to curb the occasional voluntarism of my view of performativi-ty without thereby undermining a more general theory of agency. *Gender Trouble* sometimes reads as if gender is simply a self-invention or that the psychic meaning of a gendered presentation might be read directly off its surface. Both of those postulates have had to be refined over time. Moreover, my theory sometimes waffles between under-standing performativity as linguistic and casting it as theatrical. I have come to think that the two are invariably related, chiasmically so, and that a reconsideration of the speech act as an instance of power invari-ably draws attention to both its theatrical and linguistic dimensions. In *Excitable Speech*, I sought to show that the speech act is at once per-formed (and thus theatrical, presented to an audience, subject to inter-pretation), and linguistic, inducing a set of effects through its implied relation to linguistic conventions. If one wonders how a linguistic theo-ry of the speech act relates to bodily gestures, one need only consider that speech itself is a bodily act with specific linguistic consequences. Thus speech belongs exclusively neither to corporeal presentation nor to language, and its status as word and deed is necessarily ambiguous. This ambiguity has consequences for the practice of coming out, for the insurrectionary power of the speech act, for language as a condition of both bodily seduction and the threat of injury.

If I were to rewrite this book under present circumstances, I would include a discussion of transgender and intersexuality, the way that ideal gender dimorphism works in both sorts of discourses, the different relations to surgical intervention that these related concerns sustain. I would also include a discussion on racialized sexuality and, in particular, how taboos against miscegenation (and the romanticization of cross-racial sexual exchange) are essential to the naturalized and denaturalized forms that gender takes. I continue to hope for a coalition of sexual minorities that will transcend the simple categories of identity, that will refuse the erasure of bisexuality, that will counter and dissipate the violence imposed by restrictive bodily norms. I would hope that such a coalition would be based on the irreducible complexity of sexuality and its implication in various dynamics of discursive and institutional power, and that no one will be too quick to reduce power to hierarchy and to refuse its productive political dimensions. Even as I think that gaining recognition for one's status as a sexual minority is a difficult task within reigning discourses of law, politics, and language, I continue to consider it a necessity for survival. The mobilization of identity categories for the purposes of politicization always remain threatened by the prospect of identity becoming an instrument of the power one opposes. That is no reason not to use, and be used, by identity. There is no political position purified of power, and perhaps that impurity is what produces agency as the potential interruption and reversal of regulatory regimes. Those who are deemed "unreal" nevertheless lay hold of the real, a laying hold that happens in concert, and a vital instability is produced by that performative surprise. This book is written then as part of the cultural life of a collective struggle that has had, and will continue to have, some success in increasing the possibilities for a livable life for those who live, or try to live, on the sexual margins.[15]

Judith Butler
Berkeley, California
June, 1999

Preface (1990)

Contemporary feminist debates over the meanings of gender lead time and again to a certain sense of trouble, as if the indeterminacy of gender might eventually culminate in the failure of feminism. Perhaps trouble need not carry such a negative valence. To make trouble was, within the reigning discourse of my childhood, something one should never do precisely because that would get one *in* trouble. The rebellion and its reprimand seemed to be caught up in the same terms, a phenomenon that gave rise to my first critical insight into the subtle ruse of power: the prevailing law threatened one with trouble, even put one in trouble, all to keep one out of trouble. Hence, I concluded that trouble is inevitable and the task, how best to make it, what best way to be in it. As time went by, further ambiguities arrived on the critical scene. I noted that trouble sometimes euphemized some fundamentally mysterious problem usually related to the alleged mystery of all things feminine. I read Beauvoir who explained that to be a woman within the terms of a masculinist culture is to be a source of mystery and unknowability for men, and this seemed confirmed somehow when I read Sartre for whom all desire, problematically presumed as heterosexual and masculine, was defined as *trouble*. For that masculine subject of desire, trouble became a scandal with the sudden intrusion, the unanticipated agency, of a female "object" who inexplicably returns the glance, reverses the gaze, and contests the place and authority of the masculine position. The radical dependency of the masculine subject on the female "Other" suddenly exposes his autonomy as illusory. That particular dialectical reversal of power, however, couldn't quite hold my attention—although others surely did. Power seemed to be more than an exchange between subjects or a relation of constant inversion between and subject and an Other; indeed, power appeared to operate in the production of that very binary frame for thinking about gender. I asked, what configuration of power constructs the subject and the Other, that binary relation between "men" and "women," and the internal stability of those terms? What restriction is here at work? Are those terms untroubling only to the extent that they conform to a heterosexual matrix for conceptualizing gender and desire? What happens to the subject and to the stability of gender categories when the epistemic regime of presumptive heterosexuality is unmasked as that which produces and reifies these ostensible categories of ontology?

But how can an epistemic/ontological regime be brought into question? What best way to trouble the gender categories that support gender hierarchy and compulsory heterosexuality? Consider the fate of "female trouble," that historical configuration of a nameless female indisposition, which thinly veiled the notion that being female is a natural indisposition. Serious as the medicalization of women's bodies is, the term is also laughable, and laughter in the face of serious categories is indispensable for feminism. Without a doubt, feminism continues to require its own forms of serious play. *Female Trouble* is also the title of the John Waters film that features Divine, the hero/heroine of *Hairspray* as well, whose impersonation of women implicitly suggests that gender is a kind of persistent impersonation that passes as the real. Her/his performance destabilizes the very distinctions between the natural and the artificial, depth and surface, inner and outer through which discourse about genders almost always operates. Is drag the imitation of gender, or does it dramatize the signifying gestures through which gender itself is established? Does being female constitute a "natural fact" or a cultural performance, or is "naturalness" constituted through discursively constrained performative acts that produce the body through and within the categories of sex? Divine notwithstanding, gender practices within gay and lesbian cultures often thematize "the natural" in parodic contexts that bring into relief the performative construction of an original and true sex. What other foundational categories of identity—the binary of sex, gender, and the body—can be shown as productions that create the effect of the natural, the original, and the inevitable?

To expose the foundational categories of sex, gender, and desire as effects of a specific formation of power requires a form of critical inquiry that Foucault, reformulating Nietzsche, designates as "genealogy." A genealogical critique refuses to search for the origins of gender, the inner truth of female desire, a genuine or authentic sexual identity that repression has kept from view; rather, genealogy investigates the political stakes in designating as an *origin* and *cause* those identity categories that are in fact the *effects* of institutions, practices, discourses with multiple and diffuse points of origin. The task of this inquiry is to center on—and decenter—such defining institutions: phallogocentrism and compulsory heterosexuality.

Precisely because "female" no longer appears to be a stable notion, its meaning is as troubled and unfixed as "woman," and because both terms gain their troubled significations only as relational terms, this inquiry takes as its focus gender and the relational analysis it suggests. Further, it is no longer clear that feminist theory ought to try to settle the questions of primary identity in order to get on with the task of politics. Instead, we ought to ask, what political possibilities are the consequence of a radical critique of the categories of identity. What new shape of politics emerges when identity as a common ground no longer constrains the discourse on feminist politics? And to what extent does the effort to locate a common identity as the foundation for a feminist politics preclude a radical inquiry into the political construction and regulation of identity itself?

* * *

This text is divided into three chapters that effect a critical genealogy of gender categories in very different discursive domains. Chapter 1, "Subjects of Sex/Gender/Desire," reconsiders the status of "women" as the subject of feminism and the sex/gender distinction. Compulsory heterosexuality and phallogocentrism are understood as regimes of power/discourse with often divergent ways of answering central question of gender discourse: How does language construct the categories of sex? Does "the feminine" resist representation within language? Is language understood as phallogocentric (Luce Irigaray's question)? Is "the feminine" the only sex represented within a language that conflates the female and the sexual (Monique Wittig's contention)? Where and how do compulsory heterosexuality and phallogocentrism converge? Where are the points of breakage between? How does language itself produce the fiction construction of "sex" that supports these various regimes of power? Within a language of presumptive heterosexuality, what sorts of continuities are assumed to exist among sex, gender, and desire? Are these terms discrete? What kinds of cultural practices produce subversive discontinuity and dissonance among sex, gender, and desire and call into question their alleged relations?

Chapter 2, "Prohibition, Psychoanalysis, and the Production of the Heterosexual Matrix," offers a selective reading of structuralism, psychoanalytic and feminist accounts of the incest taboo as the mechanism that tries to enforce discrete and internally coherent gender identities within a heterosexual frame. The question of homosexuality is, within some psychoanalytic discourse, invariably associated with forms of cultural unintelligibility and, in the case of lesbianism, with the desexualization of the female body. On the other hand, the uses of psychoanalytic theory for an account of complex gender "identities" is pursued through an analysis of identity, identification, and masquerade in Joan Riviere and other psychoanalytic literature. Once the incest taboo is subjected to Foucault's critique of the repressive hypothesis in *The History of Sexuality,* that prohibitive or juridical structure is shown both to instate compulsory heterosexuality within a masculinist sexual economy and to enable a critical challenge to that economy. Is psycho-analysis an antifoundationalist inquiry that affirms the kind of sexual complexity that effectively deregulates rigid and hierarchical sexual codes, or does it maintain an unacknowledged set of assumptions about the foundations of identity that work in favor of those very hierarchies?

The last chapter, "Subversive Bodily Acts," begins with a critical consideration of the construction of the maternal body in Julia Kristeva in order to show the implicit norms that govern the cultural intel-ligibility of sex and sexuality in her work. Although Foucault is engaged to provide a critique of Kristeva, a close examination of some of Foucault's own work reveals a problematic indifference to sexual dif-ference. His critique of the category of sex, however, provides an insight into the regulatory practices of some contemporary medical fic-tions designed to designate univocal sex. Monique Wittig's theory and fiction propose a "disintegration" of culturally constituted bodies, sug-gesting that morphology itself is a consequence of a hegemonic concep-tual scheme. The final section of this chapter, "Bodily Inscriptions, Performative Subversions," considers the boundary and surface of bod-ies as politically constructed, drawing on the work of Mary Douglas and Julia Kristeva. As a strategy to denaturalize and resignify bodily cat-egories, I describe and propose a set of parodic practices based in a per-formative theory of gender acts that disrupt the categories of the body, sex, gender, and sexuality and occasion their subversive resignification and proliferation beyond the binary frame.

It seems that every text has more sources than it can reconstruct within its own terms. These are sources that define and inform the very lan-guage of the text in ways that would require a thorough unraveling of the text itself to be understood, and of course there would be no guar-antee that that unraveling would ever stop. Although I have offered a childhood story to begin this preface, it is a fable irreducible to fact. Indeed, the purpose here more generally is to trace the way in which gender fables establish and circulate the misnomer of natural facts. It is clearly impossible to recover the origins of these essays, to locate the various moments that have enabled this text. The texts are assembled to facilitate a political convergence of feminism, gay and lesbian perspectives on gender, and poststructuralist theory. Philosophy is the predominant disciplinary mechanism that currently mobilizes this author-subject, although it rarely if ever appears separated from other discourses. This inquiry seeks to affirm those positions on the critical boundaries of disciplinary life. The point is not to stay marginal, but to participate in whatever network or marginal zones is spawned from other disciplinary centers and that, together, constitute a multiple displacement of those authorities. The complexity of gender requires an interdisciplinary and postdisciplinary set of discourses in order to resist the domestication of gender studies or women studies within the academy and to radicalize the notion of feminist critique.

The writing of this text was made possible by a number of institutional and individual forms of support. The American Council of Learned Societies provided a Recent Recipient of the Ph.D. Fellowship for the fall of 1987, and the School of Social Science at the Institute for Advanced Study in Princeton provided fellowship, housing, and provocative argumentation during the 1987–1988 academic year. The George Washington University Faculty Research Grant also supported my research during the summers of 1987 and 1988. Joan W. Scott has been an invaluable and incisive critic throughout various stages of this manuscript. Her commitment to a critical rethinking of the presuppositional terms of feminist politics has challenged and inspired me. The "Gender Seminar" assembled at the Institute for Advanced Study under Joan Scott's direction helped me to clarify and elaborate my views by virtue of the significant and provocative divisions in our collective thinking. Hence, I thank Lila Abu-Lughod, Yasmine Ergas, Donna Haraway, Evelyn Fox Keller, Dorinne Kondo, Rayna Rapp, Carroll Smith-Rosenberg, Louise Tilly. My students in the seminar "Gender, Identity, and Desire," offered at Wesleyan University and at Yale in 1985 and 1986, respectively, were indispensable for their willingness to imagine alternatively gendered worlds. I also appreciate the variety of critical responses that I received on presentations of parts of this work from the Princeton Women's Studies Colloquium, the Humanities Center at Johns Hopkins University, the University of Notre Dame, the University of Kansas, Amherst College, and the Yale University School of Medicine. My acknowledgment also goes to Linda Singer, whose persistent radicalism has been invaluable, Sandra Bartky for her work and her timely words of encouragement, Linda Nicholson for her editorial and critical advice, and Linda Anderson for her acute political intuitions. I also thank the following individuals, friends, and colleagues who shaped and supported my thinking: Eloise Moore Aggar, Inés Azar, Peter Caws, Nancy F. Cott, Kathy Natanson, Lois Natanson, Maurice Natanson, Stacy Pies, Josh Shapiro, Margaret Soltan, Robert V. Stone, Richard Vann, and Eszti Votaw. I thank Sandra Schmidt for her fine work in helping to prepare this manuscript, and Meg Gilbert for her assistance. I also thank Maureen MacGrogan for encouraging this project and others with her humor, patience, and fine editorial guidance.

As before, I thank Wendy Owen for her relentless imagination, keen criticism, and for the provocation of her work.

GENDER TROUBLE

1

Subjects of Sex/Gender/Desire

One is not born a woman, but rather becomes one.
> —SIMONE DE BEAUVOIR

Strictly speaking, "women" cannot be said to exist.
> —JULIA KRISTEVA

Woman does not have a sex.
> —LUCE IRIGARAY

The deployment of sexuality ... established this notion of sex.
> —MICHEL FOUCAULT

The category of sex is the political category that founds society as heterosexual.
> —MONIQUE WITTIG

I. "WOMEN" AS THE SUBJECT OF FEMINISM

For the most part, feminist theory has assumed that there is some existing identity, understood through the category of women, who not only initiates feminist interests and goals within discourse, but constitutes the subject for whom political representation is pursued. But *politics* and *representation* are controversial terms. On the one hand, *representation* serves as the operative term within a political process that seeks to extend visibility and legitimacy to women as political subjects; on the other hand, representation is the normative function of a language which is said either to reveal or to distort what is

3

assumed to be true about the category of women. For feminist theory, the development of a language that fully or adequately represents women has seemed necessary to foster the political visibility of women. This has seemed obviously important considering the pervasive cultural condition in which women's lives were either misrepresented or not represented at all.

Recently, this prevailing conception of the relation between feminist theory and politics has come under challenge from within feminist discourse. The very subject of women is no longer understood in stable or abiding terms. There is a great deal of material that not only questions the viability of "the subject" as the ultimate candidate for representation or, indeed, liberation, but there is very little agreement after all on what it is that constitutes, or ought to constitute, the category of women. The domains of political and linguistic "representation" set out in advance the criterion by which subjects themselves are formed, with the result that representation is extended only to what can be acknowledged as a subject. In other words, the qualifications for being a subject must first be met before representation can be extended.

Foucault points out that juridical systems of power *produce* the subjects they subsequently come to represent.[1] Juridical notions of power appear to regulate political life in purely negative terms—that is, through the limitation, prohibition, regulation, control, and even "protection" of individuals related to that political structure through the contingent and retractable operation of choice. But the subjects regulated by such structures are, by virtue of being subjected to them, formed, defined, and reproduced in accordance with the requirements of those structures. If this analysis is right, then the juridical formation of language and politics that represents women as "the subject" of feminism is itself a discursive formation and effect of a given version of representational politics. And the feminist subject turns out to be discursively constituted by the very political system that is supposed to facilitate its emancipation. This becomes politically problematic if that system can be shown to produce gendered subjects along a differential axis of domination or to produce subjects who are presumed to be masculine. In such cases, an uncritical appeal to such a system for the emancipation of "women" will be clearly self-defeating.

The question of "the subject" is crucial for politics, and for feminist politics in particular, because juridical subjects are invariably produced through certain exclusionary practices that do not "show" once the juridical structure of politics has been established. In other words, the political construction of the subject proceeds with certain legitimating and exclusionary aims, and these political operations are effectively concealed and naturalized by a political analysis that takes juridical structures as their foundation. Juridical power inevitably "produces" what it claims merely to represent; hence, politics must be concerned with this dual function of power: the juridical and the productive. In effect, the law produces and then conceals the notion of "a subject before the law"[2] in order to invoke that discursive formation as a naturalized foundational premise that subsequently legitimates that law's own regulatory hegemony. It is not enough to inquire into how women might become more fully represented in language and politics. Feminist critique ought also to understand how the category of "women," the subject of feminism, is produced and restrained by the very structures of power through which emancipation is sought.

Indeed, the question of women as the subject of feminism raises the possibility that there may not be a subject who stands "before" the law, awaiting representation in or by the law. Perhaps the subject, as well as the invocation of a temporal "before," is constituted by the law as the fictive foundation of its own claim to legitimacy. The prevailing assumption of the ontological integrity of the subject before the law might be understood as the contemporary trace of the state of nature hypothesis, that foundationalist fable constitutive of the juridical structures of classical liberalism. The performative invocation of a nonhistorical "before" becomes the foundational premise that guarantees a presocial ontology of persons who freely consent to be governed and, thereby, constitute the legitimacy of the social contract.

5

Apart from the foundationalist fictions that support the notion of the subject, however, there is the political problem that feminism encounters in the assumption that the term *women* denotes a common identity. Rather than a stable signifier that commands the assent of those whom it purports to describe and represent, *women,* even in the plural, has become a troublesome term, a site of contest, a cause for anxiety. As Denise Riley's title suggests, *Am I That Name?* is a question produced by the very possibility of the name's multiple significations.[3] If one "is" a woman, that is surely not all one is; the term fails to be exhaustive, not because a pregendered "person" transcends the specific paraphernalia of its gender, but because gender is not always constituted coherently or consistently in different historical contexts, and because gender intersects with racial, class, ethnic, sexual, and regional modalities of discursively constituted identities. As a result, it becomes impossible to separate out "gender" from the political and cultural intersections in which it is invariably produced and maintained.

The political assumption that there must be a universal basis for feminism, one which must be found in an identity assumed to exist cross-culturally, often accompanies the notion that the oppression of women has some singular form discernible in the universal or hegemonic structure of patriarchy or masculine domination. The notion of a universal patriarchy has been widely criticized in recent years for its failure to account for the workings of gender oppression in the concrete cultural contexts in which it exists. Where those various contexts have been consulted within such theories, it has been to find "examples" or "illustrations" of a universal principle that is assumed from the start. That form of feminist theorizing has come under criticism for its efforts to colonize and appropriate non-Western cultures to support highly Western notions of oppression, but because they tend as well to construct a "Third World" or even an "Orient" in which gender oppression is subtly explained as symptomatic of an essential, non-Western barbarism. The urgency of feminism to establish a universal status for patriarchy in order to strengthen the appearance of feminism's own

6

claims to be representative has occasionally motivated the shortcut to a categorial or fictive universality of the structure of domination, held to produce women's common subjugated experience.

Although the claim of universal patriarchy no longer enjoys the kind of credibility it once did, the notion of a generally shared conception of "women," the corollary to that framework, has been much more difficult to displace. Certainly, there have been plenty of debates: Is there some commonality among "women" that preexists their oppression, or do "women" have a bond by virtue of their oppression alone? Is there a specificity to women's cultures that is independent of their subordination by hegemonic, masculinist cultures? Are the specificity and integrity of women's cultural or linguistic practices always specified against and, hence, within the terms of some more dominant cultural formation? If there is a region of the "specifically feminine," one that is both differentiated from the masculine as such and recognizable in its difference by an unmarked and, hence, presumed universality of "women"? The masculine/feminine binary constitutes not only the exclusive framework in which that specificity can be recognized, but in every other way the "specificity" of the feminine is once again fully decontextualized and separated off analytically and politically from the constitution of class, race, ethnicity, and other axes of power relations that both constitute "identity" and make the singular notion of identity a misnomer.[4]

My suggestion is that the presumed universality and unity of the subject of feminism is effectively undermined by the constraints of the representational discourse in which it functions. Indeed, the premature insistence on a stable subject of feminism, understood as a seamless category of women, inevitably generates multiple refusals to accept the category. These domains of exclusion reveal the coercive and regulatory consequences of that construction, even when the construction has been elaborated for emancipatory purposes. Indeed, the fragmentation within feminism and the paradoxical opposition to feminism from "women" whom feminism claims to represent suggest the necessary limits of identity politics. The suggestion that feminism can seek wider representation for a subject that it itself constructs has the ironic consequence that feminist goals risk failure by refusing to take account of the constitutive powers of their own representational claims. This problem is not ameliorated through an appeal to the category of women for merely "strategic" purposes, for strategies always have meanings that exceed the purposes for which they are intended. In this case, exclusion itself might qualify as such an unintended yet consequential meaning. By conforming to a requirement of representational politics that feminism articulate a stable subject, feminism thus opens itself to charges of gross misrepresentation.

Obviously, the political task is not to refuse representational politics—as if we could. The juridical structures of language and politics constitute the contemporary field of power; hence, there is no position outside this field, but only a critical genealogy of its own legitimating practices. As such, the critical point of departure is *the historical present*, as Marx put it. And the task is to formulate within this constituted frame a critique of the categories of identity that contemporary juridical structures engender, naturalize, and immobilize.

Perhaps there is an opportunity at this juncture of cultural politics, a period that some would call "postfeminist," to reflect from within a feminist perspective on the injunction to construct a subject of feminism. Within feminist political practice, a radical rethinking of the ontological constructions of identity appears to be necessary in order to formulate a representational politics that might revive feminism on other grounds. On the other hand, it may be time to entertain a radical critique that seeks to free feminist theory from the necessity of having to construct a single or abiding ground which is invariably contested by those identity positions or anti-identity positions that it invariably excludes. Do the exclusionary practices that ground feminist theory in a notion of "women" as subject paradoxically undercut feminist goals to extend its claims to "representation"?[5]

Perhaps the problem is even more serious. Is the construction of the category of women as a coherent and stable subject an unwitting regulation and reification of gender relations? And is not such a reification precisely contrary to feminist aims? To what extent does the category of women achieve stability and coherence only in the context of the heterosexual matrix?[6] If a stable notion of gender no longer proves to be the foundational premise of feminist politics, perhaps a new sort of feminist politics is now desirable to contest the very reifications of gender and identity, one that will take the variable construction of identity as both a methodological and normative prerequisite, if not a political goal.

To trace the political operations that produce and conceal what qualifies as the juridical subject of feminism is precisely the task of *a feminist genealogy* of the category of women. In the course of this effort to question "women" as the subject of feminism, the unproblematic invocation of that category may prove to *preclude* the possibility of feminism as a representational politics. What sense does it make to extend representation to subjects who are constructed through the exclusion of those who fail to conform to unspoken normative requirements of the subject? What relations of domination and exclusion are inadvertently sustained when representation becomes the sole focus of politics? The identity of the feminist subject ought not to be the foundation of feminist politics, if the formation of the subject takes place within a field of power regularly buried through the assertion of that foundation. Perhaps, paradoxically, "representation" will be shown to make sense for feminism only when the subject of "women" is nowhere presumed.

II. The Compulsory Order of Sex/Gender/Desire

Although the unproblematic unity of "women" is often invoked to construct a solidarity of identity, a split is introduced in the feminist subject by the distinction between sex and gender. Originally intended to dispute the biology-is-destiny formulation, the distinction between sex and gender serves the argument that whatever biological intractability sex appears to have, gender is culturally constructed: hence, gender is neither the causal result of sex nor as seemingly fixed as sex. The unity of the subject is thus already potentially contested by the distinction that permits of gender as a multiple interpretation of sex. [7]

If gender is the cultural meanings that the sexed body assumes, then a gender cannot be said to follow from a sex in any one way. Taken to its logical limit, the sex/gender distinction suggests a radical discontinuity between sexed bodies and culturally constructed genders. Assuming for the moment the stability of binary sex, it does not follow that the construction of "men" will accrue exclusively to the bodies of males or that "women" will interpret only female bodies. Further, even if the sexes appear to be unproblematically binary in their morphology and constitution (which will become a question), there is no reason to assume that genders ought also to remain as two. [8] The presumption of a binary gender system implicitly retains the belief in a mimetic relation of gender to sex whereby gender mirrors sex or is otherwise restricted by it. When the constructed status of gender is theorized as radically independent of sex, gender itself becomes a free-floating artifice, with the consequence that *man* and *masculine* might just as easily signify a female body as a male one, and *woman* and *feminine* a male body as easily as a female one.

This radical splitting of the gendered subject poses yet another set of problems. Can we refer to a "given" sex or a "given" gender without first inquiring into how sex and/or gender is given, through what means? And what is "sex" anyway? Is it natural, anatomical, chromosomal, or hormonal, and how is a feminist critic to assess the scientific discourses which purport to establish such "facts" for us? [9] Does sex have a history? [10] Does each sex have a different history, or histories? Is there a history of how the duality of sex was established, a genealogy that might expose the binary options as a variable construction? Are the ostensibly natural facts of sex discursively produced by various scientific discourses in the service of other political and social interests? If the immutable character of sex is contested, perhaps this construct called "sex" is as culturally constructed as gender; indeed, perhaps it was always already gender, with the consequence that the distinction between sex and gender turns out to be no distinction at all.[11]

It would make no sense, then, to define gender as the cultural interpretation of sex, if sex itself is a gendered category. Gender ought not to be conceived merely as the cultural inscription of meaning on a pregiven sex (a juridical conception); gender must also designate the very apparatus of production whereby the sexes themselves are established. As a result, gender is not to culture as sex is to nature; gender is also the discursive/cultural means by which "sexed nature" or "a natural sex" is produced and established as "prediscursive," prior to culture, a politically neutral surface *on which* culture acts. This construction of "sex" as the radically unconstructed will concern us again in the discussion of Lévi-Strauss and structuralism in chapter 2. At this juncture it is already clear that one way the internal stability and binary frame for sex is effectively secured is by casting the duality of sex in a prediscursive domain. This production of sex as the prediscursive ought to be understood as the effect of the apparatus of cultural construction designated by *gender.* How, then, does gender need to be reformulated to encompass the power relations that produce the effect of a prediscursive sex and so conceal that very operation of discursive production?

III. Gender: The Circular Ruins of Contemporary Debate

Is there "a" gender which persons are said to *have,* or is it an essential attribute that a person is said to *be,* as implied in the question "What gender are you?" When feminist theorists claim that gender is the cultural interpretation of sex or that gender is culturally constructed, what is the manner or mechanism of this construction? If gender is constructed, could it be constructed differently, or does its constructedness imply some form of social determinism, foreclosing the possibility of agency and transformation? Does "construction" suggest that certain laws generate gender differences along universal axes of sexual difference? How and where does the construction of gender take place? What

11

sense can we make of a construction that cannot assume a human constructor prior to that construction? On some accounts, the notion that gender is constructed suggests a certain determinism of gender meanings inscribed on anatomically differentiated bodies, where those bodies are understood as passive recipients of an inexorable cultural law. When the relevant "culture" that "constructs" gender is understood in terms of such a law or set of laws, then it seems that gender is as determined and fixed as it was under the biology-is-destiny formulation. In such a case, not biology, but culture, becomes destiny.

On the other hand, Simone de Beauvoir suggests in *The Second Sex* that "one is not born a woman, but, rather, becomes one."[12] For Beauvoir, gender is "constructed," but implied in her formulation is an agent, a *cogito,* who somehow takes on or appropriates that gender and could, in principle, take on some other gender. Is gender as variable and volitional as Beauvoir's account seems to suggest? Can "construction" in such a case be reduced to a form of choice? Beauvoir is clear that one "becomes" a woman, but always under a cultural compulsion to become one. And clearly, the compulsion does not come from "sex." There is nothing in her account that guarantees that the "one" who becomes a woman is necessarily female. If "the body is a situation,"[13] as she claims, there is no recourse to a body that has not always already been interpreted by cultural meanings; hence, sex could not qualify as a prediscursive anatomical facticity. Indeed, sex, by definition, will be shown to have been gender all along.[14]

The controversy over the meaning of *construction* appears to founder on the conventional philosophical polarity between free will and determinism. As a consequence, one might reasonably suspect that some common linguistic restriction on thought both forms and limits the terms of the debate. Within those terms, "the body" appears as a passive medium on which cultural meanings are inscribed or as the instrument through which an appropriative and interpretive will determines a cultural meaning for itself. In either case, the body is figured as a mere *instrument* or *medium* for which a set of cultural meanings are only externally related. But "the body" is itself a construction, as are the myriad "bodies" that constitute the domain of gendered subjects. Bodies cannot be said to have a signifiable existence prior to the mark of their gender; the question then emerges: To what extent does the body *come into being* in and through the mark(s) of gender? How do we reconceive the body no longer as a passive medium or instrument awaiting the enlivening capacity of a distinctly immaterial will?[15]

Whether gender or sex is fixed or free is a function of a discourse which, it will be suggested, seeks to set certain limits to analysis or to safeguard certain tenets of humanism as presuppositional to any analysis of gender. The locus of intractability, whether in "sex" or "gender" or in the very meaning of "construction," provides a clue to what cultural possibilities can and cannot become mobilized through any further analysis. The limits of the discursive analysis of gender presuppose and preempt the possibilities of imaginable and realizable gender configurations within culture. This is not to say that any and all gendered possibilities are open, but that the boundaries of analysis suggest the limits of a discursively conditioned experience. These limits are always set within the terms of a hegemonic cultural discourse predicated on binary structures that appear as the language of universal rationality. Constraint is thus built into what that language constitutes as the imaginable domain of gender.

Although social scientists refer to gender as a "factor" or a "dimension" of an analysis, it is also applied to embodied persons as "a mark" of biological, linguistic, and/or cultural difference. In these latter cases, gender can be understood as a signification that an (already) sexually differentiated body assumes, but even then that signification exists only *in relation* to another, opposing signification. Some feminist theorists claim that gender is "a relation," indeed, a set of relations, and not an individual attribute. Others, following Beauvoir, would argue that only the feminine gender is marked, that the universal person and the masculine gender are conflated, thereby defining women in terms of

13

their sex and extolling men as the bearers of a body-transcendent universal personhood.

In a move that complicates the discussion further, Luce Irigaray argues that women constitute a paradox, if not a contradiction, within the discourse of identity itself. Women are the "sex" which is not "one." Within a language pervasively masculinist, a phallogocentric language, women constitute the *unrepresentable*. In other words, women represent the sex that cannot be thought, a linguistic absence and opacity. Within a language that rests on univocal signification, the female sex constitutes the unconstrainable and undesignatable. In this sense, women are the sex which is not "one," but multiple.[16] In opposition to Beauvoir, for whom women are designated as the Other, Irigaray argues that both the subject and the Other are masculine mainstays of a closed phallogocentric signifying economy that achieves its totalizing goal through the exclusion of the feminine altogether. For Beauvoir, women are the negative of men, the lack against which masculine identity differentiates itself; for Irigaray, that particular dialectic constitutes a system that excludes an entirely different economy of signification. Women are not only represented falsely within the Sartrian frame of signifying-subject and signified-Other, but the falsity of the signification points out the entire structure of representation as inadequate. The sex which is not one, then, provides a point of departure for a criticism of hegemonic Western representation and of the metaphysics of substance that structures the very notion of the subject.

What is the metaphysics of substance, and how does it inform thinking about the categories of sex? In the first instance, humanist conceptions of the subject tend to assume a substantive person who is the bearer of various essential and nonessential attributes. A humanist feminist position might understand gender as an *attribute* of a person who is characterized essentially as a pregendered substance or "core," called the person, denoting a universal capacity for reason, moral deliberation, or language. The universal conception of the person, however, is displaced as a point of departure for a social theory of gender by those historical and anthropological positions that understand gender as a relation among socially constituted subjects in specifiable contexts. This relational or contextual point of view suggests that what the person "is," and, indeed, what gender "is," is always relative to the constructed relations in which it is determined.[17] As a shifting and contextual phenomenon, gender does not denote a substantive being, but a relative point of convergence among culturally and historically specific sets of relations.

Irigaray would maintain, however, that the feminine "sex" is a point of linguistic *absence,* the impossibility of a grammatically denoted substance, and, hence, the point of view that exposes that substance as an abiding and foundational illusion of a masculinist discourse. This absence is not marked as such within the masculine signifying economy—a contention that reverses Beauvoir's argument (and Wittig's) that the female sex is marked, while the male sex is not. For Irigaray, the female sex is not a "lack" or an "Other" that immanently and negatively defines the subject in its masculinity. On the contrary, the female sex eludes the very requirements of representation, for she is neither "Other" nor the "lack," those categories remaining relative to the Sartrian subject, immanent to that phallogocentric scheme. Hence, for Irigaray, the feminine could never be the *mark of a subject,* as Beauvoir would suggest. Further, the feminine could not be theorized in terms of a determinate *relation* between the masculine and the feminine within any given discourse, for discourse is not a relevant notion here. Even in their variety, discourses constitute so many modalities of phallogocentric language. The female sex is thus also *the subject* that is not one. The relation between masculine and feminine cannot be represented in a signifying economy in which the masculine constitutes the closed circle of signifier and signified. Paradoxically enough, Beauvoir prefigured this impossibility in *The Second Sex* when she argued that men could not settle the question of women because they would then be acting as both judge and party to the case.[18]

The distinctions among the above positions are far from discrete;

each of them can be understood to problematize the locality and meaning of both the "subject" and "gender" within the context of socially instituted gender asymmetry. The interpretive possibilities of gender are in no sense exhausted by the alternatives suggested above. The problematic circularity of a feminist inquiry into gender is underscored by the presence of positions which, on the one hand, presume that gender is a secondary characteristic of persons and those which, on the other hand, argue that the very notion of the person, positioned within language as a "subject," is a masculinist construction and prerogative which effectively excludes the structural and semantic possibility of a feminine gender. The consequence of such sharp disagreements about the meaning of gender (indeed, whether *gender* is the term to be argued about at all, or whether the discursive construction of *sex* is, indeed, more fundamental, or perhaps *women* or *woman* and / or *men* and *man*) establishes the need for a radical rethinking of the categories of identity within the context of relations of radical gender asymmetry.

For Beauvoir, the "subject" within the existential analytic of misogyny is always already masculine, conflated with the universal, differentiating itself from a feminine "Other" outside the universalizing norms of personhood, hopelessly "particular," embodied, condemned to immanence. Although Beauvoir is often understood to be calling for the right of women, in effect, to become existential subjects and, hence, for inclusion within the terms of an abstract universality, her position also implies a fundamental critique of the very disembodiment of the abstract masculine epistemological subject.[19] That subject is abstract to the extent that it disavows its socially marked embodiment and, further, projects that disavowed and disparaged embodiment on to the feminine sphere, effectively renaming the body as female. This association of the body with the female works along magical relations of reciprocity whereby the female sex becomes restricted to its body, and the male body, fully disavowed, becomes, paradoxically, the incorporeal instrument of an ostensibly radical freedom. Beauvoir's analysis implicitly poses the question: Through what act of

negation and disavowal does the masculine pose as a disembodied universality and the feminine get constructed as a disavowed corporeality?
The dialectic of master-slave, here fully reformulated within the non-
reciprocal terms of gender asymmetry, prefigures what Irigaray will
later describe as the masculine signifying economy that includes both
the existential subject and its Other.

Beauvoir proposes that the female body ought to be the situation
and instrumentality of women's freedom, not a defining and limiting
essence.[20] The theory of embodiment informing Beauvoir's analysis is
clearly limited by the uncritical reproduction of the Cartesian distinction between freedom and the body. Despite my own previous efforts
to argue the contrary, it appears that Beauvoir maintains the mind/
body dualism, even as she proposes a synthesis of those terms.[21] The
preservation of that very distinction can be read as symptomatic of the
very phallogocentrism that Beauvoir underestimates. In the philosophical tradition that begins with Plato and continues through Descartes,
Husserl, and Sartre, the ontological distinction between soul (consciousness, mind) and body invariably supports relations of political
and psychic subordination and hierarchy. The mind not only subjugates
the body, but occasionally entertains the fantasy of fleeing its embodiment altogether. The cultural associations of mind with masculinity
and body with femininity are well documented within the field of philosophy and feminism.[22] As a result, any uncritical reproduction of the
mind/body distinction ought to be rethought for the implicit gender
hierarchy that the distinction has conventionally produced, maintained, and rationalized.

The discursive construction of "the body" and its separation from
"freedom" in Beauvoir fails to mark along the axis of gender the very
mind-body distinction that is supposed to illuminate the persistence of
gender asymmetry. Officially, Beauvoir contends that the female body
is marked within masculinist discourse, whereby the masculine body,
in its conflation with the universal, remains unmarked. Irigaray clearly suggests that both marker and marked are maintained within a

17

masculinist mode of signification in which the female body is "marked off," as it were, from the domain of the signifiable. In post-Hegelian terms, she is "cancelled," but not preserved. On Irigaray's reading, Beauvoir's claim that woman "is sex" is reversed to mean that she is not the sex she is designated to be, but, rather, the masculine sex *encore* (and *en corps*) parading in the mode of otherness. For Irigaray, that phallogo-centric mode of signifying the female sex perpetually reproduces phan-tasms of its own self-amplifying desire. Instead of a self-limiting linguistic gesture that grants alterity or difference to women, phallogo-centrism offers a name to eclipse the feminine and take its place.

iv. Theorizing the Binary, the Unitary, and Beyond

Beauvoir and Irigaray clearly differ over the fundamental structures by which gender asymmetry is reproduced; Beauvoir turns to the failed reciprocity of an asymmetrical dialectic, while Irigaray suggests that the dialectic itself is the monologic elaboration of a masculinist signify-ing economy. Although Irigaray clearly broadens the scope of feminist critique by exposing the epistemological, ontological, and logical structures of a masculinist signifying economy, the power of her analy-sis is undercut precisely by its globalizing reach. Is it possible to identi-fy a monolithic as well as a monologic masculinist economy that traverses the array of cultural and historical contexts in which sexual difference takes place? Is the failure to acknowledge the specific cul-tural operations of gender oppression itself a kind of epistemological imperialism, one which is not ameliorated by the simple elaboration of cultural differences as "examples" of the selfsame phallogocentrism? The effort to *include* "Other" cultures as variegated amplifications of a global phallogocentrism constitutes an appropriative act that risks a repetition of the self-aggrandizing gesture of phallogocentrism, colo-nizing under the sign of the same those differences that might other-wise call that totalizing concept into question.[23]

Feminist critique ought to explore the totalizing claims of a mas-culinist signifying economy, but also remain self-critical with respect to the totalizing gestures of feminism. The effort to identify the enemy as singular in form is a reverse-discourse that uncritically mimics the strategy of the oppressor instead of offering a different set of terms. That the tactic can operate in feminist and antifeminist contexts alike suggests that the colonizing gesture is not primarily or irreducibly masculinist. It can operate to effect other relations of racial, class, and heterosexist subordination, to name but a few. And clearly, listing the varieties of oppression, as I began to do, assumes their discrete, sequential coexistence along a horizontal axis that does not describe their convergences within the social field. A vertical model is similarly insufficient; oppressions cannot be summarily ranked, causally related, distributed among planes of "originality" and "derivativeness."[24] Indeed, the field of power structured in part by the imperializing gesture of dialectical appropriation exceeds and encompasses the axis of sexual difference, offering a mapping of intersecting differentials which cannot be summarily hierarchized either within the terms of phallogocentrism or any other candidate for the position of "primary condition of oppression." Rather than an exclusive tactic of masculinist signifying economies, dialectical appropriation and suppression of the Other is one tactic among many, deployed centrally but not exclusively in the service of expanding and rationalizing the masculinist domain.

The contemporary feminist debates over essentialism raise the question of the universality of female identity and masculinist oppression in other ways. Universalistic claims are based on a common or shared epistemological standpoint, understood as the articulated consciousness or shared structures of oppression or in the ostensibly transcultural structures of femininity, maternity, sexuality, and/or *écriture féminine*. The opening discussion in this chapter argued that this globalizing gesture has spawned a number of criticisms from women who claim that the category of "women" is normative and exclusionary and is invoked with the unmarked dimensions of class and racial privilege intact. In other words, the insistence upon the coherence and unity of the category of women has effectively refused the multiplicity of cultural, social, and political intersections in which the concrete array of "women" are constructed.

Some efforts have been made to formulate coalitional politics which do not assume in advance what the content of "women" will be. They propose instead a set of dialogic encounters by which variously positioned women articulate separate identities within the framework of an emergent coalition. Clearly, the value of coalitional politics is not to be underestimated, but the very form of coalition, of an emerging and unpredictable assemblage of positions, cannot be figured in advance. Despite the clearly democratizing impulse that motivates coalition building, the coalitional theorist can inadvertently reinsert herself as sovereign of the process by trying to assert an ideal form for coalitional structures *in advance,* one that will effectively guarantee unity as the outcome. Related efforts to determine what is and is not the true shape of a dialogue, what constitutes a subject-position, and, most importantly, when "unity" has been reached, can impede the self-shaping and self-limiting dynamics of coalition.

The insistence in advance on coalitional "unity" as a goal assumes that solidarity, whatever its price, is a prerequisite for political action. But what sort of politics demands that kind of advance purchase on unity? Perhaps a coalition needs to acknowledge its contradictions and take action with those contradictions intact. Perhaps also part of what dialogic understanding entails is the acceptance of divergence, break-age, splinter, and fragmentation as part of the often tortuous process of democratization. The very notion of "dialogue" is culturally specific and historically bound, and while one speaker may feel secure that a conversation is happening, another may be sure it is not. The power relations that condition and limit dialogic possibilities need first to be interrogated. Otherwise, the model of dialogue risks relapsing into a liberal model that assumes that speaking agents occupy equal positions of power and speak with the same presuppositions about what constitutes "agreement" and "unity" and, indeed, that those are the goals to be sought. It would be wrong to assume in advance that there is a cate-

gory of "women" that simply needs to be filled in with various components of race, class, age, ethnicity, and sexuality in order to become
complete. The assumption of its essential incompleteness permits that
category to serve as a permanently available site of contested meanings. The definitional incompleteness of the category might then serve
as a normative ideal relieved of coercive force.

Is "unity" necessary for effective political action? Is the premature
insistence on the goal of unity precisely the cause of an ever more bit-
ter fragmentation among the ranks? Certain forms of acknowledged
fragmentation might facilitate coalitional action precisely because the
"unity" of the category of women is neither presupposed nor desired.
Does "unity" set up an exclusionary norm of solidarity at the level of
identity that rules out the possibility of a set of actions which disrupt
the very borders of identity concepts, or which seek to accomplish
precisely that disruption as an explicit political aim? Without the presupposition or goal of "unity," which is, in either case, always instituted
at a conceptual level, provisional unities might emerge in the context
of concrete actions that have purposes other than the articulation of
identity. Without the compulsory expectation that feminist actions
must be instituted from some stable, unified, and agreed-upon identity, those actions might well get a quicker start and seem more conge-
nial to a number of "women" for whom the meaning of the category is
permanently moot.

This antifoundationalist approach to coalitional politics assumes
neither that "identity" is a premise nor that the shape or meaning of a
coalitional assemblage can be known prior to its achievement. Because
the articulation of an identity within available cultural terms instates a
definition that forecloses in advance the emergence of new identity
concepts in and through politically engaged actions, the foundationalist
tactic cannot take the transformation or expansion of existing identity
concepts as a normative goal. Moreover, when agreed-upon identities
or agreed-upon dialogic structures, through which already established identities are communicated, no longer constitute the theme or

subject of politics, then identities can come into being and dissolve depending on the concrete practices that constitute them. Certain political practices institute identities on a contingent basis in order to accomplish whatever aims are in view. Coalitional politics requires neither an expanded category of "women" nor an internally multiplicitous self that offers its complexity at once.

Gender is a complexity whose totality is permanently deferred, never fully what it is at any given juncture in time. An open coalition, then, will affirm identities that are alternately instituted and relinquished according to the purposes at hand; it will be an open assemblage that permits of multiple convergences and divergences without obedience to a normative telos of definitional closure.

v. Identity, Sex, and the Metaphysics of Substance

What can be meant by "identity," then, and what grounds the presumption that identities are self-identical, persisting through time as the same, unified and internally coherent? More importantly, how do these assumptions inform the discourses on "gender identity"? It would be wrong to think that the discussion of "identity" ought to proceed prior to a discussion of gender identity for the simple reason that "persons" only become intelligible through becoming gendered in conformity with recognizable standards of gender intelligibility. Sociological discussions have conventionally sought to understand the notion of the person in terms of an agency that claims ontological priority to the various roles and functions through which it assumes social visibility and meaning. Within philosophical discourse itself, the notion of "the person" has received analytic elaboration on the assumption that whatever social context the person is "in" remains somehow externally related to the definitional structure of personhood, be that consciousness, the capacity for language, or moral deliberation. Although that literature is not examined here, one premise of such inquiries is the focus of critical exploration and inversion. Whereas the question of what constitutes "personal identity" within philosophical accounts

22

almost always centers on the question of what internal feature of the person establishes the continuity or self-identity of the person through time, the question here will be: To what extent do *regulatory practices* of gender formation and division constitute identity, the internal coherence of the subject, indeed, the self-identical status of the person? To what extent is "identity" a normative ideal rather than a descriptive feature of experience? And how do the regulatory practices that govern gender also govern culturally intelligible notions of identity? In other words, the "coherence" and "continuity" of "the person" are not logical or analytic features of personhood, but, rather, socially instituted and maintained norms of intelligibility. Inasmuch as "identity" is assured through the stabilizing concepts of sex, gender, and sexuality, the very notion of "the person" is called into question by the cultural emergence of those "incoherent" or "discontinuous" gendered beings who appear to be persons but who fail to conform to the gendered norms of cultural intelligibility by which persons are defined.

"Intelligible" genders are those which in some sense institute and maintain relations of coherence and continuity among sex, gender, sexual practice, and desire. In other words, the spectres of discontinuity and incoherence, themselves thinkable only in relation to existing norms of continuity and coherence, are constantly prohibited and produced by the very laws that seek to establish causal or expressive lines of connection among biological sex, culturally constituted genders, and the "expression" or "effect" of both in the manifestation of sexual desire through sexual practice.

The notion that there might be a "truth" of sex, as Foucault ironically terms it, is produced precisely through the regulatory practices that generate coherent identities through the matrix of coherent gender norms. The heterosexualization of desire requires and institutes the production of discrete and asymmetrical oppositions between "feminine" and "masculine," where these are understood as expressive attributes of "male" and "female." The cultural matrix through which gender identity has become intelligible requires that certain kinds of

"identities" cannot "exist"—that is, those in which gender does not follow from sex and those in which the practices of desire do not "follow"
from either sex or gender. "Follow" in this context is a political relation
of entailment instituted by the cultural laws that establish and regulate
the shape and meaning of sexuality. Indeed, precisely because certain
kinds of "gender identities" fail to conform to those norms of cultural
intelligibility, they appear only as developmental failures or logical
impossibilities from within that domain. Their persistence and proliferation, however, provide critical opportunities to expose the limits and
regulatory aims of that domain of intelligibility and, hence, to open up
within the very terms of that matrix of intelligibility rival and subversive matrices of gender disorder.

Before such disordering practices are considered, however, it seems
crucial to understand the "matrix of intelligibility." Is it singular? Of
what is it composed? What is the peculiar alliance presumed to exist
between a system of compulsory heterosexuality and the discursive categories that establish the identity concepts of sex? If "identity" is an *effect*
of discursive practices, to what extent is gender identity, construed as a
relationship among sex, gender, sexual practice, and desire, the effect of
a regulatory practice that can be identified as compulsory heterosexuality? Would that explanation return us to yet another totalizing frame in
which compulsory heterosexuality merely takes the place of phallogocentrism as the monolithic cause of gender oppression?

Within the spectrum of French feminist and poststructuralist theory, very different regimes of power are understood to produce the
identity concepts of sex. Consider the divergence between those positions, such as Irigaray's, that claim there is only one sex, the masculine,
that elaborates itself in and through the production of the "Other," and
those positions, Foucault's, for instance, that assume that the category
of sex, whether masculine or feminine, is a production of a diffuse regulatory economy of sexuality. Consider also Wittig's argument that the
category of sex is, under the conditions of compulsory heterosexuality,
always feminine (the masculine remaining unmarked and, hence, syn-

onymous with the "universal"). Wittig concurs, however paradoxically, with Foucault in claiming that the category of sex would itself disappear and, indeed, *dissipate* through the disruption and displacement of heterosexual hegemony.

The various explanatory models offered here suggest the very different ways in which the category of sex is understood depending on how the field of power is articulated. Is it possible to maintain the complexity of these fields of power and think through their productive capacities together? On the one hand, Irigaray's theory of sexual difference suggests that women can never be understood on the model of a "subject" within the conventional representational systems of Western culture precisely because they constitute the fetish of representation and, hence, the unrepresentable as such. Women can never "be," according to this ontology of substances, precisely because they are the relation of difference, the excluded, by which that domain marks itself off. Women are also a "difference" that cannot be understood as the simple negation or "Other" of the always-already-masculine subject. As discussed earlier, they are neither the subject nor its Other, but a difference from the economy of binary opposition, itself a ruse for a monologic elaboration of the masculine.

Central to each of these views, however, is the notion that sex appears within hegemonic language as a *substance,* as, metaphysically speaking, a self-identical being. This appearance is achieved through a performative twist of language and/or discourse that conceals the fact that "being" a sex or a gender is fundamentally impossible. For Irigaray, grammar can never be a true index of gender relations precisely because it supports the substantial model of gender as a binary relation between two positive and representable terms.[25] In Irigaray's view, the substantive grammar of gender, which assumes men and women as well as their attributes of masculine and feminine, is an example of a binary that effectively masks the univocal and hegemonic discourse of the masculine, phallogocentrism, silencing the feminine as a site of subversive multiplicity. For Foucault, the substantive grammar of sex imposes an

25

artificial binary relation between the sexes, as well as an artificial internal coherence within each term of that binary. The binary regulation of sexuality suppresses the subversive multiplicity of a sexuality that disrupts heterosexual, reproductive, and medicojuridical hegemonies.

For Wittig, the binary restriction on sex serves the reproductive aims of a system of compulsory heterosexuality; occasionally, she claims that the overthrow of compulsory heterosexuality will inaugurate a true humanism of "the person" freed from the shackles of sex. In other contexts, she suggests that the profusion and diffusion of a nonphallocentric erotic economy will dispel the illusions of sex, gender, and identity. At yet other textual moments it seems that "the lesbian" emerges as a third gender that promises to transcend the binary restriction on sex imposed by the system of compulsory heterosexuality. In her defense of the "cognitive subject," Wittig appears to have no metaphysical quarrel with hegemonic modes of signification or representation; indeed, the subject, with its attribute of self-determination, appears to be the rehabilitation of the agent of existential choice under the name of the lesbian: "the advent of individual subjects demands first destroying the categories of sex . . . the lesbian is the only concept I know of which is beyond the categories of sex."[26] She does not criticize "the subject" as invariably masculine according to the rules of an inevitably patriarchal Symbolic, but proposes in its place the equivalent of a lesbian subject as language-user.[27]

The identification of women with "sex," for Beauvoir as for Wittig, is a conflation of the category of women with the ostensibly sexualized features of their bodies and, hence, a refusal to grant freedom and autonomy to women as it is purportedly enjoyed by men. Thus, the destruction of the category of sex would be the destruction of an *attribute,* sex, that has, through a misogynist gesture of synecdoche, come to take the place of the person, the self-determining *cogito.* In other words, only men are "persons," and there is no gender but the feminine:

26

Gender is the linguistic index of the political opposition between the sexes. Gender is used here in the singular because indeed there are not two genders. There is only one: the feminine, the "masculine" not being a gender. For the masculine is not the masculine, but the general.[28]

Hence, Wittig calls for the destruction of "sex" so that women can assume the status of a universal subject. On the way toward that destruction, "women" must assume both a particular and a universal point of view.[29] As a subject who can realize concrete universality through freedom, Wittig's lesbian confirms rather than contests the normative promise of humanist ideals premised on the metaphysics of substance. In this respect, Wittig is distinguished from Irigaray, not only in terms of the now familiar oppositions between essentialism and materialism,[30] but in terms of the adherence to a metaphysics of substance that confirms the normative model of humanism as the framework for feminism. Where it seems that Wittig has subscribed to a radical project of lesbian emancipation and enforced a distinction between "lesbian" and "woman," she does this through the defense of the pregendered "person," characterized as freedom. This move not only confirms the presocial status of human freedom, but subscribes to that metaphysics of substance that is responsible for the production and naturalization of the category of sex itself.

The *metaphysics of substance* is a phrase that is associated with Nietzsche within the contemporary criticism of philosophical discourse. In a commentary on Nietzsche, Michel Haar argues that a number of philosophical ontologies have been trapped within certain illusions of "Being" and "Substance" that are fostered by the belief that the grammatical formulation of subject and predicate reflects the prior ontological reality of substance and attribute. These constructs, argues Haar, constitute the artificial philosophical means by which simplicity, order, and identity are effectively instituted. In no sense, however, do they reveal or represent some true order of things. For our purposes, this Nietzschean criticism becomes instructive when it is applied to the psychological categories that govern much popular and theoretical thinking about gender identity. According to Haar, the critique of the metaphysics of substance implies a critique of the very notion of the psychological person as a substantive thing:

> The destruction of logic by means of its genealogy brings with it as well the ruin of the psychological categories founded upon this logic. All psychological categories (the ego, the individual, the person) derive from the illusion of substantial identity. But this illusion goes back basically to a superstition that deceives not only common sense but also philosophers—namely, the belief in language and, more precisely, in the truth of grammatical categories. It was grammar (the structure of subject and predicate) that inspired Descartes' certainty that "I" is the subject of "think," whereas it is rather the thoughts that come to "me": at bottom, faith in grammar simply conveys the will to be the "cause" of one's thoughts. The subject, the self, the individual, are just so many false concepts, since they transform into substances fictitious unities having at the start only a linguistic reality.[31]

Wittig provides an alternative critique by showing that persons cannot be signified within language without the mark of gender. She provides a political analysis of the grammar of gender in French. According to Wittig, gender not only designates persons, "qualifies" them, as it were, but constitutes a conceptual episteme by which binary gender is universalized. Although French gives gender to all sorts of nouns other than persons, Wittig argues that her analysis has consequences for English as well. At the outset of "The Mark of Gender" (1984), she writes:

> The mark of gender, according to grammarians, concerns substantives. They talk about it in terms of function. If they question its meaning, they may joke about it, calling gender a "fictive sex." . . . as

28

far as the categories of the person are concerned, both [English and French] are bearers of gender to the same extent. Both indeed give way to a primitive ontological concept that enforces in language a division of beings into sexes. . . . As an ontological concept that deals with the nature of Being, along with a whole nebula of other primitive concepts belonging to the same line of thought, gender seems to belong primarily to philosophy.[32]

For gender to "belong to philosophy" is, for Wittig, to belong to "that body of self-evident concepts without which philosophers believe they cannot develop a line of reasoning and which for them go without saying, for they exist prior to any thought, any social order, in nature."[33] Wittig's view is corroborated by that popular discourse on gender identity that uncritically employs the inflectional attribution of "being" to genders and to "sexualities." The unproblematic claim to "be" a woman and "be" heterosexual would be symptomatic of that metaphysics of gender substances. In the case of both "men" and "women," this claim tends to subordinate the notion of gender under that of identity and to lead to the conclusion that a person *is* a gender and *is* one in virtue of his or her sex, psychic sense of self, and various expressions of that psychic self, the most salient being that of sexual desire. In such a prefeminist context, gender, naively (rather than critically) confused with sex, serves as a unifying principle of the embodied self and maintains that unity over and against an "opposite sex" whose structure is presumed to maintain a parallel but oppositional internal coherence among sex, gender, and desire. The articulation "I feel like a woman" by a female or "I feel like a man" by a male presupposes that in neither case is the claim meaninglessly redundant. Although it might appear unproblematic *to be* a given anatomy (although we shall later consider the way in which that project is also fraught with difficulty), the experience of a gendered psychic disposition or cultural identity is considered an achievement. Thus, "I feel like a woman" is true to the extent that Aretha Franklin's invocation of the defining Other is assumed: "You make me feel like a natural woman."[34] This achievement requires a differentiation from the opposite gender. Hence, one is one's gender to the extent that one is not the other gender, a formulation that presupposes and enforces the restriction of gender within that binary pair.

Gender can denote a *unity* of experience, of sex, gender, and desire, only when sex can be understood in some sense to necessitate gender—where gender is a psychic and/or cultural designation of the self—and desire—where desire is heterosexual and therefore differentiates itself through an oppositional relation to that other gender it desires. The internal coherence or unity of either gender, man or woman, thereby requires both a stable and oppositional heterosexuality. That institutional heterosexuality both requires and produces the univocity of each of the gendered terms that constitute the limit of gendered possibilities within an oppositional, binary gender system. This conception of gender presupposes not only a causal relation among sex, gender, and desire, but suggests as well that desire reflects or expresses gender and that gender reflects or expresses desire. The metaphysical unity of the three is assumed to be truly known and expressed in a differentiating desire for an oppositional gender—that is, in a form of oppositional heterosexuality. Whether as a naturalistic paradigm which establishes a causal continuity among sex, gender, and desire, or as an authentic-expressive paradigm in which some true self is said to be revealed simultaneously or successively in sex, gender, and desire, here "the old dream of symmetry," as Irigaray has called it, is presupposed, reified, and rationalized.

This rough sketch of gender gives us a clue to understanding the political reasons for the substantializing view of gender. The institution of a compulsory and naturalized heterosexuality requires and regulates gender as a binary relation in which the masculine term is differentiated from a feminine term, and this differentiation is accomplished through the practices of heterosexual desire. The act of differentiating the two oppositional moments of the binary results in a consolidation of each term, the respective internal coherence of sex, gender, and desire.

The strategic displacement of that binary relation and the metaphysics of substance on which it relies presuppose that the categories of female and male, woman and man, are similarly produced within the binary frame. Foucault implicitly subscribes to such an explanation. In the closing chapter of the first volume of *The History of Sexuality* and in his brief but significant introduction to *Herculine Barbin, Being the Recently Discovered Journals of a Nineteenth-Century Hermaphrodite,*[35] Foucault suggests that the category of sex, prior to any categorization of sexual difference, is itself constructed through a historically specific mode of *sexuality*. The tactical production of the discrete and binary categorization of sex conceals the strategic aims of that very apparatus of production by postulating "sex" as "a cause" of sexual experience, behavior, and desire. Foucault's genealogical inquiry exposes this ostensible "cause" as "an effect," the production of a given regime of sexuality that seeks to regulate sexual experience by instating the discrete categories of sex as foundational and causal functions within any discursive account of sexuality.

Foucault's introduction to the journals of the hermaphrodite, Herculine Barbin, suggests that the genealogical critique of these reified categories of sex is the inadvertent consequence of sexual practices that cannot be accounted for within the medicolegal discourse of a naturalized heterosexuality. Herculine is not an "identity," but the sexual impossibility of an identity. Although male and female anatomical elements are jointly distributed in and on this body, that is not the true source of scandal. The linguistic conventions that produce intelligible gendered selves find their limit in Herculine precisely because she/he occasions a convergence and disorganization of the rules that govern sex/gender/desire. Herculine deploys and redistributes the terms of a binary system, but that very redistribution disrupts and proliferates those terms outside the binary itself. According to Foucault, Herculine is not categorizable within the gender binary as it stands; the

31

disconcerting convergence of heterosexuality and homosexuality in her/his person are only occasioned, but never caused, by his/her anatomical discontinuity. Foucault's appropriation of Herculine is suspect,[36] but his analysis implies the interesting belief that sexual heterogeneity (paradoxically foreclosed by a naturalized "hetero"-sexuality) implies a critique of the metaphysics of substance as it informs the identitarian categories of sex. Foucault imagines Herculine's experience as "a world of pleasures in which grins hang about without the cat."[37] Smiles, happinesses, pleasures, and desires are figured here as qualities without an abiding substance to which they are said to adhere. As free-floating attributes, they suggest the possibility of a gendered experience that cannot be grasped through the substantializing and hierarchizing grammar of nouns (*res extensa*) and adjectives (attributes, essential and accidental). Through his cursory reading of Herculine, Foucault proposes an ontology of accidental attributes that exposes the postulation of identity as a culturally restricted principle of order and hierarchy, a regulatory fiction.

If it is possible to speak of a "man" with a masculine attribute and to understand that attribute as a happy but accidental feature of that man, then it is also possible to speak of a "man" with a feminine attribute, whatever that is, but still to maintain the integrity of the gender. But once we dispense with the priority of "man" and "woman" as abiding substances, then it is no longer possible to subordinate dissonant gendered features as so many secondary and accidental characteristics of a gender ontology that is fundamentally intact. If the notion of an abiding substance is a fictive construction produced through the compulsory ordering of attributes into coherent gender sequences, then it seems that gender as substance, the viability of *man* and *woman* as nouns, is called into question by the dissonant play of attributes that fail to conform to sequential or causal models of intelligibility.

The appearance of an abiding substance or gendered self, what the psychiatrist Robert Stoller refers to as a "gender core,"[38] is thus produced by the regulation of attributes along culturally established lines

32

of coherence. As a result, the exposure of this fictive production is conditioned by the deregulated play of attributes that resist assimilation into the ready made framework of primary nouns and subordinate adjectives. It is of course always possible to argue that dissonant adjectives work retroactively to redefine the substantive identities they are said to modify and, hence, to expand the substantive categories of gender to include possibilities that they previously excluded. But if these substances are nothing other than the coherences contingently created through the regulation of attributes, it would seem that the ontology of substances itself is not only an artificial effect, but essentially superfluous.

In this sense, *gender* is not a noun, but neither is it a set of free-floating attributes, for we have seen that the substantive effect of gender is performatively produced and compelled by the regulatory practices of gender coherence. Hence, within the inherited discourse of the metaphysics of substance, gender proves to be performative—that is, constituting the identity it is purported to be. In this sense, gender is always a doing, though not a doing by a subject who might be said to preexist the deed. The challenge for rethinking gender categories outside of the metaphysics of substance will have to consider the relevance of Nietzsche's claim in *On the Genealogy of Morals* that "there is no 'being' behind doing, effecting, becoming; 'the doer' is merely a fiction added to the deed—the deed is everything."[39] In an application that Nietzsche himself would not have anticipated or condoned, we might state as a corollary: There is no gender identity behind the expressions of gender; that identity is performatively constituted by the very "expressions" that are said to be its results.

VI. LANGUAGE, POWER, AND THE STRATEGIES OF DISPLACEMENT

A great deal of feminist theory and literature has nevertheless assumed that there is a "doer" behind the deed. Without an agent, it is argued, there can be no agency and hence no potential to initiate a transformation of relations of domination within society. Wittig's radical feminist theory occupies an ambiguous position within the continuum of theories on the question of the subject. On the one hand, Wittig appears to dispute the metaphysics of substance, but on the other hand, she retains the human subject, the individual, as the metaphysical locus of agency. While Wittig's humanism clearly presupposes that there is a doer behind the deed, her theory nevertheless delineates the performative construction of gender within the material practices of culture, disputing the temporality of those explanations that would confuse "cause" with "result." In a phrase that suggests the intertextual space that links Wittig with Foucault (and reveals the traces of the Marxist notion of reification in both of their theories), she writes:

> A materialist feminist approach shows that what we take for the cause or origin of oppression is in fact only the *mark* imposed by the oppressor; the "myth of woman," plus its material effects and manifestations in the appropriated consciousness and bodies of women. Thus, this mark does not preexist oppression ... sex is taken as an "immediate given," a "sensible given," "physical features," belonging to a natural order. But what we believe to be a physical and direct perception is only a sophisticated and mythic construction, an "imaginary formation."[40]

Because this production of "nature" operates in accord with the dictates of compulsory heterosexuality, the emergence of homosexual desire, in her view, transcends the categories of sex: "If desire could liberate itself, it would have nothing to do with the preliminary marking by sexes."[41]

Wittig refers to "sex" as a mark that is somehow applied by an institutionalized heterosexuality, a mark that can be erased or obfuscated through practices that effectively contest that institution. Her view, of course, differs radically from Irigaray's. The latter would understand the "mark" of gender to be part of the hegemonic signifying economy of the masculine that operates through the self-elaborating

34

mechanisms of specularization that have virtually determined the field of ontology within the Western philosophical tradition. For Wittig, language is an instrument or tool that is in no way misogynist in its structures, but only in its applications.[42] For Irigaray, the possibility of another language or signifying economy is the only chance at escaping the "mark" of gender which, for the feminine, is nothing but the phallogocentric erasure of the female sex. Whereas Irigaray seeks to expose the ostensible "binary" relation between the sexes as a masculinist ruse that excludes the feminine altogether, Wittig argues that positions like Irigaray's reconsolidate the binary between masculine and feminine and recirculate a mythic notion of the feminine. Clearly drawing on Beauvoir's critique of the myth of the feminine in *The Second Sex,* Wittig asserts, "there is no 'feminine writing.'"[43]

Wittig is clearly attuned to the power of language to subordinate and exclude women. As a "materialist," however, she considers language to be "another order of materiality,"[44] an institution that can be radically transformed. Language ranks among the concrete and contingent practices and institutions maintained by the choices of individuals and, hence, weakened by the collective actions of choosing individuals. The linguistic fiction of "sex," she argues, is a category produced and circulated by the system of compulsory heterosexuality in an effort to restrict the production of identities along the axis of heterosexual desire. In some of her work, both male and female homosexuality, as well as other positions independent of the heterosexual contract, provide the occasion either for the overthrow or the proliferation of the category of sex. In *The Lesbian Body* and elsewhere, however, Wittig appears to take issue with genitally organized sexuality *per se* and to call for an alternative economy of pleasures which would both contest the construction of female subjectivity marked by women's supposedly distinctive reproductive function.[45] Here the proliferation of pleasures outside the reproductive economy suggests both a specifically feminine form of erotic diffusion, understood as a counterstrategy to the reproductive construction of genitality. In a sense, *The Lesbian Body* can be understood, for Wittig, as an "inverted" reading of Freud's *Three Essays on the Theory of Sexuality,* in which he argues for the developmental superiority of genital sexuality over and against the less restricted and more diffuse infantile sexuality. Only the "invert," the medical classification invoked by Freud for "the homosexual," fails to "achieve" the genital norm. In waging a political critique against genitality, Wittig appears to deploy "inversion" as a critical reading practice, valorising precisely those features of an undeveloped sexuality designated by Freud and effectively inaugurating a "post-genital politics."[46] Indeed, the notion of development can be read only as normalization within the heterosexual matrix. And yet, is this the only reading of Freud possible? And to what extent is Wittig's practice of "inversion" committed to the very model of normalization that she seeks to dismantle? In other words, if the model of a more diffuse and antigenital sexuality serves as the singular, oppositional alternative to the hegemonic structure of sexuality, to what extent is that binary relation fated to reproduce itself endlessly? What possibility exists for the disruption of the oppositional binary itself?

Wittig's oppositional relationship to psychoanalysis produces the unexpected consequence that her theory presumes precisely that psychoanalytic theory of development, now fully "inverted," that she seeks to overcome. Polymorphous perversity, assumed to exist prior to the marking by sex, is valorised as the telos of human sexuality.[47] One possible feminist psychoanalytic response to Wittig might argue that she both undertheorizes and underestimates the meaning and function of *the language* in which "the mark of gender" occurs. She understands that marking practice as contingent, radically variable, and even dispensable. The status of a primary *prohibition* in Lacanian theory operates more forcefully and less contingently than the notion of a *regulatory practice* in Foucault or a materialist account of a system of heterosexist oppression in Wittig.

In Lacan, as in Irigaray's post-Lacanian reformulation of Freud, sexual difference is not a simple binary that retains the metaphysics of substance as its foundation. The masculine "subject" is a fictive con-

36

struction produced by the law that prohibits incest and forces an infinite displacement of a heterosexualizing desire. The feminine is never a
mark of the subject; the feminine could not be an "attribute" of a gender. Rather, the feminine is the signification of lack, signified by the
Symbolic, a set of differentiating linguistic rules that effectively create
sexual difference. The masculine linguistic position undergoes individuation and heterosexualization required by the founding prohibitions
of the Symbolic law, the law of the Father. The incest taboo that bars
the son from the mother and thereby instates the kinship relation
between them is a law enacted "in the name of the Father." Similarly,
the law that refuses the girl's desire for both her mother and father
requires that she take up the emblem of maternity and perpetuate the
rules of kinship. Both masculine and feminine positions are thus instituted through prohibitive laws that produce culturally intelligible genders, but only through the production of an unconscious sexuality that
reemerges in the domain of the imaginary.[48]

The feminist appropriation of sexual difference, whether written in
opposition to the phallogocentrism of Lacan (Irigaray) or as a critical
reelaboration of Lacan, attempts to theorize the feminine, not as an
expression of the metaphysics of substance, but as the unrepresentable
absence effected by (masculine) denial that grounds the signifying economy through exclusion. The feminine as the repudiated/excluded within that system constitutes the possibility of a critique and disruption of
that hegemonic conceptual scheme. The works of Jacqueline Rose[49] and
Jane Gallop[50] underscore in different ways the constructed status of
sexual difference, the inherent instability of that construction, and the
dual consequentiality of a prohibition that at once institutes a sexual
identity and provides for the exposure of that construction's tenuous
ground. Although Wittig and other materialist feminists within the
French context would argue that sexual difference is an unthinking
replication of a reified set of sexed polarities, these criticisms neglect
the critical dimension of the unconscious which, as a site of repressed
sexuality, reemerges within the discourse of the subject as the very

impossibility of its coherence. As Rose points out very clearly, the construction of a coherent sexual identity along the disjunctive axis of the feminine/masculine is bound to fail;[51] the disruptions of this coherence through the inadvertent reemergence of the repressed reveal not only that "identity" is constructed, but that the prohibition that constructs identity is inefficacious (the paternal law ought to be understood not as a deterministic divine will, but as a perpetual bumbler, preparing the ground for the insurrections against him).

The differences between the materialist and Lacanian (and post-Lacanian) positions emerge in a normative quarrel over whether there is a retrievable sexuality either "before" or "outside" the law in the mode of the unconscious or "after" the law as a postgenital sexuality. Paradoxically, the normative trope of polymorphous perversity is understood to characterize both views of alternative sexuality. There is no agreement, however, on the manner of delimiting that "law" or set of "laws." The psychoanalytic critique succeeds in giving an account of the construction of "the subject"—and perhaps also the illusion of substance—within the matrix of normative gender relations. In her existential-materialist mode, Wittig presumes the subject, the person, to have a presocial and pregendered integrity. On the other hand, "the paternal Law" in Lacan, as well as the monologic mastery of phallogocentrism in Irigaray, bear the mark of a monotheistic singularity that is perhaps less unitary and culturally universal than the guiding structuralist assumptions of the account presume.[52]

But the quarrel seems also to turn on the articulation of a temporal trope of a subversive sexuality that flourishes *prior* to the imposition of a law, *after* its overthrow, or during its reign as a constant challenge to its authority. Here it seems wise to reinvoke Foucault who, in claiming that sexuality and power are coextensive, implicitly refutes the postulation of a subversive or emancipatory sexuality which could be free of the law. We can press the argument further by pointing out that "the before" of the law and "the after" are discursively and performatively instituted modes of temporality that are invoked within the terms of a normative

framework which asserts that subversion, destabilization, or displacement requires a sexuality that somehow escapes the hegemonic prohibitions on sex. For Foucault, those prohibitions are invariably and
inadvertently productive in the sense that "the subject" who is supposed
to be founded and produced in and through those prohibitions does not
have access to a sexuality that is in some sense "outside," "before," or
"after" power itself. Power, rather than the law, encompasses both the
juridical (prohibitive and regulatory) and the productive (inadvertently
generative) functions of differential relations. Hence, the sexuality that
emerges within the matrix of power relations is not a simple replication
or copy of the law itself, a uniform repetition of a masculinist economy
of identity. The productions swerve from their original purposes and
inadvertently mobilize possibilities of "subjects" that do not merely
exceed the bounds of cultural intelligibility, but effectively expand the
boundaries of what is, in fact, culturally intelligible.

The feminist norm of a postgenital sexuality became the object of
significant criticism from feminist theorists of sexuality, some of whom
have sought a specifically feminist and/or lesbian appropriation of
Foucault. This utopian notion of a sexuality freed from heterosexual
constructs, a sexuality beyond "sex," failed to acknowledge the ways in
which power relations continue to construct sexuality for women even
within the terms of a "liberated" heterosexuality or lesbianism.[53] The
same criticism is waged against the notion of a specifically feminine sexual pleasure that is radically differentiated from phallic sexuality.
Irigaray's occasional efforts to derive a specific feminine sexuality from
a specific female anatomy have been the focus of anti-essentialist arguments for some time.[54] The return to biology as the ground of a specific
feminine sexuality or meaning seems to defeat the feminist premise that
biology is not destiny. But whether feminine sexuality is articulated here
through a discourse of biology for purely strategic reasons,[55] or whether
it is, in fact, a feminist return to biological essentialism, the characterization of female sexuality as radically distinct from a phallic organization
of sexuality remains problematic. Women who fail either to recognize

that sexuality as their own or understand their sexuality as partially constructed within the terms of the phallic economy are potentially written off within the terms of that theory as "male-identified" or "unenlightened." Indeed, it is often unclear within Irigaray's text whether sexuality is culturally constructed, or whether it is only culturally constructed within the terms of the phallus. In other words, is specifically feminine pleasure "outside" of culture as its prehistory or as its utopian future? If so, of what use is such a notion for negotiating the contemporary struggles of sexuality within the terms of its construction?

The pro-sexuality movement within feminist theory and practice has effectively argued that sexuality is always constructed within the terms of discourse and power, where power is partially understood in terms of heterosexual and phallic cultural conventions. The emergence of a sexuality constructed (not determined) in these terms within lesbian, bisexual, and heterosexual contexts is, therefore, *not* a sign of a masculine identification in some reductive sense. It is not the failed project of criticizing phallogocentrism or heterosexual hegemony, as if a political critique could effectively undo the cultural construction of the feminist critic's sexuality. If sexuality is culturally constructed within existing power relations, then the postulation of a normative sexuality that is "before," "outside," or "beyond" power is a cultural impossibility and a politically impracticable dream, one that postpones the concrete and contemporary task of rethinking subversive possibilities for sexuality and identity within the terms of power itself. This critical task presumes, of course, that to operate within the matrix of power is not the same as to replicate uncritically relations of domination. It offers the possibility of a repetition of the law which is not its consolidation, but its displacement. In the place of a "male-identified" sexuality in which "male" serves as the cause and irreducible meaning of that sexuality, we might develop a notion of sexuality constructed in terms of phallic relations of power that replay and redistribute the possibilities of that phallicism precisely through the subversive operation of "identifications" that are, within the power field of sexuality, inevitable.

40

If "identifications," following Jacqueline Rose, can be exposed as phantasmatic, then it must be possible to enact an identification that displays its phantasmatic structure. If there is no radical repudiation of a culturally constructed sexuality, what is left is the question of how to acknowledge and "do" the construction one is invariably in. Are there forms of repetition that do not constitute a simple imitation, reproduction, and, hence, consolidation of the law (the anachronistic notion of "male identification" that ought to be discarded from a feminist vocabulary)? What possibilities of gender configurations exist among the various emergent and occasionally convergent matrices of cultural intelligibility that govern gendered life?

Within the terms of feminist sexual theory, it is clear that the presence of power dynamics within sexuality is in no sense the same as the simple consolidation or augmentation of a heterosexist or phallogocentric power regime. The "presence" of so-called heterosexual conventions within homosexual contexts as well as the proliferation of specifically gay discourses of sexual difference, as in the case of "butch" and "femme" as historical identities of sexual style, cannot be explained as chimerical representations of originally heterosexual identities. And neither can they be understood as the pernicious insistence of heterosexist constructs within gay sexuality and identity. The repetition of heterosexual constructs within sexual cultures both gay and straight may well be the inevitable site of the denaturalization and mobilization of gender categories. The replication of heterosexual constructs in non-heterosexual frames brings into relief the utterly constructed status of the so-called heterosexual original. Thus, gay is to straight *not* as copy is to original, but, rather, as copy is to copy. The parodic repetition of "the original," discussed in the final sections of chapter 3 of this text, reveals the original to be nothing other than a parody of the *idea* of the natural and the original.[56] Even if heterosexist constructs circulate as the available sites of power/discourse from which to do gender at all, the question remains: What possibilities of recirculation exist? Which possibilities of doing gender repeat and displace through hyperbole, dissonance, internal confusion, and proliferation the very constructs by which they are mobilized?

Consider not only that the ambiguities and incoherences within and among heterosexual, homosexual, and bisexual practices are suppressed and redescribed within the reified framework of the disjunctive and asymmetrical binary of masculine/feminine, but that these cultural configurations of gender confusion operate as sites for intervention, exposure, and displacement of these reifications. In other words, the "unity" of gender is the effect of a regulatory practice that seeks to render gender identity uniform through a compulsory heterosexuality. The force of this practice is, through an exclusionary apparatus of production, to restrict the relative meanings of "heterosexuality," "homosexuality," and "bisexuality" as well as the subversive sites of their convergence and resignification. That the power regimes of heterosexism and phallogocentrism seek to augment themselves through a constant repetition of their logic, their metaphysic, and their naturalized ontologies does not imply that repetition itself ought to be stopped—as if it could be. If repetition is bound to persist as the mechanism of the cultural reproduction of identities, then the crucial question emerges: What kind of subversive repetition might call into question the regulatory practice of identity itself?

If there is no recourse to a "person," a "sex," or a "sexuality" that escapes the matrix of power and discursive relations that effectively produce and regulate the intelligibility of those concepts for us, what constitutes the possibility of effective inversion, subversion, or displacement within the terms of a constructed identity? What possibilities exist *by virtue of* the constructed character of sex and gender? Whereas Foucault is ambiguous about the precise character of the "regulatory practices" that produce the category of sex, and Wittig appears to invest the full responsibility of the construction to sexual reproduction and its instrument, compulsory heterosexuality, yet other discourses converge to produce this categorial fiction for reasons not always clear or consistent with one another. The power relations that infuse the biological sciences are not easily reduced, and the medico-legal alliance emerging in nineteenth-century Europe has spawned cat-egorial fictions that could not be anticipated in advance. The very complexity of the discursive map that constructs gender appears to hold out the promise of an inadvertent and generative convergence of these discursive and regulatory structures. If the regulatory fictions of sex and gender are themselves multiply contested sites of meaning, then the very multiplicity of their construction holds out the possibility of a disruption of their univocal posturing.

Clearly this project does not propose to lay out within traditional philosophical terms an *ontology* of gender whereby the meaning of *being* a woman or a man is elucidated within the terms of phenomenology. The presumption here is that the "being" of gender is *an effect,* an object of a genealogical investigation that maps out the political parameters of its construction in the mode of ontology. To claim that gender is con-structed is not to assert its illusoriness or artificiality, where those terms are understood to reside within a binary that counterposes the "real" and the "authentic" as oppositional. As a genealogy of gender ontology, this inquiry seeks to understand the discursive production of the plausibility of that binary relation and to suggest that certain cultur-al configurations of gender take the place of "the real" and consolidate and augment their hegemony through that felicitous self-naturalization.

If there is something right in Beauvoir's claim that one is not born, but rather *becomes* a woman, it follows that *woman* itself is a term in process, a becoming, a constructing that cannot rightfully be said to originate or to end. As an ongoing discursive practice, it is open to inter-vention and resignification. Even when gender seems to congeal into the most reified forms, the "congealing" is itself an insistent and insidious practice, sustained and regulated by various social means. It is, for Beauvoir, never possible finally to become a woman, as if there were a *telos* that governs the process of acculturation and construction. Gender is the repeated stylization of the body, a set of repeated acts within a highly rigid regulatory frame that congeal over time to produce the

43

appearance of substance, of a natural sort of being. A political genealogy of gender ontologies, if it is successful, will deconstruct the substantive appearance of gender into its constitutive acts and locate and account for those acts within the compulsory frames set by the various forces that police the social appearance of gender. To expose the contingent acts that create the appearance of a naturalistic necessity, a move which has been a part of cultural critique at least since Marx, is a task that now takes on the added burden of showing how the very notion of the subject, intelligible only through its appearance as gendered, admits of possibilities that have been forcibly foreclosed by the various reifications of gender that have constituted its contingent ontologies.

The following chapter investigates some aspects of the psychoanalytic structuralist account of sexual difference and the construction of sexuality with respect to its power to contest the regulatory regimes outlined here as well as its role in uncritically reproducing those regimes. The univocity of sex, the internal coherence of gender, and the binary framework for both sex and gender are considered throughout as regulatory fictions that consolidate and naturalize the convergent power regimes of masculine and heterosexist oppression. The final chapter considers the very notion of "the body," not as a ready surface awaiting signification, but as a set of boundaries, individual and social, politically signified and maintained. No longer believable as an interior "truth" of dispositions and identity, sex will be shown to be a performatively enacted signification (and hence not "to be"), one that, released from its naturalized interiority and surface, can occasion the parodic proliferation and subversive play of gendered meanings. This text continues, then, as an effort to think through the possibility of subverting and displacing those naturalized and reified notions of gender that support masculine hegemony and heterosexist power, to make gender trouble, not through the strategies that figure a utopian beyond, but through the mobilization, subversive confusion, and proliferation of precisely those constitutive categories that seek to keep gender in its place by posturing as the foundational illusions of identity.

2

Prohibition, Psychoanalysis, and the Production of the Heterosexual Matrix

The straight mind continues to affirm that incest, and not homosexuality,
represents its major interdiction. Thus, when thought by the straight
mind, homosexuality is nothing but heterosexuality.
—Monique Wittig, "The Straight Mind"

On occasion feminist theory has been drawn to the thought of an origin, a time before what some would call "patriarchy" that would provide an imaginary perspective from which to establish the contingency of the history of women's oppression. Debates have emerged over whether prepatriarchal cultures have existed, whether they were matriarchal or matrilineal in structure, whether patriarchy could be shown to have a beginning and, hence, be subject to an end. The critical impetus behind these kinds of inquiry sought understandably to show that the antifeminist argument in favor of the inevitability of patriarchy constituted a reification and naturalization of a *historical* and contingent phenomenon.

Although the turn to a prepatriarchal state of culture was intended to expose the self-reification of patriarchy, that prepatriarchal scheme has proven to be a different sort of reification. More recently, some feminists have offered a reflexive critique of some reified constructs within feminism itself. The very notion of "patriarchy" has threatened to become a universalizing concept that overrides or reduces distinct

45

articulations of gender asymmetry in different cultural contexts. As feminism has sought to become integrally related to struggles against racial and colonialist oppression, it has become increasingly important to resist the colonizing epistemological strategy that would subordinate different configurations of domination under the rubric of a transcultural notion of patriarchy. The articulation of the law of patriarchy as a repressive and regulatory structure also requires reconsideration from this critical perspective. The feminist recourse to an imaginary past needs to be cautious not to promote a politically problematic reification of women's experience in the course of debunking the self-reifying claims of masculinist power.

The self-justification of a repressive or subordinating law almost always grounds itself in a story about what it was like *before* the advent of the law, and how it came about that the law emerged in its present and necessary form.[1] The fabrication of those origins tends to describe a state of affairs before the law that follows a necessary and unilinear narrative that culminates in, and thereby justifies, the constitution of the law. The story of origins is thus a strategic tactic within a narrative that, by telling a single, authoritative account about an irrecoverable past, makes the constitution of the law appear as a historical inevitability.

Some feminists have found in the prejuridical past traces of a utopian future, a potential resource for subversion or insurrection that promises to lead to the destruction of the law and the instatement of a new order. But if the imaginary "before" is inevitably figured within the terms of a prehistorical narrative that serves to legitimate the present state of the law or, alternatively, the imaginary future beyond the law, then this "before" is always already imbued with the self-justificatory fabrications of present and future interests, whether feminist or antifeminist. The postulation of the "before" within feminist theory becomes politically problematic when it constrains the future to materialize an idealized notion of the past or when it supports, even inadvertently, the reification of a precultural sphere of the authentic feminine. This recourse to an original or genuine femininity is a nostal-

46

gic and parochial ideal that refuses the contemporary demand to formulate an account of gender as a complex cultural construction. This
ideal tends not only to serve culturally conservative aims, but to constitute an exclusionary practice within feminism, precipitating precisely the kind of fragmentation that the ideal purports to overcome.

Throughout the speculation of Engels, socialist feminism, those
feminist positions rooted in structuralist anthropology, there emerge
various efforts to locate moments or structures within history or culture that establish gender hierarchy. The isolation of such structures or
key periods is pursued in order to repudiate those reactionary theories
which would naturalize or universalize the subordination of women.
As significant efforts to provide a critical displacement of the universalizing gestures of oppression, these theories constitute part of the
contemporary theoretical field in which a further contestation of
oppression is taking place. The question needs to be pursued, however,
whether these powerful critiques of gender hierarchy make use of presuppositional fictions that entail problematic normative ideals.

Lévi-Strauss's structuralist anthropology, including the problematic nature/culture distinction, has been appropriated by some feminist
theorists to support and elucidate the sex/gender distinction: the position that there is a natural or biological female who is subsequently
transformed into a socially subordinate "woman," with the consequence that "sex" is to nature or "the raw" as gender is to culture or
"the cooked." If Lévi-Strauss's framework were true, it would be possible to trace the transformation of sex into gender by locating that stable mechanism of cultures, the exchange rules of kinship, which effect
that transformation in fairly regular ways. Within such a view, "sex" is
before the law in the sense that it is culturally and political undetermined, providing the "raw material" of culture, as it were, that begins
to signify only through and after its subjection to the rules of kinship.

This very concept of sex-as-matter, sex-as-instrument-of-cultural-
signification, however, is a discursive formation that acts as a naturalized
foundation for the nature/culture distinction and the strategies of

domination that that distinction supports. The binary relation between culture and nature promotes a relationship of hierarchy in which culture freely "imposes" meaning on nature, and, hence, renders it into an "Other" to be appropriated to its own limitless uses, safeguarding the ideality of the signifier and the structure of signification on the model of domination.

Anthropologists Marilyn Strathern and Carol MacCormack have argued that nature/culture discourse regularly figures nature as female, in need of subordination by a culture that is invariably figured as male, active, and abstract.[2] As in the existential dialectic of misogyny, this is yet another instance in which reason and mind are associated with masculinity and agency, while the body and nature are considered to be the mute facticity of the feminine, awaiting signification from an opposing masculine subject. As in that misogynist dialectic, materiality and meaning are mutually exclusive terms. The sexual politics that construct and maintain this distinction are effectively concealed by the discursive production of a nature and, indeed, a natural sex that postures as the unquestioned foundation of culture. Critics of structuralism such as Clifford Geertz have argued that its universalizing framework discounts the multiplicity of cultural configurations of "nature." The analysis that assumes nature to be singular and prediscursive cannot ask, what qualifies as "nature" within a given cultural context, and for what purposes? Is the dualism necessary at all? How are the sex/gender and nature/culture dualisms constructed and naturalized in and through one another? What gender hierarchies do they serve, and what relations of subordination do they reify? If the very designation of sex is political, then "sex," that designation supposed to be most in the raw, proves to be always already "cooked," and the central distinctions of structuralist anthropology appear to collapse.[3]

The effort to locate a sexed nature before the law seems to be rooted understandably in the more fundamental project to be able to think that the patriarchal law is not universally true and all-determining. Indeed, if constructed gender is all there is, then there appears to be no "outside," no epistemic anchor in a precultural "before" that might serve as an alternative epistemic point of departure for a critical assessment of existing gender relations. Locating the mechanism whereby sex is transformed into gender is meant to establish not only the constructedness of gender, its unnatural and nonnecessary status, but the cultural universality of oppression in nonbiologistic terms. How is this mechanism formulated? Can it be found or merely imagined? Is the designation of its ostensible universality any less of a reification than the position that grounds universal oppression in biology?

Only when the mechanism of gender construction implies the *contingency* of that construction does "constructedness" *per se* prove useful to the political project to enlarge the scope of possible gender configurations. If, however, it is a life of the body beyond the law or a recovery of the body before the law which then emerges as the normative goal of feminist theory, such a norm effectively takes the focus of feminist theory away from the concrete terms of contemporary cultural struggle. Indeed, the following sections on psychoanalysis, structuralism, and the status and power of their gender-instituting prohibitions centers precisely on this notion of the law: What is its ontological status—is it juridical, oppressive, and reductive in its workings, or does it inadvertently create the possibility of its own cultural displacement? To what extent does the articulation of a body prior to articulation performatively contradict itself and spawn alternatives in its place?

I. STRUCTURALISM'S CRITICAL EXCHANGE

Structuralist discourse tends to refer to the Law in the singular, in accord with Lévi-Strauss's contention that there is a universal structure of regulating exchange that characterizes all systems of kinship. According to *The Elementary Structures of Kinship*, the object of exchange that both consolidates and differentiates kinship relations is *women*, given as gifts from one patrilineal clan to another through the institution of marriage.[4] The bride, the gift, the object of exchange constitutes "a sign and a value" that opens a channel of exchange that not only serves the *functional* purpose of facilitating trade but performs the *symbolic* or *ritualistic* purpose of consolidating the internal bonds, the collective identity, of each clan differentiated through the act.[5] In other words, the bride functions as a relational term between groups of men; she does not *have* an identity, and neither does she exchange one identity for another. She *reflects* masculine identity precisely through being the site of its absence. Clan members, invariably male, invoke the prerogative of identity through marriage, a repeated act of symbolic differentiation. Exogamy distinguishes and binds patronymically specific kinds of men. Patrilineality is secured through the ritualistic expulsion of women and, reciprocally, the ritualistic importation of women. As wives, women not only secure the reproduction of the *name* (the functional purpose), but effect a symbolic intercourse between clans of men. As the site of a patronymic exchange, women are and are not the patronymic sign, excluded from the signifier, the very patronym they bear. The woman in marriage qualifies not as an identity, but only as a relational term that both distinguishes and binds the various clans to a common but internally differentiated patrilineal identity.

The structural systematicity of Lévi-Strauss's explanation of kinship relations appeals to a universal logic that appears to structure human relations. Although Lévi-Strauss reports in *Tristes tropiques* that he left philosophy because anthropology provided a more concrete cultural texture to the analysis of human life, he nevertheless assimilates that cultural texture to a totalizing logical structure that effectively returns his analyses to the decontextualized philosophical structures he purported to leave. Although a number of questions can be raised about the presumptions of universality in Lévi-Strauss's work (as they are in anthropologist Clifford Geertz's *Local Knowledge)*, the questions here concern the place of identitarian assumptions in this universal logic and the relationship of that identitarian logic to the subordinate status of women within the cultural reality that this logic describes. If the symbolic nature of exchange is its universally human character as well, and if that universal structure distributes "identity" to male persons and a subordinate and relational "negation" or "lack" to women, then this logic might well be contested by a position or set of positions excluded from its very terms. What might an alternative logic of kinship be like? To what extent do identitarian logical systems always require the construction of socially impossible identities to occupy an unnamed, excluded, but presuppositional relation subsequently concealed by the logic itself? Here the impetus for Irigaray's marking off of the phallogocentric economy becomes clear, as does a major poststructuralist impulse within feminism that questions whether an effective critique of phallogocentrism requires a displacement of the Symbolic as defined by Lévi-Strauss.

The *totality* and *closure* of language is both presumed and contested within structuralism. Although Saussure understands the relationship of signifier and signified to be arbitrary, he places this arbitrary relation within a necessarily complete linguistic system. All linguistic terms presuppose a linguistic totality of structures, the entirety of which is presupposed and implicitly recalled for any one term to bear meaning. This quasi-Leibnizian view, in which language figures as a systematic totality, effectively suppresses the moment of difference between signifier and signified, relating and unifying that moment of arbitrariness within a totalizing field. The poststructuralist break with Saussure and with the identitarian structures of exchange found in Lévi-Strauss refutes the claims of totality and universality and the presumption of binary structural oppositions that implicitly operate to quell the insistent ambiguity and openness of linguistic and cultural signification.[6] As a result, the discrepancy between signifier and signified becomes the operative and limitless *différance* of language, rendering all referentiality into a potentially limitless displacement.

For Lévi-Strauss, the masculine cultural identity is established through an overt act of differentiation between patrilineal clans, where the "difference" in this relation is Hegelian—that is, one which simultaneously distinguishes and binds. But the "difference" established between men and the women who effect the differentiation between men eludes the dialectic altogether. In other words, the differentiating moment of social exchange appears to be a social bond between men, a Hegelian unity between masculine terms that are simultaneously specified and individualized.[7] On an abstract level, this is an identity-in-difference, since both clans retain a similar identity: male, patriarchal, and patrilineal. Bearing different names, they particularize themselves within this all-encompassing masculine cultural identity. But what relation instates women as the object of exchange, clothed first in one patronym and then another? What kind of differentiating mechanism distributes gender functions in this way? What kind of differentiating *différance* is presupposed and excluded by the explicit, male-mediating negation of Lévi-Strauss's Hegelian economy? As Irigaray argues, this phallogocentric economy depends essentially on an economy of *différance* that is never manifest, but always both presupposed and disavowed. In effect, the relations among patrilineal clans are based in homosocial desire (what Irigaray punningly calls "hommo-sexuality"),[8] a repressed and, hence, disparaged sexuality, a relationship between men which is, finally, about the bonds of men, but which takes place through the heterosexual exchange and distribution of women.[9]

In a passage that reveals the homoerotic unconscious of the phallogocentric economy, Lévi-Strauss offers the link between the incest taboo and the consolidation of homoerotic bonds:

> Exchange—and consequently the rule of exogamy—is not simply that of goods exchanged. Exchange—and consequently the rule of exogamy that expresses it—has in itself a social value. It provides the means of binding men together.

The taboo generates exogamic heterosexuality which Lévi-Strauss understands as the artificial accomplishment of a nonincestuous heterosexuality extracted through prohibition from a more natural and unconstrained sexuality (an assumption shared by Freud in *Three Essays on the Theory of Sexuality*).

The relation of reciprocity established between men, however, is the condition of a relation of radical nonreciprocity between men and women and a relation, as it were, of nonrelation between women. Lévi-Strauss's notorious claim that "the emergence of symbolic thought must have required that women, like words, should be things that were exchanged," suggests a necessity that Lévi-Strauss himself induces from the presumed universal structures of culture from the retrospective position of a transparent observer. But the "must have" appears as an inference only to function as a performative; since the moment in which the symbolic emerged could not be one that Lévi-Strauss witnessed, he conjectures a necessary history: The report thereby becomes an injunction. His analysis prompted Irigaray to reflect on what would happen if "the goods got together" and revealed the unanticipated agency of an alternative sexual economy. Her recent work, *Sexes et parentés,*[10] offers a critical exegesis of how this construction of reciprocal exchange between men presupposes a nonreciprocity between the sexes inarticulable within that economy, as well as the unnameability of the female, the feminine, and lesbian sexuality.

If there is a sexual domain that is *excluded* from the Symbolic and can potentially expose the Symbolic as hegemonic rather than totalizing in its reach, it must then be possible to locate this excluded domain either within or outside that economy and to strategize its intervention in terms of that placement. The following rereading of the structuralist law and the narrative that accounts for the production of sexual difference within its terms centers on the presumed fixity and universality of that law and, through a genealogical critique, seeks to expose that law's powers of inadvertent and self-defeating generativity. Does "the Law" produce these positions unilaterally or invariably? Can it produce configurations of sexuality that effectively contest the law itself, or are those contests inevitably phantasmatic? Can the *generativity* of that law be specified as variable or even subversive?

The law forbidding incest is the locus of this economy of kinship that forbids endogamy. Lévi-Strauss maintains that the centrality of the incest taboo establishes the significant nexus between structuralist anthropology and psychoanalysis. Although Lévi-Strauss acknowledges that Freud's *Totem and Taboo* has been discredited on empirical grounds, he considers that repudiating gesture as paradoxical evidence in support of Freud's thesis. Incest, for Lévi-Strauss, is not a social fact, but a pervasive cultural fantasy. Presuming the heterosexual masculinity of the subject of desire, Lévi-Strauss maintains that "the desire for the mother or the sister, the murder of the father and the sons' repentance undoubtedly do not correspond to any fact or group of facts occupying a given place in history. But perhaps they symbolically express an ancient and lasting dream."[11]

In an effort to affirm the psychoanalytic insight into unconscious incestuous fantasy, Lévi-Strauss refers to the "magic of this dream, its power to mould men's thoughts unbeknown to them ... the acts it evokes have never been committed, because culture opposes them at all times and all places."[12] This rather astonishing statement provides insight not only into Lévi-Strauss's apparent powers of denial (acts of incest "have never been committed" !), but the central difficulty with assuming the efficacy of that prohibition. That the prohibition exists in no way suggests that it works. Rather, its existence appears to suggest that desires, actions, indeed, pervasive social practices of incest are generated precisely in virtue of the eroticization of that taboo. That incestuous desires are phantasmatic in no way implies that they are not also "social facts." The question is, rather, how do such phantasms become generated and, indeed, instituted as a consequence of their prohibition? Further, how does the social conviction, here symptomatically articulated through Lévi-Strauss, that the prohibition *is* efficacious disavow and, hence, clear a social space in which incestuous practices are free to reproduce themselves without proscription?

For Lévi-Strauss, the taboo against the act of heterosexual incest between son and mother as well as that incestuous fantasy are instated as universal truths of culture. How is incestuous heterosexuality constituted as the ostensibly natural and pre-artificial matrix for desire, and how is desire established as a heterosexual male prerogative? The naturalization of both heterosexuality and masculine sexual agency are discursive constructions nowhere accounted for but everywhere assumed within this founding structuralist frame.

The Lacanian appropriation of Lévi-Strauss focuses on the prohibition against incest and the rule of exogamy in the reproduction of culture, where culture is understood primarily as a set of linguistic structures and significations. For Lacan, the Law which forbids the incestuous union between boy and mother initiates the structures of kinship, a series of highly regulated libidinal displacements that take place through language. Although the structures of language, collectively understood as the Symbolic, maintain an ontological integrity apart from the various speaking agents through whom they work, the Law reasserts and individuates itself within the terms of every infantile entrance into culture. Speech emerges only upon the condition of dissatisfaction, where dissatisfaction is instituted through incestuous prohibition; the original *jouissance* is lost through the primary repression that founds the subject. In its place emerges the sign which is similarly barred from the signifier and which seeks in what it signifies a recovery of that irrecoverable pleasure. Founded through that prohibition, the subject speaks only to displace desire onto the metonymic substitutions for that irretrievable pleasure. Language is the residue and alternative accomplishment of dissatisfied desire, the variegated cultural production of a sublimation that never really satisfies. That language inevitably fails to signify is the necessary consequence of the prohibition which grounds the possibility of language and marks the vanity of its referential gestures.

II. LACAN, RIVIERE, AND THE STRATEGIES OF MASQUERADE

To ask after the "being" of gender and/or sex in Lacanian terms is to confound the very purpose of Lacan's theory of language. Lacan disputes the primacy given to ontology within the terms of Western metaphysics and insists upon the subordination of the question

"What is/has being?" to the prior question "How is 'being' instituted and allocated through the signifying practices of the paternal economy?" The ontological specification of being, negation, and their relations is understood to be determined by a language structured by the paternal law and its mechanisms of differentiation. A thing takes on the characterization of "being" and becomes mobilized by that ontological gesture only within a structure of signification that, as the Symbolic, is itself pre-ontological.

There is no inquiry, then, into ontology *per se*, no access to being, without a prior inquiry into the "being" of the Phallus, the authorizing signification of the Law that takes sexual difference as a presupposition of its own intelligibility. "Being" the Phallus and "having" the Phallus denote divergent sexual positions, or nonpositions (impossible positions, really), within language. To "be" the Phallus is to be the "signifier" of the desire of the Other and *to appear* as this signifier. In other words, it is to be the object, the Other of a (heterosexualized) masculine desire, but also to represent or reflect that desire. This is an Other that constitutes, not the limit of masculinity in a feminine alterity, but the site of a masculine self-elaboration. For women to "be" the Phallus means, then, to reflect the power of the Phallus, to signify that power, to "embody" the Phallus, to supply the site to which it penetrates, and to signify the Phallus through "being" its Other, its absence, its lack, the dialectical confirmation of its identity. By claiming that the Other that lacks the Phallus is the one who *is* the Phallus, Lacan clearly suggests that power is wielded by this feminine position of not-having, that the masculine subject who "has" the Phallus requires this Other to confirm and, hence, be the Phallus in its "extended" sense.[13]

This ontological characterization presupposes that the appearance or effect of being is always produced through the structures of signification. The Symbolic order creates cultural intelligibility through the mutually exclusive positions of "having" the Phallus (the position of men) and "being" the Phallus (the paradoxical position of women). The interdependency of these positions recalls the Hegelian structure of failed reciprocity between master and slave, in particular, the unexpected dependency of the master on the slave in order to establish his own identity through reflection.[14] Lacan casts that drama, however, in a phantasmatic domain. Every effort to establish identity within the terms of this binary disjunction of "being" and "having" returns to the inevitable "lack" and "loss" that ground their phantasmatic construction and mark the incommensurability of the Symbolic and the real.

If the Symbolic is understood as a culturally universal structure of signification that is nowhere fully instantiated in the real, it makes sense to ask: What or who is it that signifies what or whom in this ostensibly crosscultural affair? This question, however, is posed within a frame that presupposes a subject as signifier and an object as signified, the traditional epistemological dichotomy within philosophy prior to the structuralist displacement of the subject. Lacan calls into question this scheme of signification. He poses the relation between the sexes in terms that reveal the speaking "I" as a masculinized effect of repression, one which postures as an autonomous and self-grounding subject, but whose very coherence is called into question by the sexual positions that it excludes in the process of identity formation. For Lacan, the subject comes into being—that is, begins to posture as a self-grounding signifier within language—only on the condition of a primary repression of the pre-individuated incestuous pleasures associated with the (now repressed) maternal body.

The masculine subject only *appears* to originate meanings and thereby to signify. His seemingly self-grounded autonomy attempts to conceal the repression which is both its ground and the perpetual possibility of its own ungrounding. But that process of meaning-constitution requires that women reflect that masculine power and everywhere reassure that power of the reality of its illusory autonomy. This task is confounded, to say the least, when the demand that women reflect the autonomous power of masculine subject/signifier becomes essential to the construction of that autonomy and, thus, becomes the basis of a radical dependency that effectively undercuts the function it serves. But further, this dependency, although denied, is also *pursued* by the masculine subject, for the woman as reassuring sign is the displaced maternal body, the vain but persistent promise of the recovery of pre-individuated *jouissance*. The conflict of masculinity appears, then, to be precisely the demand for a full recognition of autonomy that will also and nevertheless promise a return to those full pleasures prior to repression and individuation.

Women are said to "be" the Phallus in the sense that they maintain the power to reflect or represent the "reality" of the self-grounding postures of the masculine subject, a power which, if withdrawn, would break up the foundational illusions of the masculine subject position. In order to "be" the Phallus, the reflector and guarantor of an apparent masculine subject position, women must become, must "be" (in the sense of "posture as if they were") precisely what men are not and, in their very lack, establish the essential function of men. Hence, "being" the Phallus is always a "being for" a masculine subject who seeks to reconfirm and augment his identity through the recognition of that "being for." In a strong sense, Lacan disputes the notion that *men* signify the meaning of *women* or that *women* signify the meaning of *men*. The division and exchange between this "being" and "having" the Phallus is established by the Symbolic, the paternal law. Part of the comedic dimension of this failed model of reciprocity, of course, is that both masculine and feminine positions are signified, the signifier belonging to the Symbolic that can never be assumed in more than token form by either position.

To *be* the Phallus is to be signified by the paternal law, to be both its object and its instrument and, in structuralist terms, the "sign" and promise of its power. Hence, as the constituted or signified object of exchange through which the paternal law extends its power and the mode in which it appears, women are said to be the Phallus, that is, the emblem of its continuing circulation. But this "being" the Phallus is necessarily dissatisfying to the extent that women can never fully reflect that law; some feminists argue that it requires a renunciation of women's own desire (a double renunciation, in fact, corresponding to the "double wave" of repression that Freud claimed founds femininity),[15] which is the expropriation of that desire as the desire to be nothing other than a reflection, a guarantor of the pervasive necessity of the Phallus.

On the other hand, men are said to "have" the Phallus, yet never to "be" it, in the sense that the penis is not equivalent to that Law and can never fully symbolize that Law. Hence, there is a necessary or presuppositional impossibility to any effort to occupy the position of "having" the Phallus, with the consequence that both positions of "having" and "being" are, in Lacan's terms, finally to be understood as comedic failures that are nevertheless compelled to articulate and enact these repeated impossibilities.

But how does a woman "appear" to be the Phallus, the lack that embodies and affirms the Phallus? According to Lacan, this is done through masquerade, the effect of a melancholy that is essential to the feminine position as such. In his early essay, "The Meaning of the Phallus," he writes of "the relations between the sexes":

> Let us say that these relations will revolve around a being and a having which, because they refer to a signifier, the phallus, have the contradictory effect of on the one hand lending reality to the subject in that signifier, and on the other making unreal the relations to be signified.[16]

In the lines that directly follow this sentence, Lacan appears to refer to the appearance of the "reality" of the masculine subject as well as to the "unreality" of heterosexuality. He also appears to refer to the position of women (my interruption is within brackets): "This follows from the intervention of an 'appearing' which gets substituted for the 'having' [a substitution is required, no doubt, because women are said not "to have"] so as to protect it on one side and to mask its lack on the other." Although there is no grammatical gender here, it seems that Lacan is describing the position of women for whom "lack" is characteristic and, hence, in need of masking and who are in some unspecified sense in need of protection. Lacan then states that this situation produces "the effect that the ideal or typical manifestations of behaviour in both sexes, up to and including the act of sexual copulation, are entirely propelled into comedy" (84).

Lacan continues this exposition of heterosexual comedy by explaining that this "appearing as being" the Phallus that women are compelled to do is inevitably *masquerade*. The term is significant because it suggests contradictory meanings: On the one hand, if the "being," the ontological specification of the Phallus, is masquerade, then it would appear to reduce all being to a form of appearing, the appearance of being, with the consequence that all gender ontology is reducible to the play of appearances. On the other hand, masquerade suggests that there is a "being" or ontological specification of femininity *prior to* the masquerade, a feminine desire or demand that is masked and capable of disclosure, that, indeed, might promise an eventual disruption and displacement of the phallogocentric signifying economy.

At least two very different tasks can be discerned from the ambiguous structure of Lacan's analysis. On the one hand, masquerade may be understood as the performative production of a sexual ontology, an appearing that makes itself convincing as a "being"; on the other hand, masquerade can be read as a denial of a feminine desire that presupposes some prior ontological femininity regularly unrepresented by the phallic economy. Irigaray remarks in such a vein that "the masquerade . . . is what women do . . . in order to participate in man's desire, but at the cost of giving up their own."[17] The former task would engage a critical reflection on gender ontology as parodic (de)construction and, perhaps, pursue the mobile possibilities of the slippery distinction between "appearing" and "being," a radicalization of the "comedic" dimension of sexual ontology only partially pursued by Lacan. The latter would initiate feminist strategies of unmasking in order to recover or release whatever feminine desire has remained suppressed within the terms of the phallic economy.[18]

Perhaps these alternative directions are not as mutually exclusive as they appear, since appearances become more suspect all the time. Reflections on the meaning of masquerade in Lacan as well as in Joan Riviere's "Womanliness as a Masquerade" have differed greatly in their interpretations of what precisely is masked by masquerade. Is masquerade the consequence of a feminine desire that must be negated and, thus, made into a lack that, nevertheless, must appear in some way? Is masquerade the consequence of a denial *of* this lack for the purpose of appearing to be the Phallus? Does masquerade construct femininity as the reflection of the Phallus in order to disguise bisexual possibilities that otherwise might disrupt the seamless construction of a heterosexualized femininity? Does masquerade, as Riviere suggests, transform aggression and the fear of reprisal into seduction and flirtation? Does it serve primarily to conceal or repress a pregiven femininity, a feminine desire which would establish an insubordinate alterity to the masculine subject and expose the necessary failure of masculinity? Or is masquerade the means by which femininity itself is *first* established, the exclusionary practice of identity formation in which the masculine is effectively excluded and instated as outside the boundaries of a feminine gendered position?

Lacan continues the quotation cited above:

> Paradoxical as this formulation might seem, it is in order to be the phallus, that is, the signifier of the desire of the Other, that the woman will reject an essential part of her femininity, notably all its attributes through masquerade. It is for what she is not that she expects to be desired as well as loved. But she finds the signifier of her own desire in the body of the one to whom she addresses her demand for love. Certainly we should not forget that the organ invested with this signifying function takes on the value of a fetish. (84)

If this unnamed "organ," presumably the penis (treated like the Hebraic *Yahweh,* never to be spoken), is a fetish, why should it be that we might so easily forget it, as Lacan himself assumes? And what is the "essential part of her femininity" that must be rejected? Is it the, again, unnamed part which, once rejected, appears as a lack? Or is it the lack itself that must be rejected, so that she might appear as the Phallus itself? Is the unnameability of this "essential part" the same unnameability that attends the male "organ" that we are always in danger of forgetting? Is this precisely that forgetfulness that constitutes the repression at the core of feminine masquerade? Is it a presumed masculinity that must be forfeited in order to appear as the lack that confirms and, therefore, is the Phallus, or is it a phallic possibility, that must be negated in order to be that lack that confirms?

Lacan clarifies his own position as he remarks that "the function of the mask . . . dominates the identifications through which refusals of love are resolved" (85). In other words, the mask is part of the incorporative strategy of melancholy, the taking on of attributes of the object/Other that is lost, where loss is the consequence of a refusal of love.[19] That the mask "dominates" as well as "resolves" these refusals suggests that appropriation is the strategy through which those refusals are themselves refused, a double negation that redoubles the structure of identity through the melancholic absorption of the one who is, in effect, twice lost.

Significantly, Lacan locates the discussion of the mask in conjunction with an account of female homosexuality. He claims that "the orientation of feminine homosexuality, as observation shows, follows from a disappointment which reenforces the side of the demand for love" (85). Who is observing and what is being observed are conveniently elided here, but Lacan takes his commentary to be obvious to anyone who cares to look. What one sees through "observation" is the founding disappointment of the female homosexual, where this disappointment recalls the refusals that are dominated/resolved through masquerade. One also "observes" somehow that the female homosexual is subject to a strengthened idealization, a demand for love that is pursued at the expense of desire.

Lacan continues this paragraph on "feminine homosexuality" with

the statement partially quoted above: "These remarks should be qualified by going back to the function of the mask [which is] to dominate
the identifications through which refusals of love are resolved," and if
female homosexuality is understood as a *consequence* of a disappointment "as observation shows," then this disappointment must appear,
and appear clearly, in order to be observed. If Lacan presumes that
female homosexuality issues from a disappointed heterosexuality, as
observation is said to show, could it not be equally clear to the observer that heterosexuality issues from a disappointed homosexuality? Is it
the mask of the female homosexual that is "observed," and if so, what
clearly readable expression gives evidence of that "disappointment"
and that "orientation" as well as the displacement of desire by the (idealized) demand for love? Lacan is perhaps suggesting that what is clear
to observation is the desexualized status of the lesbian, the incorporation of a refusal that appears as the absence of desire.[20] But we can
understand this conclusion to be the necessary result of a heterosexualized and masculine observational point of view that takes lesbian sexuality to be a refusal of sexuality *per se* only because sexuality is
presumed to be heterosexual, and the observer, here constructed as
the heterosexual male, is clearly being refused. Indeed, is this account
not the consequence of a refusal that disappoints the observer, and
whose disappointment, disavowed and projected, is made into the
essential character of the women who effectively refuse him?

In a characteristic gliding over pronominal locations, Lacan fails to
make clear who refuses whom. As readers, we are meant, however, to
understand that this free-floating "refusal" is linked in a significant way
to the mask. If every refusal is, finally, a loyalty to some other bond in
the present or the past, refusal is simultaneously preservation as well.
The mask thus conceals this loss, but preserves (and negates) this
loss through its concealment. The mask has a double function which
is the double function of melancholy. The mask is taken on through
the process of incorporation which is a way of inscribing and then
wearing a melancholic identification in and on the body; in effect, it is

the signification of the body in the mold of the Other who has been refused. Dominated through appropriation, every refusal fails, and the refuser becomes part of the very identity of the refused, indeed, becomes the psychic refuse of the refused. The loss of the object is never absolute because it is redistributed within a psychic/corporeal boundary that expands to incorporate that loss. This locates the process of gender incorporation within the wider orbit of melancholy.

Published in 1929, Joan Riviere's essay, "Womanliness as a Masquerade,"[21] introduces the notion of femininity as masquerade in terms of a theory of aggression and conflict resolution. This theory appears at first to be far afield from Lacan's analysis of masquerade in terms of the comedy of sexual positions. She begins with a respectful review of Ernest Jones's typology of the development of female sexuality into heterosexual and homosexual forms. She focuses, however, on the "intermediate types" that blur the boundaries between the heterosexual and the homosexual and, implicitly, contest the descriptive capacity of Jones's classificatory system. In a remark that resonates with Lacan's facile reference to "observation," Riviere seeks recourse to mundane perception or experience to validate her focus on these "intermediate types": "In daily life types of men and women are constantly met with who, while mainly heterosexual in their development, plainly display strong features of the other sex" (35). What is here most plain is the classifications that condition and structure the perception of this mix of attributes. Clearly, Riviere begins with set notions about what it is to display characteristics of one's sex, and how it is that those plain characteristics are understood to express or reflect an ostensible sexual orientation.[22] This perception or observation not only assumes a correlation among characteristics, desires, and "orientations,"[23] but creates that unity through the perceptual act itself. Riviere's postulated unity between gender attributes and a naturalized "orientation" appears as an instance of what Wittig refers to as the "imaginary formation" of sex.

And yet, Riviere calls into question these naturalized typologies through an appeal to a psychoanalytic account that locates the meaning of mixed gender attributes in the "interplay of conflicts" (35). Significantly, she contrasts this kind of psychoanalytic theory with one that would reduce the presence of ostensibly "masculine" attributes in a woman to a "radical or fundamental tendency." In other words, the acquisition of such attributes and the accomplishment of a heterosexual or homosexual orientation are produced through the resolution of conflicts that have as their aim the suppression of anxiety. Citing Ferenczi in order to establish an analogy with her own account, Riviere writes:

> Ferenczi pointed out . . . that homosexual men exaggerate their heterosexuality as a "defence" against their homosexuality. I shall attempt to show that women who wish for masculinity may put on a mask of womanliness to avert anxiety and the retribution feared from men. (35)

It is unclear what is the "exaggerated" form of heterosexuality the homosexual man is alleged to display, but the phenomenon under notice here might simply be that gay men simply may not look much different from their heterosexual counterparts. This lack of an overt differentiating style or appearance may be diagnosed as a symptomatic "defense" only because the gay man in question does not conform to the idea of the homosexual that the analyst has drawn and sustained from cultural stereotypes. A Lacanian analysis might argue that the supposed "exaggeration" in the homosexual man of whatever attributes count as apparent heterosexuality is the attempt to "have" the Phallus, the subject position that entails an active and heterosexualized desire. Similarly, the "mask" of the "women who wish for masculinity" can be interpreted as an effort to renounce the "having" of the Phallus in order to avert retribution by those from whom it must have been procured through castration. Riviere explains the fear of retribution as the consequence of a woman's fantasy to take the place of men, more precisely, of the father. In the case that she herself examines, which some consider to be autobiographical, the rivalry with the father is not over the desire of the mother, as one might expect, but over the place of the father in public discourse as speaker, lecturer, writer—that is, as a user of signs rather than a sign-object, an item of exchange. This castrating desire might be understood as the desire to relinquish the status of woman-as-sign in order to appear as a subject within language.

Indeed, the analogy that Riviere draws between the homosexual man and the masked woman is not, in her view, an analogy between male and female homosexuality. Femininity is taken on by a woman who "wishes for masculinity," but fears the retributive consequences of taking on the public appearance of masculinity. Masculinity is taken on by the male homosexual who, presumably, seeks to hide—not from others, but from himself—an ostensible femininity. The woman takes on a masquerade knowingly in order to conceal her masculinity from the masculine audience she wants to castrate. But the homosexual man is said to exaggerate his "heterosexuality" (meaning a masculinity that allows him to pass as heterosexual?) as a "defense," unknowingly, because he cannot acknowledge his own homosexuality (or is it that the analyst would not acknowledge it, if it were his?). In other words, the homosexual man takes unconscious retribution on himself, both desiring and fearing the consequences of castration. The male homosexual does not "know" his homosexuality, although Ferenczi and Riviere apparently do.

But does Riviere know the homosexuality of the woman in masquerade that she describes? When it comes to the counterpart of the analogy that she herself sets up, the woman who "wishes for masculinity" is homosexual only in terms of sustaining a masculine identification, but not in terms of a sexual orientation or desire. Invoking Jones's typology once again, as if it were a phallic shield, she formulates a "defense" that designates as asexual a class of female homosexuals understood as the masquerading type: "his first group of homosexual women who, while taking no interest in other women, wish for 'recognition' of their masculinity from men and claim to be the equals of men, or in other words, to be men themselves" (37). As in Lacan, the lesbian is here signified as an asexual position, as indeed, a position that refuses sexuality. For the earlier analogy with Ferenzci to become complete, it would seem that this description enacts the "defense" against female homosexuality *as sexuality* that is nevertheless understood as the reflexive structure of the "homosexual man." And yet, there is no clear way to read this description of a female homosexuality that is not about a sexual desire for women. Riviere would have us believe that this curious typological anomaly cannot be reduced to a repressed female homosexuality or heterosexuality. What is hidden is not sexuality, but rage.

One possible interpretation is that the woman in masquerade wishes for masculinity in order to engage in public discourse with men and as a man as part of a male homoerotic exchange. And precisely because that male homoerotic exchange would signify castration, she fears the same retribution that motivates the "defenses" of the homosexual man. Indeed, perhaps femininity as masquerade is meant to deflect from male homosexuality—that being the erotic presupposition of hegemonic discourse, the "hommo-sexuality" that Irigaray suggests. In any case, Riviere would have us consider that such women sustain masculine identifications not to occupy a position in a sexual exchange, but, rather, to pursue a rivalry that has no sexual object or, at least, that has none that she will name.

Riviere's text offers a way to reconsider the question: What is masked by masquerade? In a key passage that marks a departure from the restricted analysis demarcated by Jones's classificatory system, she suggests that "masquerade" is more than the characteristic of an "intermediate type," that it is central to all "womanliness":

> The reader may now ask how I define womanliness or where I draw the line between genuine womanliness and the "masquerade". My suggestion is not, however, that there is any such difference; whether radical or superficial, they are the same thing. (38)

This refusal to postulate a femininity that is prior to mimicry and the mask is taken up by Stephen Heath in "Joan Riviere and the

Masquerade" as evidence for the notion that "authentic womanliness is such a mimicry, *is* the masquerade." Relying on the postulated characterization of libido as masculine, Heath concludes that femininity is the denial of that libido, the "dissimulation of a fundamental masculinity."[24]

Femininity becomes a mask that dominates/resolves a masculine identification, for a masculine identification would, within the presumed heterosexual matrix of desire, produce a desire for a female object, the Phallus; hence, the donning of femininity as mask may reveal a refusal of a female homosexuality and, at the same time, the hyperbolic incorporation of that female Other who is refused—an odd form of preserving and protecting that love within the circle of the melancholic and negative narcissism that results from the psychic inculcation of compulsory heterosexuality.

One might read Riviere as fearful of her own phallicism[25]—that is, of the phallic identity she risks exposing in the course of her lecture, her writing, indeed, the writing of this phallicism that the essay itself both conceals and enacts. It may, however, be less her own masculine identity than the masculine heterosexual desire that is its signature that she seeks both to deny and enact by becoming the object she forbids herself to love. This is the predicament produced by a matrix that accounts for all desire for women by subjects of whatever sex or gender as originating in a masculine, heterosexual position. The libido-as-masculine is the source from which all possible sexuality is presumed to come.[26]

Here the typology of gender and sexuality needs to give way to a discursive account of the cultural production of gender. If Riviere's analysand is a homosexual without homosexuality, that may be because that option is already refused her; the cultural existence of this prohibition is there in the lecture space, determining and differentiating her as speaker and her mainly male audience. Although she fears that her castrating wish might be understood, she denies that there is a contest over a common object of desire without which the masculine identification that she does acknowledge would lack its confirmation and essential sign. Indeed, her account presupposes the primacy of aggression over sexuality, the desire to castrate and take the place of the masculine subject, a desire avowedly rooted in a rivalry, but one which, for her, exhausts itself in the act of displacement. But the question might usefully be asked: What sexual fantasy does this aggression serve, and what sexuality does it authorize? Although the right to occupy the position of a language user is the ostensible purpose of the analysand's aggression, we can ask whether there is not a repudiation of the feminine that prepares this position within speech and which, invariably, reemerges as the Phallic-Other that will phantasmatically confirm the authority of the speaking subject?

We might then rethink the very notions of masculinity and femininity constructed here as rooted in unresolved homosexual cathexes. The melancholy refusal/domination of homosexuality culminates in the incorporation of the same-sexed object of desire and reemerges in the construction of discrete sexual "natures" that require and institute their opposites through exclusion. To presume the primacy of bisexuality or the primary characterization of the libido as masculine is still not to account for the construction of these various "primacies." Some psychoanalytic accounts would argue that femininity is based in the exclusion of the masculine, where the masculine is one "part" of a bisexual psychic composition. The coexistence of the binary is assumed, and then repression and exclusion intercede to craft discretely gendered "identities" out of this binary, with the result that identity is always already inherent in a bisexual disposition that is, through repression, severed into its component parts. In a sense, the binary restriction on culture postures as the precultural bisexuality that sunders into heterosexual familiarity through its advent into "culture." From the start, however, the binary restriction on sexuality shows clearly that culture in no way postdates the bisexuality that it purports to repress: It constitutes the matrix of intelligibility through which primary bisexuality itself becomes thinkable. The "bisexuality" that is posited as a psychic foundation and is said to be repressed at a later date is a discursive production that claims to be prior to all discourse, effected through the compulsory and generative exclusionary practices of normative heterosexuality.

Lacanian discourse centers on the notion of "a divide," a primary or fundamental split that renders the subject internally divided and that establishes the duality of the sexes. But why this exclusive focus on the fall into twoness? Within Lacanian terms, it appears that division is always the *effect* of the law, and not a preexisting condition on which the law acts. Jacqueline Rose writes that "for both sexes, sexuality will necessarily touch on the duplicity which undermines its fundamental divide,"[27] suggesting that sexual division, effected through repression, is invariably undermined by the very ruse of identity. But is it not a prediscursive doubleness that comes to undermine the univocal posturing of each position within the field of sexual difference? Rose writes compellingly that "for Lacan, as we have seen, there is no prediscursive reality ('How return, other than by means of a special discourse, to a prediscursive reality?', SXX, p. 33), no place prior to the law which is available and can be retrieved." As an indirect critique of Irigaray's efforts to mark a place for feminine writing outside the phallic economy, Rose then adds, "And there is no feminine outside language."[28] If prohibition creates the "fundamental divide" of sexuality, and if this "divide" is shown to be duplicitous precisely because of the artificiality of its division, then there must be a division that *resists* division, a psychic doubleness or inherent bisexuality that comes to undermine every effort of severing. To consider this psychic doubleness as the *effect* of the Law is Lacan's stated purpose, but the point of resistance within his theory as well.

Rose is no doubt right to claim that every identification, precisely because it has a phantasm as its ideal, is bound to fail. Any psychoanalytic theory that prescribes a developmental process that presupposes the accomplishment of a given father-son or mother-daughter identification mistakenly conflates the Symbolic with the real and misses the critical point of incommensurability that exposes "identification" and the drama of "being" and "having" the Phallus as invariably phantasmatic.[29] And yet, what determines the domain of the phantasmatic, the rules that regulate the incommensurability of the Symbolic with the real? It is clearly not enough to claim that this drama holds for Western, late capitalist household dwellers and that perhaps in some yet to be defined epoch some other Symbolic regime will govern the language of sexual ontology. By instituting the Symbolic as invariably phantasmatic, the "invariably" wanders into an "inevitably," generating a description of sexuality in terms that promote cultural stasis as its result.

The rendition of Lacan that understands the prediscursive as an impossibility promises a critique that conceptualizes the Law as prohibitive and generative at once. That the language of physiology or disposition does not appear here is welcome news, but binary restrictions nevertheless still operate to frame and formulate sexuality and delimit in advance the forms of its resistance to the "real." In marking off the very domain of what is subject to repression, exclusion operates prior to repression—that is, in the delimitation of the Law and its objects of subordination. Although one can argue that for Lacan repression creates the repressed through the prohibitive and paternal law, that argument does not account for the pervasive nostalgia for the lost fullness of *jouissance* in his work. Indeed, the loss could not be understood as loss unless the very irrecoverability of that pleasure did not designate a past that is barred from the present through the prohibitive law. That we cannot know that past from the position of the founded subject is not to say that that past does not reemerge within that subject's speech as *fêlure*, discontinuity, metonymic slippage. As the truer noumenal reality existed for Kant, the prejuridical past of *jouissance* is unknowable from within spoken language; that does not mean, however, that this past has no reality. The very inaccessibility of the past, indicated by metonymic slippage in contemporary speech, confirms that original fullness as the ultimate reality.

The further question emerges: What plausibility can be given to an account of the Symbolic that requires a conformity to the Law that

71

proves impossible to perform and that makes no room for the flexibility of the Law itself, its cultural reformulation in more plastic forms? The injunction to become sexed in the ways prescribed by the Symbolic always leads to failure and, in some cases, to the exposure of the phantasmatic nature of sexual identity itself. The Symbolic's claim to be cultural intelligibility in its present and hegemonic form effectively consolidates the power of those phantasms as well as the various dramas of identificatory failures. The alternative is not to suggest that identification should become a viable accomplishment. But there does seem to be a romanticization or, indeed, a religious idealization of "failure," humility and limitation before the Law, which makes the Lacanian narrative ideologically suspect. The dialectic between a juridical imperative that cannot be fulfilled and an inevitable failure "before the law" recalls the tortured relationship between the God of the Old Testament and those humiliated servants who offer their obedience without reward. That sexuality now embodies this religious impulse in the form of the demand for love (considered to be an "absolute" demand) that is distinct from both need and desire (a kind of ecstatic transcendence that eclipses sexuality altogether) lends further credibility to the Symbolic as that which operates for human subjects as the inaccessible but all-determining deity.

This structure of religious tragedy in Lacanian theory effectively undermines any strategy of cultural politics to configure an alternative imaginary for the play of desires. If the Symbolic guarantees the failure of the tasks it commands, perhaps its purposes, like those of the Old Testament God, are altogether unteleological—not the accomplishment of some goal, but obedience and suffering to enforce the "subject's" sense of limitation "before the law." There is, of course, the comic side to this drama that is revealed through the disclosure of the permanent impossibility of the realization of identity. But even this comedy is the inverse expression of an enslavement to the God that it claims to be unable to overcome.

Lacanian theory must be understood as a kind of "slave morality."

How would Lacanian theory be reformulated after the appropriation of Nietzsche's insight in *On the Genealogy of Morals* that God, the inaccessible Symbolic, *is rendered inaccessible* by a power (the will-to-power) that regularly institutes its own powerlessness?[30] This figuration of the paternal law as the inevitable and unknowable authority before which the sexed subject is bound to fail must be read for the theological impulse that motivates it as well as for the critique of theology that points beyond it. The construction of the law that guarantees failure is symptomatic of a slave morality that disavows the very generative powers it uses to construct the "Law" as a permanent impossibility. What is the power that creates this fiction that reflects inevitable subjection? What are the cultural stakes in keeping power within that self-negating circle, and how might that power be reclaimed from the trappings of a prohibitive law that is that power in its dissimulation and self-subjection?

III. Freud and the Melancholia of Gender

Although Irigaray maintains that the structure of femininity and melancholy "cross-check"[31] and Kristeva identifies motherhood with melancholy in "Motherhood According to Bellini" as well as *Soleil noir: Dépression et mélancolie,*[32] there has been little effort to understand the melancholic denial/preservation of homosexuality in the production of gender within the heterosexual frame. Freud isolates the mechanism of melancholia as essential to "ego formation" and "character," but only alludes to the centrality of melancholia to gender. In *The Ego and the Id* (1923), he elaborates on the structure of mourning as the incipient structure of ego formation, a thesis whose traces can be found in the 1917 essay "Mourning and Melancholia."[33] In the experience of losing another human being whom one has loved, Freud argues, the ego is said to incorporate that other into the very structure of the ego, taking on attributes of the other and "sustaining" the other through magical acts of imitation. The loss of the other whom one desires and loves is overcome through a specific act of identification that seeks to harbor that other within the very structure of the self: "So by taking flight into the ego, love escapes annihilation" (178). This identification is not simply momentary or occasional, but becomes a new structure of identity; in effect, the other becomes part of the ego through the permanent internalization of the other's attributes.[34] In cases in which an ambivalent relationship is severed through loss, that ambivalence becomes internalized as a self-critical or self-debasing disposition in which the role of the other is now occupied and directed by the ego itself: "The narcissistic identification with the object then becomes a substitute for the erotic cathexis, the result of which is that in spite of the conflict with the loved person the love-relation need not be given up" (170). Later, Freud makes clear that the process of internalizing and sustaining lost loves is crucial to the formation of the ego and its "object-choice."

In *The Ego and the Id,* Freud refers to this process of internalization described in "Mourning and Melancholia" and remarks:

> we succeeded in explaining the painful disorder of melancholia by supposing that [in those suffering from it] an object which was lost has been set up again inside the ego—that is, that an object-cathexis has been replaced by an identification. At that time, however, we did not appreciate the full significance of this process and did not know how common and how typical it is. Since then we have come to understand that this kind of substitution has a great share in determining the form taken by the ego and that it makes an essential contribution towards building up what is called its "character." (18)

As this chapter on "The Ego and the Super-Ego (Ego-Ideal)" proceeds, however, it is not merely "character" that is being described, but the acquisition of gender identity as well. In claiming that "it may be that this identification is the sole condition under which the id can give up its objects," Freud suggests that the internalizing strategy of melancholia does not *oppose* the work of mourning, but may be the only way in which the ego can survive the loss of its essential emotional ties to others. Freud goes on to claim that "the character of the ego is a precipitate of abandoned object-cathexes and that it contains the history of those object-choices" (19). This process of internalizing lost loves becomes pertinent to gender formation when we realize that the incest taboo, among other functions, initiates a loss of a love-object for the ego and that this ego recuperates from this loss through the internalization of the tabooed object of desire. In the case of a prohibited heterosexual union, it is the object which is denied, but not the modality of desire, so that the desire is deflected from that object onto other objects of the opposite sex. But in the case of a prohibited homosexual union, it is clear that both the desire and the object require renunciation and so become subject to the internalizing strategies of melancholia. Hence, "the young boy deals with his father by identifying himself with him" (21).

In the first formation of the boy-father identification, Freud speculates that the identification takes place without the prior object cathexis (21), meaning that the identification is not the consequence of a love lost or prohibited of the son for the father. Later, however, Freud does postulate primary bisexuality as a complicating factor in the process of character and gender formation. With the postulation of a bisexual set of libidinal dispositions, there is no reason to deny an original sexual love of the son for the father, and yet Freud implicitly does. The boy does, however, sustain a primary cathexis for the mother, and Freud remarks that bisexuality there makes itself known in the masculine and feminine behavior with which the boy-child attempts to seduce the mother.

Although Freud introduces the Oedipal complex to explain why the boy must repudiate the mother and adopt an ambivalent attitude toward the father, he remarks shortly afterward that, "It may even be that the ambivalence displayed in the relations to the parents should be attributed entirely to bisexuality and that it is not, as I have represented above, developed out of identification in consequence of rivalry" (23, n.1). But what would condition the ambivalence in such a case? Clearly, Freud means to suggest that the boy must choose not only between the two object choices, but the two sexual dispositions, masculine and feminine. That the boy usually chooses the heterosexual would, then, be the result, not of the fear of castration by the father, but of the fear of castration—that is, the fear of "feminization" associated within heterosexual cultures with male homosexuality. In effect, it is not primarily the heterosexual lust for the mother that must be punished and sublimated, but the homosexual cathexis that must be subordinated to a culturally sanctioned heterosexuality. Indeed, if it is primary bisexuality rather than the Oedipal drama of rivalry which produces the boy's repudiation of femininity and his ambivalence toward his father, then the primacy of the maternal cathexis becomes increasingly suspect and, consequently, the primary heterosexuality of the boy's object cathexis.

Regardless of the reason for the boy's repudiation of the mother (do we construe the punishing father as a rival or as an object of desire who forbids himself as such?), the repudiation becomes the founding moment of what Freud calls gender "consolidation." Forfeiting the mother as object of desire, the boy either internalizes the loss through identification with her, or displaces his heterosexual attachment, in which case he fortifies his attachment to his father and thereby "consolidates" his masculinity. As the metaphor of consolidation suggests, there are clearly bits and pieces of masculinity to be found within the psychic landscape, dispositions, sexual trends, and aims, but they are diffuse and disorganized, unbounded by the exclusivity of a heterosexual object choice. Indeed, if the boy renounces both aim and object and, therefore, heterosexual cathexis altogether, he internalizes the mother and sets up a feminine superego which dissolves and disorganizes masculinity, consolidating feminine libidinal dispositions in its place.

For the young girl as well, the Oedipal complex can be either "positive" (same-sex identification) or "negative" (opposite-sex identification); the loss of the father initiated by the incest taboo may result either in an identification with the object lost (a consolidation of masculinity) or a deflection of the aim from the object, in which case heterosexuality triumphs over homosexuality, and a substitute object is found. At the close of his brief paragraph on the negative Oedipal complex in the young girl, Freud remarks that the factor that decides which identification is accomplished is the strength or weakness of masculinity and femininity in her disposition. Significantly, Freud avows his confusion about what precisely a masculine or feminine disposition is when he interrupts his statement midway with the hyphenated doubt: "—whatever that may consist in—" (22).

What are these primary dispositions on which Freud himself apparently founders? Are these attributes of an unconscious libidinal organization, and how precisely do the various identifications set up in consequence of the Oedipal conflict work to reinforce or dissolve each of these dispositions? What aspect of "femininity" do we call dispositional, and which is the consequence of identification? Indeed, what is to keep us from understanding the "dispositions" of bisexuality as the *effects* or *productions* of a series of internalizations? Moreover, how do we identify a "feminine" or a "masculine" disposition at the outset? By what traces is it known, and to what extent do we assume a "feminine" or a "masculine" disposition as the precondition of a heterosexual object choice? In other words, to what extent do we read the desire for the father as evidence of a feminine disposition only because we begin, despite the postulation of primary bisexuality, with a heterosexual matrix for desire?

The conceptualization of bisexuality in terms of *dispositions,* feminine and masculine, which have heterosexual aims as their intentional correlates, suggests that for Freud *bisexuality is the coincidence of two heterosexual desires within a single psyche.* The masculine disposition is, in effect, never oriented toward the father as an object of sexual love, and neither is the feminine disposition oriented toward the mother (the young girl may be so oriented, but this is before she has renounced that "masculine" side of her dispositional nature). In repudiating the mother as an object of sexual love, the girl of necessity repudiates her masculinity and, paradoxically, "fixes" her femininity as a consequence. Hence, within Freud's thesis of primary bisexuality, there is no homosexuality, and only opposites attract.

But what is the proof Freud gives us for the existence of such dispositions? If there is no way to distinguish between the femininity acquired through internalizations and that which is strictly dispositional, then what is to preclude the conclusion that all gender-specific affinities are the consequence of internalizations? On what basis are dispositional sexualities and identities ascribed to individuals, and what meaning can we give to "femininity" and "masculinity" at the outset? Taking the problematic of internalization as a point of departure, let us consider the status of internalized identifications in the formation of gender and, secondarily, the relation between an internalized gender affinity and the self-punishing melancholia of internalized identifications.

In "Mourning and Melancholia," Freud interprets the self-critical attitudes of the melancholic to be the result of the internalization of a lost object of love. Precisely because that object is lost, even though the relationship remains ambivalent and unresolved, the object is "brought inside" the ego where the quarrel magically resumes as an interior dialogue between two parts of the psyche. In "Mourning and Melancholia," the lost object is set up within the ego as a critical voice or agency, and the anger originally felt for the object is reversed so that the internalized object now berates the ego:

> If one listens patiently to the many and various self-accusations of the melancholic, one cannot in the end avoid the impression that often the most violent of them are hardly applicable to the patient himself, but that with insignificant modifications they do fit someone else, some person whom the patient loves, has loved or ought to love. . . . the self-reproaches are reproaches against a loved object which have been shifted onto the patient's own ego. (169)

The melancholic refuses the loss of the object, and internalization becomes a strategy of magically resuscitating the lost object, not only because the loss is painful, but because the ambivalence felt toward the object requires that the object be retained until differences are settled. In this early essay, Freud understands grief to be the withdrawal of libidinal cathexis from the object and the successful transferral of that cathexis onto a fresh object. In *The Ego and the Id,* however, Freud revises this distinction between mourning and melancholia and suggests that the identification process associated with melancholia may be "the sole condition under which the id can give up its objects" (19). In other words, the identification with lost loves characteristic of melancholia becomes the precondition for the work of mourning. The two processes, originally conceived as oppositional, are now understood as integrally related aspects of the grieving process.[35] In his later view, Freud remarks that the internalization of loss is compensatory: "When the ego assumes the features of the object, it is forcing itself, so to speak, upon the id's loss by saying: 'Look, you can love me too—I am so like the object' "(20). Strictly speaking, the giving up of the object is not a negation of the cathexis, but its internalization and, hence, preservation.

What precisely is the topology of the psyche in which the ego and its lost loves reside in perpetual habitation? Clearly, Freud conceptualizes the ego in the perpetual company of the ego ideal which acts as a moral agency of various kinds. The internalized losses of the ego are reestablished as part of this agency of moral scrutiny, the internalization of anger and blame originally felt for the object in its external mode. In the act of internalization, that anger and blame, inevitably heightened by the loss itself, are turned inward and sustained; the ego changes place with the internalized object, thereby investing this internalized externality with moral agency and power. Thus, the ego forfeits its anger and efficacy to the ego ideal which turns against the very ego by which it is sustained; in other words, the ego constructs a way to turn against itself. Indeed, Freud warns of the hypermoral possibilities of this ego ideal, which, taken to its extreme, can motivate suicide.[36]

The construction of the interior ego ideal involves the internalization of gender identities as well. Freud remarks that the ego ideal is a solution to the Oedipal complex and is thus instrumental in the successful consolidation of masculinity and femininity:

> The super-ego is, however, not simply a residue of the earliest object-choices of the id: it also represents an energetic reaction-formation against these choices. Its relation to the ego is not exhausted by the precept: "You ought to be like this (like your father.)" It also comprises the prohibition: "You *may not be* like this (like your father)—that is, you may not do all that he does; some things are his prerogative." (24)

The ego ideal thus serves as an interior agency of sanction and taboo which, according to Freud, works to consolidate gender identity through the appropriate rechanneling and sublimation of desire. The internalization of the parent as object of love suffers a necessary inversion of meaning. The parent is not only prohibited as an object of love, but is internalized as a *prohibiting* or withholding object of love. The prohibitive function of the ego ideal thus works to inhibit or, indeed, repress the expression of desire for that parent, but also founds an interior "space" in which that love can be *preserved*. Because the solution to the Oedipal dilemma can be either "positive" or "negative," the prohibition of the opposite-sexed parent can either lead to an identification with the sex of the parent lost or a refusal of that identification and, consequently, a deflection of heterosexual desire.

As a set of sanctions and taboos, the ego ideal regulates and determines masculine and feminine identification. Because identifications substitute for object relations, and identifications are the consequence of loss, gender identification is a kind of melancholia in which the sex of the prohibited object is internalized as a prohibition. This prohibition sanctions and regulates discrete gendered identity and the law of heterosexual desire. The resolution of the Oedipal complex affects gender identification through not only the incest taboo, but, prior to that, the taboo against homosexuality. The result is that one identifies with the same-sexed object of love, thereby internalizing both the aim and object of the homosexual cathexis. The identifications consequent to melancholia are modes of preserving unresolved object relations, and in the case of same-sexed gender identification, the unresolved object relations are invariably homosexual. Indeed, the stricter and more stable the gender affinity, the less resolved the original loss, so that rigid gender boundaries inevitably work to conceal the loss of an original love that, unacknowledged, fails to be resolved.

But clearly not all gender identification is based on the successful implementation of the taboo against homosexuality. If feminine and masculine dispositions are the result of the effective internalization of that taboo, and if the melancholic answer to the loss of the same-sexed object is to incorporate and, indeed, *to become* that object through the construction of the ego ideal, then gender identity appears primarily to be the internalization of a prohibition that proves to be formative of identity. Further, this identity is constructed and maintained by the consistent application of this taboo, not only in the stylization of the body in compliance with discrete categories of sex, but in the production and "disposition" of sexual desire. The language of disposition moves from a verb formation (*to be disposed*) into a noun formation, whereupon it becomes congealed (*to have dispositions*); the language of "dispositions" thus arrives as a false foundationalism, the results of affectivity being formed or "fixed" through the effects of the prohibition. As a consequence, dispositions are not the primary sexual facts of the psyche, but produced effects of a law imposed by culture and by the complicitous and transvaluating acts of the ego ideal.

In melancholia, the loved object is lost through a variety of means: separation, death, or the breaking of an emotional tie. In the Oedipal situation, however, the loss is dictated by a *prohibition* attended by a set of punishments. The melancholia of gender identification which "answers" the Oedipal dilemma must be understood, then, as the internalization of an interior moral directive which gains its structure and energy from an externally enforced taboo. Although Freud does not explicitly argue in its favor, it would appear that the taboo against homosexuality must *precede* the heterosexual incest taboo; the taboo against homosexuality in effect creates the heterosexual "dispositions" by which the Oedipal conflict becomes possible. The young boy and young girl who enter into the Oedipal drama with incestuous hetero-sexual aims have already been subjected to prohibitions which "dis-pose" them in distinct sexual directions. Hence, the dispositions that Freud assumes to be primary or constitutive facts of sexual life are effects of a law which, internalized, produces and regulates discrete gender identity and heterosexuality.

Far from foundational, these dispositions are the result of a process whose aim is to disguise its own genealogy. In other words, "disposi-tions" are traces of a history of enforced sexual prohibitions which is untold and which the prohibitions seek to render untellable. The nar-rative account of gender acquisition that begins with the postulation of dispositions effectively forecloses the narrative point of departure which would expose the narrative as a self-amplifying tactic of the pro-hibition itself. In the psychoanalytic narrative, the dispositions are trained, fixed, and consolidated by a prohibition which later and in the name of culture arrives to quell the disturbance created by an unre-strained homosexual cathexis. Told from the point of view which takes the prohibitive law to be the founding moment of the narrative, the law both produces sexuality in the form of "dispositions" and appears disingenuously at a later point in time to transform these ostensibly "natural" dispositions into culturally acceptable structures of exogamic kinship. In order to conceal the genealogy of the law as productive of the very phenomenon it later claims only to channel or repress, the law performs a third function: Instating itself as the principle of logical continuity in a narrative of causal relations which takes psychic facts as its point of departure, this configuration of the law forecloses the pos-sibility of a more radical genealogy into the cultural origins of sexuali-ty and power relations.

What precisely does it mean to reverse Freud's causal narrative and to think of primary dispositions as effects of the law? In the first volume of *The History of Sexuality,* Foucault criticizes the repressive hypothesis for the presumption of an original desire (not "desire" in Lacan's terms, but *jouissance*) that maintains ontological integrity and temporal priority with respect to the repressive law.[37] This law, according to Foucault, subsequently silences or transmutes that desire into a secondary and inevitably dissatisfying form or expression (displacement). Foucault argues that the desire which is conceived as both original and repressed is the effect of the subjugating law itself. In consequence, the law produces the conceit of the repressed desire in order to rationalize its own self-amplifying strategies, and, rather than exercise a repressive function, the juridical law, here as elsewhere, ought to be reconceived as a discursive practice which is productive or generative—discursive in that it produces the linguistic fiction of repressed desire in order to maintain its own position as a teleological instrument. The desire in question takes on the meaning of "repressed" to the extent that the law constitutes its contextualizing frame; indeed, the law identifies and invigorates "repressed desire" as such, circulates the term, and, in effect, carves out the discursive space for the self-conscious and linguistically elaborated experience called "repressed desire."

The taboo against incest and, implicitly, against homosexuality is a repressive injunction which presumes an original desire localized in the notion of "dispositions," which suffers a repression of an originally homosexual libidinal directionality and produces the displaced phenomenon of heterosexual desire. The structure of this particular metanarrative of infantile development figures sexual dispositions as the prediscursive, temporally primary, and ontologically discrete drives which have a purpose and, hence, a meaning prior to their emergence into language and culture. The very entry into the cultural field deflects that desire from its original meaning, with the consequence that desire within culture is, of necessity, a series of displacements. Thus, the repressive law effectively produces heterosexuality, and acts not merely as a negative or exclusionary code, but as a sanction and, most pertinently, as a law of discourse, distinguishing the speakable from the unspeakable (delimiting and constructing the domain of the unspeakable), the legitimate from the illegitimate.

IV. GENDER COMPLEXITY AND THE LIMITS
OF IDENTIFICATION

The foregoing analyses of Lacan, Riviere, and Freud's *The Ego and the Id* offer competing versions of how gender identifications work—indeed, of whether they can be said to "work" at all. Can gender complexity and dissonance be accounted for by the multiplication and convergence of a variety of culturally dissonant identifications? Or is all identification constructed through the exclusion of a sexuality that puts those identifications into question? In the first instance, multiple identifications can constitute a nonhierarchical configuration of shifting and overlapping identifications that call into question the primacy of any univocal gender attribution. In the Lacanian framework, identification is understood to be fixed within the binary disjunction of "having" or "being" the Phallus, with the consequence that the excluded term of the binary continually haunts and disrupts the coherent posturing of any one. The excluded term is an excluded sexuality that contests the self-grounding pretensions of the subject as well as its claims to know the source and object of its desire.

For the most part, feminist critics concerned with the psychoanalytic problematic of identification have often focused on the question of a maternal identification and sought to elaborate a feminist epistemological position from that maternal identification and/or a maternal discourse evolved from the point of view of that identification and its difficulties. Although much of that work is extremely significant and clearly influential, it has come to occupy a hegemonic position within the emerging canon of feminist theory. Further, it tends to reinforce precisely the binary, heterosexist framework that carves up genders into masculine and feminine and forecloses an adequate description of the kinds of subversive and parodic convergences that characterize gay and lesbian cultures. As a very partial effort to come to terms with that maternalist discourse, however, Julia Kristeva's description of the semiotic as a maternal subversion of the Symbolic will be examined in the following chapter.

What critical strategies and sources of subversion appear as the consequence of the psychoanalytic accounts considered so far? The recourse to the unconscious as a source of subversion makes sense, it seems, only if the paternal law is understood as a rigid and universal determinism which makes of "identity" a fixed and phantasmatic affair. Even if we accept the phantasmatic content of identity, there is no reason to assume that the law which fixes the terms of that fantasy is impervious to historical variability and possibility.

As opposed to the founding Law of the Symbolic that fixes identity in advance, we might reconsider the history of constitutive identifications without the presupposition of a fixed and founding Law. Although the "universality" of the paternal law may be contested within anthropological circles, it seems important to consider that the *meaning* that the law sustains in any given historical context is less univocal and less deterministically efficacious than the Lacanian account appears to acknowledge. It should be possible to offer a schematic of the ways in which a constellation of identifications conforms or fails to conform to culturally imposed standards of gender integrity. The constitutive identifications of an autobiographical narrative are always partially fabricated in the telling. Lacan claims that we can never tell the story of our origins, precisely because language bars the speaking subject from the repressed libidinal origins of its speech; however, the foundational moment in which the paternal law institutes the subject seems to function as a metahistory which we not only can but ought to tell, even though the founding moments of the subject, the institution of the law, is as equally prior to the speaking subject as the unconscious itself.

The alternative perspective on identification that emerges from psychoanalytic theory suggests that multiple and coexisting identifications produce conflicts, convergences, and innovative dissonances within gender configurations which contest the fixity of masculine and feminine placements with respect to the paternal law. In effect, the possibility of multiple identifications (which are not finally reducible to primary or founding identifications that are fixed within masculine and feminine positions) suggests that the Law is not deterministic and that "the" law may not even be singular.

The debate over the meaning or subversive possibilities of identifications so far has left unclear exactly where those identifications are to be found. The interior psychic space in which identifications are said to be preserved makes sense only if we can understand that interior space as a phantasized locale that serves yet another psychic function. In agreement with Nicolas Abraham and Maria Torok it seems, psychoanalyst Roy Schafer argues that "incorporation" is a fantasy and not a process; the interior space into which an object is taken is imagined, and imagined within a language that can conjure and reify such spaces.[38] If the identifications sustained through melancholy are "incorporated," then the question remains: Where is this incorporated space? If it is not literally within the body, perhaps it is *on* the body as its surface signification such that the body must itself be understood *as* an incorporated space.

Abraham and Torok have argued that introjection is a process that serves the work of mourning (where the object is not only lost, but acknowledged as lost).[39] Incorporation, on the other hand, belongs more properly to melancholy, the state of disavowed or suspended grief in which the object is magically sustained "in the body" in some way. Abraham and Torok suggest that introjection of the loss characteristic of mourning establishes *an empty space,* literalized by the empty mouth which becomes the condition of speech and signification. The successful displacement of the libido from the lost object is achieved through the formation of *words* which both signify and displace that object; this displacement from the original object is an essentially metaphorical activity in which words "figure" the absence and surpass it. Introjection is understood to be the work of mourning, but incorporation, which denotes a *magical* resolution of loss, characterizes melancholy. Whereas introjection founds the possibility of metaphorical signification, incorporation is antimetaphorical precisely because it maintains the loss as radically unnameable; in other words, incorporation is not only a failure to name or avow the loss, but erodes the conditions of metaphorical signification itself.

As in the Lacanian perspective, for Abraham and Torok the repudiation of the maternal body is the condition of signification within the Symbolic. They argue further that this primary repression founds the possibility of individuation and of significant speech, where speech is necessarily metaphorical, in the sense that the referent, the object of desire, is a perpetual displacement. In effect, the loss of the maternal body as an object of love is understood to establish the empty space out of which words originate. But the refusal of this loss—melancholy— results in the failure to displace into words; indeed, the place of the maternal body is established in the body, "encrypted," to use their term, and given permanent residence there as a dead and deadening part of the body or one inhabited or possessed by phantasms of various kinds.

When we consider gender identity as a melancholic structure, it makes sense to choose "incorporation" as the manner by which that identification is accomplished. Indeed, according to the scheme above, gender identity would be established through a refusal of loss that encrypts itself in the body and that determines, in effect, the living versus the dead body. As an antimetaphorical activity, incorporation *literalizes* the loss *on* or *in* the body and so appears as the facticity of the body, the means by which the body comes to bear "sex" as its literal truth. The localization and/or prohibition of pleasures and desires in given "erotogenic" zones is precisely the kind of gender-differentiating melancholy that suffuses the body's surface. The loss of the pleasurable object is resolved through the incorporation of that very pleasure with the result that pleasure is both determined and prohibited through the compulsory effects of the gender-differentiating law.

The incest taboo is, of course, more inclusive than the taboo against homosexuality, but in the case of the heterosexual incest taboo through which heterosexual identity is established, the loss is borne as grief. In the case of the prohibition against homosexual incest through which heterosexual identity is established, however, the loss is sustained through a melancholic structure. The loss of the heterosexual object, argues Freud, results in the displacement of that object, but not the heterosexual aim; on the other hand, the loss of the homosexual object requires the loss of the aim *and* the object. In other words, the object is not only lost, but the desire fully denied, such that "I never lost that person and I never loved that person, indeed never felt that kind of love at all." The melancholic preservation of that love is all the more securely safeguarded through the totalizing trajectory of the denial.

Irigaray's argument that in Freud's work the structures of melancholy and of developed femininity are very similar refers to the denial of both object and aim that constitutes the "double wave" of repression characteristic of a fully developed femininity. For Irigaray, it is the recognition of castration that initiates the young girl into "a 'loss' that radically escapes any representation."[40] Melancholia is thus a psychoanalytic norm for women, one that rests upon her ostensible desire to have the penis, a desire which, conveniently, can no longer be felt or known.

Irigaray's reading, full of mocking citations, is right to debunk the developmental claims regarding sexuality and femininity that clearly pervade Freud's text. As she also shows, there are possible readings of that theory that exceed, invert, and displace Freud's stated aims. Consider that the refusal of the homosexual cathexis, desire and aim together, a refusal both compelled by social taboo and appropriated through developmental stages, results in a melancholic structure which effectively encloses that aim and object within the corporeal space or "crypt" established through an abiding denial. If the heterosexual denial of homosexuality results in melancholia and if melancholia operates through incorporation, then the disavowed homosexual love is preserved through the cultivation of an oppositionally defined gender identity. In other words, disavowed male homosexuality culminates in a heightened or consolidated masculinity, one which maintains the feminine as the unthinkable and unnameable. The acknowledgment of heterosexual desire, however, leads to a displacement from an original to a secondary object, precisely the kind of libidinal detachment and reattachment that Freud affirms as the character of normal grief.

Clearly, a homosexual for whom heterosexual desire is unthinkable may well maintain that heterosexuality through a melancholic structure of incorporation, an identification and embodiment of the love that is neither acknowledged nor grieved. But here it becomes clear that the heterosexual refusal to acknowledge the primary homosexual attachment is culturally enforced by a prohibition on homosexuality which is in no way paralleled in the case of the melancholic homosexual. In other words, heterosexual melancholy is culturally instituted and maintained as the price of stable gender identities related through oppositional desires.

But what language of surface and depth adequately expresses this incorporating effect of melancholy? A preliminary answer to this question is possible within the psychoanalytic discourse, but a fuller understanding will lead in the last chapter to a consideration of gender as an enactment that performatively constitutes the appearance of its own interior fixity. At this point, however, the contention that incorporation is a fantasy suggests that the incorporation of an identification is a fantasy of literalization or a *literalizing fantasy*.[41] Precisely by virtue of its melancholic structure, this literalization of the body conceals its genealogy and offers itself under the category of "natural fact."

What does it mean to sustain a literalizing fantasy? If gender differentiation follows upon the incest taboo and the prior taboo on homosexuality, then "becoming" a gender is a laborious process of becoming *naturalized*, which requires a differentiation of bodily pleasures and parts on the basis of gendered meanings. Pleasures are said to reside in the penis, the vagina, and the breasts or to emanate from them, but such descriptions correspond to a body which has already been constructed or naturalized as gender-specific. In other words, some parts of the body become conceivable foci of pleasure precisely because they correspond to a normative ideal of a gender-specific body. Pleasures are in some sense determined by the melancholic structure of gender whereby some organs are deadened to pleasure, and others brought to life. Which pleasures shall live and which shall die is often a matter of which serve the legitimating practices of identity formation that take place within the matrix of gender norms.[42]

Transsexuals often claim a radical discontinuity between sexual pleasures and bodily parts. Very often what is wanted in terms of pleasure requires an imaginary participation in body parts, either appendages or orifices, that one might not actually possess, or, similarly, pleasure may require imagining an exaggerated or diminished set of parts. The imaginary status of desire, of course, is not restricted to the transsexual identity; the phantasmatic nature of desire reveals the body not as its ground or cause, but as its *occasion* and its *object*. The strategy of desire is in part the transfiguration of the desiring body itself. Indeed, in order to desire at all it may be necessary to believe in an altered bodily ego[43] which, within the gendered rules of the imaginary, might fit the requirements of a body capable of desire. This imaginary condition of desire always exceeds the physical body through or on which it works.

Always already a cultural sign, the body sets limits to the imaginary meanings that it occasions, but is never free of an imaginary construction. The fantasized body can never be understood in relation to the body as real; it can only be understood in relation to another culturally instituted fantasy, one which claims the place of the "literal" and the "real." The limits to the "real" are produced within the naturalized heterosexualization of bodies in which physical facts serve as causes and desires reflect the inexorable effects of that physicality.

The conflation of desire with the real—that is, the belief that it is parts of the body, the "literal" penis, the "literal" vagina, which cause pleasure and desire—is precisely the kind of literalizing fantasy char-

acteristic of the syndrome of melancholic heterosexuality. The disavowed homosexuality at the base of melancholic heterosexuality
reemerges as the self-evident anatomical facticity of sex, where "sex"
designates the blurred unity of anatomy, "natural identity," and "natural
desire." The loss is denied and incorporated, and the genealogy of that
transmutation fully forgotten and repressed. The sexed surface of the
body thus emerges as the necessary sign of a natural(ized) identity and
desire. The loss of homosexuality is refused and the love sustained or
encrypted in the parts of the body itself, literalized in the ostensible
anatomical facticity of sex. Here we see the general strategy of literalization as a form of forgetfulness, which, in the case of a literalized
sexual anatomy, "forgets" the imaginary and, with it, an imaginable
homosexuality. In the case of the melancholic heterosexual male, he
never loved another man, he *is* a man, and he can seek recourse to the
empirical facts that will prove it. But the literalization of anatomy not
only proves nothing, but is a literalizing restriction of pleasure in the
very organ that is championed as the sign of masculine identity. The
love for the father is stored in the penis, safeguarded through an
impervious denial, and the desire which now centers on that penis has
that continual denial as its structure and its task. Indeed, the woman-
as-object must be the sign that he not only never felt homosexual
desire, but never felt the grief over its loss. Indeed, the woman-as-sign
must effectively displace and conceal that preheterosexual history in
favor of one that consecrates a seamless heterosexuality.

v. Reformulating Prohibition as Power

Although Foucault's genealogical critique of foundationalism has
guided this reading of Lévi-Strauss, Freud, and the heterosexual
matrix, an even more precise understanding is needed of how the
juridical law of psychoanalysis, repression, produces and proliferates
the genders it seeks to control. Feminist theorists have been drawn to
the psychoanalytic account of sexual difference in part because the
Oedipal and pre-Oedipal dynamics appear to offer a way to trace the

primary construction of gender. Can the prohibition against incest that proscribes and sanctions hierarchial and binary gendered positions be reconceived as a productive power that inadvertently generates several cultural configurations of gender? Is the incest taboo subject to the critique of the repressive hypothesis that Foucault provides? What would a feminist deployment of that critique look like? Would such a critique mobilize the project to confound the binary restrictions on sex/gender imposed by the heterosexual matrix? Clearly, one of the most influential feminist readings of Lévi-Strauss, Lacan, and Freud is Gayle Rubin's "The Traffic of Women: The 'Political Economy' of Sex," published in 1975.[44] Although Foucault does not appear in that article, Rubin effectively sets the stage for a Foucaultian critique. That she herself later appropriates Foucault for her own work in radical sexual theory[45] retrospectively raises the question of how that influential article might be rewritten within a Foucaultian frame.

Foucault's analysis of the culturally productive possibilities of the prohibitive law clearly takes its bearing within the existing theory on sublimation articulated by Freud in *Civilization and its Discontents* and reinterpreted by Marcuse in *Eros and Civilization*. Both Freud and Marcuse identify the productive effects of sublimation, arguing that cultural artifacts and institutions are the effects of sublimated Eros. Although Freud saw the sublimation of sexuality as producing a general "discontent," Marcuse subordinates Eros to Logos in Platonic fashion and saw in the act of sublimation the most satisfying expression of the human spirit. In a radical departure from these theories of sublimation, however, Foucault argues on behalf of a productive law without the postulation of an original desire; the operation of this law is justified and consolidated through the construction of a narrative account of its own genealogy which effectively masks its own immersion in power relations. The incest taboo, then, would repress no primary dispositions, but effectively create the distinction between "primary" and "secondary" dispositions to describe and reproduce the distinction between a legitimate heterosexuality and an illegitimate homosexuality. Indeed, if we conceive of the incest taboo as primarily productive in its effects, then the prohibition that founds the "subject" and survives as the law of its desire becomes the means by which identity, particularly gender identity, is constituted.

Underscoring the incest taboo as both a prohibition and a sanction, Rubin writes:

> the incest taboo imposes the social aim of exogamy and alliance upon the biological events of sex and procreation. The incest taboo divides the universe of sexual choice into categories of permitted and prohibited sexual partners. (173)

Because all cultures seek to reproduce themselves, and because the particular social identity of the kinship group must be preserved, exogamy is instituted and, as its presupposition, so is exogamic heterosexuality. Hence, the incest taboo not only forbids sexual union between members of the same kinship line, but involves a taboo against homosexuality as well. Rubin writes:

> the incest taboo presupposes a prior, less articulate taboo on homosexuality. A prohibition against *some* heterosexual unions assumes a taboo against *non*heterosexual unions. Gender is not only an identification with one sex; it also entails that sexual desire be directed toward the other sex. The sexual division of labor is implicated in both aspects of gender—male and female it creates them, and it creates them heterosexual. (180)

Rubin understands psychoanalysis, especially in its Lacanian incarnation, to complement Lévi-Strauss's description of kinship relations. In particular, she understands that the "sex/gender system," the regulated cultural mechanism of transforming biological males and females into discrete and hierarchized genders, is at once mandated by cultural institutions (the family, the residual forms of "the exchange of women," obligatory heterosexuality) and inculcated through the laws which structure and propel individual psychic development. Hence, the Oedipal complex instantiates and executes the cultural taboo against incest and results in discrete gender identification and a corollary heterosexual disposition. In this essay, Rubin further maintains that before the transformation of a biological male or female into a gendered man or woman, "each child contains all of the sexual possibilities available to human expression" (189).

The effort to locate and describe a sexuality "before the law" as a primary bisexuality or as an ideal and unconstrained polymorphousness implies that the law is antecedent to sexuality. As a restriction of an originary fullness, the law prohibits some set of prepunitive sexual possibilities and the sanctioning of others. But if we apply the Foucaultian critique of the repressive hypothesis to the incest taboo, that paradigmatic law of repression, then it would appear that the law produces *both* sanctioned heterosexuality and transgressive homosexuality. Both are indeed *effects,* temporally and ontologically later than the law itself, and the illusion of a sexuality before the law is itself the creation of that law.

Rubin's essay remains committed to a distinction between sex and gender which assumes the discrete and prior ontological reality of a "sex" which is done over in the name of the law, that is, transformed subsequently into "gender."This narrative of gender acquisition requires a certain temporal ordering of events which assumes that the narrator is in some position to "know" both what is before and after the law. And yet the narration takes place within a language which, strictly speaking, is after the law, the consequence of the law, and so proceeds from a belated and retrospective point of view. If this language is structured by the law, and the law is exemplified, indeed, enacted in the language, then the description, the narration, not only cannot know what is outside itself—that is, prior to the law—but its description of that "before" will always be in the service of the "after." In other words, not only does the narration claim access to a "before" from which it is definitionally (by virtue of its linguisticality) precluded, but the description of the "before" takes place within the terms of the "after" and, hence, becomes an attenuation of the law itself into the site of its absence.

Although Rubin claims that the unlimited universe of sexual possibilities exists for the pre-Oedipal child, she does not subscribe to a primary bisexuality. Indeed, bisexuality is the consequence of child-rearing practices in which parents of both sexes are present and presently occupied with child care and in which the repudiation of femininity no longer serves as a precondition of gender identity for both men and women (199). When Rubin calls for a "revolution in kinship," she envisions the eradication of the exchange of women, the traces of which are evident not only in the contemporary institutionalization of heterosexuality, but in the residual psychic norms (the institutionalization of the psyche) which sanction and construct sexuality and gender identity in heterosexual terms. With the loosening of the compulsory character of heterosexuality and the simultaneous emergence of bisexual and homosexual cultural possibilities for behavior and identity, Rubin envisions the overthrow of gender itself (204). Inasmuch as gender is the cultural transformation of a biological polysexuality into a culturally mandated heterosexuality and inasmuch as that heterosexuality deploys discrete and hierarchized gender identities to accomplish its aim, then the breakdown of the compulsory character of heterosexuality would imply, for Rubin, the corollary breakdown of gender itself. Whether or not gender can be fully eradicated and in what sense its "breakdown" is culturally imaginable remain intriguing but unclarified implications of her analysis.

Rubin's argument rests on the possibility that the law can be effectively overthrown and that the cultural interpretation of differently sexed bodies can proceed, ideally, without reference to gender disparity. That systems of compulsory heterosexuality may alter, and indeed have changed, and that the exchange of women, in whatever residual form, need not always determine heterosexual exchange, seems clear; in this sense, Rubin recognizes the misogynist implications of Lévi-

Strauss's notoriously nondiachronic structuralism. But what leads her to the conclusion that gender is merely a function of compulsory heterosexuality and that without that compulsory status, the field of bodies would no longer be marked in gendered terms? Clearly, Rubin has already envisioned an alternative sexual world, one which is attributed to a utopian stage in infantile development, a "before" the law which promises to reemerge "after" the demise or dispersal of that law. If we accept the Foucaultian and Derridean criticisms of the viability of knowing or referring to such a "before," how would we revise this narrative of gender acquisition? If we reject the postulation of an ideal sexuality prior to the incest taboo, and if we also refuse to accept the structuralist premise of the cultural permanence of that taboo, what relation between sexuality and the law remains for the description of gender? Do we need recourse to a happier state before the law in order to maintain that contemporary gender relations and the punitive production of gender identities are oppressive?

Foucault's critique of the repressive-hypothesis in *The History of Sexuality, Volume I* argues that (a) the structuralist "law" might be understood as one formation of *power*, a specific historical configuration and that (b) the law might be understood to produce or generate the desire it is said to repress. The object of repression is not *the desire* it takes to be its ostensible object, but the multiple configurations of power itself, the very plurality of which would displace the seeming universality and necessity of the juridical or repressive law. In other words, desire and its repression are an occasion for the consolidation of juridical structures; desire is manufactured and forbidden as a ritual symbolic gesture whereby the juridical model exercises and consolidates its own power.

The incest taboo is the juridical law that is said both to prohibit incestuous desires and to construct certain gendered subjectivities through the mechanism of compulsory identification. But what is to guarantee the universality or necessity of this law? Clearly, there are anthropological debates that seek to affirm and to dispute the universality of the incest taboo,[46] and there is a second-order dispute over what, if anything, the claim to universality might imply about the meaning of social processes.[47] To claim that a law is universal is not to claim that it operates in the same way crossculturally or that it determines social life in some unilateral way. Indeed, the attribution of universality to a law may simply imply that it operates as a dominant framework within which social relations take place. Indeed, to claim the universal presence of a law in social life is in no way to claim that it exists in every aspect of the social form under consideration; minimally, it means that it exists and operates somewhere in every social form.

My task here is not to show that there are cultures in which the incest taboo as such does not operate, but rather to underscore the generativity of that taboo, where it does operate, and not merely its juridical status. In other words, not only does the taboo forbid and dictate sexuality in certain forms, but it inadvertently produces a variety of substitute desires and identities that are in no sense constrained in advance, except insofar as they are "substitutes" in some sense. If we extend the Foucaultian critique to the incest taboo, then it seems that the taboo and the original desire for mother/father can be historicized in ways that resist the formulaic universality of Lacan. The taboo might be understood to create and sustain the desire for the mother/father as well as the compulsory displacement of that desire. The notion of an "original" sexuality forever repressed and forbidden thus becomes a production of the law which subsequently functions as its prohibition. If the mother is the original desire, and that may well be true for a wide range of late-capitalist household dwellers, then that is a desire both produced and prohibited within the terms of that cultural context. In other words, the law which prohibits that union is the selfsame law that invites it, and it is no longer possible to isolate the repressive from the productive function of the juridical incest taboo.

Clearly, psychoanalytic theory has always recognized the productive function of the incest taboo; it is what creates heterosexual desire and discrete gender identity. Psychoanalysis has also been clear that the incest taboo does not always operate to produce gender and desire in the ways intended. The example of the negative Oedipal complex is but one occasion in which the prohibition against incest is clearly stronger with respect to the opposite-sexed parent than the same-sexed parent, and the parent prohibited becomes the figure of identification. But how would this example be redescribed within the conception of the incest taboo as both juridical and generative? The desire for the parent who, tabooed, becomes the figure of identification is both produced and denied by the same mechanism of power. But for what end? If the incest taboo regulates the production of discrete gender identities, and if that production requires the prohibition and sanction of heterosexuality, then homosexuality emerges as a desire which must be produced in order to remain repressed. In other words, for heterosexuality to remain intact as a distinct social form, it *requires* an intelligible conception of homosexuality and also requires the prohibition of that conception in rendering it culturally unintelligible. Within psychoanalysis, bisexuality and homosexuality are taken to be primary libidinal dispositions, and heterosexuality is the laborious construction based upon their gradual repression. While this doctrine seems to have a subversive possibility to it, the discursive construction of both bisexuality and homosexuality within the psychoanalytic literature effectively refutes the claim to its precultural status. The discussion of the language of bisexual dispositions above is a case in point.[48]

The bisexuality that is said to be "outside" the Symbolic and that serves as the locus of subversion is, in fact, a construction within the terms of that constitutive discourse, the construction of an "outside" that is nevertheless fully "inside," not a possibility beyond culture, but a concrete cultural possibility that is refused and redescribed as impossible. What remains "unthinkable" and "unsayable" within the terms of an existing cultural form is not necessarily what is excluded from the matrix of intelligibility within that form; on the contrary, it is the marginalized, not the excluded, the cultural possibility that calls for dread or, mini-

mally, the loss of sanctions. Not to have social recognition as an effective heterosexual is to lose one possible social identity and perhaps to
gain one that is radically less sanctioned. The "unthinkable" is thus fully
within culture, but fully excluded from *dominant* culture. The theory
which presumes bisexuality or homosexuality as the "before" to culture and then locates that "priority" as the source of a prediscursive
subversion, effectively forbids from within the terms of the culture the
very subversion that it ambivalently defends and defends against. As I
will argue in the case of Kristeva, subversion thus becomes a futile gesture, entertained only in a derealized aesthetic mode which can never
be translated into other cultural practices.

In the case of the incest taboo, Lacan argues that desire (as opposed
to need) is instituted through that law. "Intelligible" existence within the
terms of the Symbolic requires both the institutionalization of desire
and its dissatisfaction, the necessary consequence of the repression of
the *original* pleasure and need associated with the maternal body. This
full pleasure that haunts desire as that which it can never attain is the
irrecoverable memory of pleasure before the law. Lacan is clear that
that pleasure before the law is only fantasized, that it recurs in the infinite phantasms of desire. But in what sense is the phantasm, itself forbidden from the literal recovery of an original pleasure, the constitution
of a fantasy of "originality" that may or may not correspond to a literal
libidinal state? Indeed, to what extent is such a question decidable within the terms of Lacanian theory? A displacement or substitution can
only be understood as such in relation to an original, one which in this
case can never be recovered or known. This speculative origin is always
speculated about from a retrospective position, from which it assumes
the character of an ideal. The sanctification of this pleasurable "beyond"
is instituted through the invocation of a Symbolic order that is essentially unchangeable.[49] Indeed, one needs to read the drama of the
Symbolic, of desire, of the institution of sexual difference as a self-
supporting signifying economy that wields power in the marking off of

what can and cannot be thought within the terms of cultural intelligibility. Mobilizing the distinction between what is "before" and what is "during" culture is one way to foreclose cultural possibilities from the start. The "order of appearances," the founding temporality of the account, as much as it contests narrative coherence by introducing the split into the subject and the *fêlure* into desire, reinstitutes a coherence at the level of temporal exposition. As a result, this narrative strategy, revolving upon the distinction between an irrecoverable origin and a perpetually displaced present, makes all effort at recovering that origin in the name of subversion inevitably belated.

3

Subversive Bodily Acts

The Body Politics of Julia Kristeva

Kristeva's theory of the semiotic dimension of language at first appears to engage Lacanian premises only to expose their limits and to offer a specifically feminine locus of subversion of the paternal law within language.[1] According to Lacan, the paternal law structures all linguistic signification, termed "the Symbolic," and so becomes a universal organizing principle of culture itself. This law creates the possibility of meaningful language and, hence, meaningful experience, through the repression of primary libidinal drives, including the radical dependency of the child on the maternal body. Hence, the Symbolic becomes possible by repudiating the primary relationship to the maternal body. The "subject" who emerges as a consequence of this repression becomes a bearer or proponent of this repressive law. The libidinal chaos characteristic of that early dependency is now fully constrained by a unitary agent whose language is structured by that law. This language, in turn, structures the world by suppressing multiple meanings (which always recall the libidinal multiplicity which characterized the primary relation to the maternal body) and instating univocal and discrete meanings in their place.

Kristeva challenges the Lacanian narrative which assumes cultural meaning requires the repression of that primary relationship to the maternal body. She argues that the "semiotic" is a dimension of language occasioned by that primary maternal body, which not only refutes Lacan's primary premise, but serves as a perpetual source of subversion within the Symbolic. For Kristeva, the semiotic expresses that original

101

libidinal multiplicity within the very terms of culture, more precisely, within poetic language in which multiple meanings and semantic non-closure prevail. In effect, poetic language is the recovery of the maternal body within the terms of language, one that has the potential to disrupt, subvert, and displace the paternal law.

Despite her critique of Lacan, however, Kristeva's strategy of subversion proves doubtful. Her theory appears to depend upon the stability and reproduction of precisely the paternal law that she seeks to displace. Although she effectively exposes the limits of Lacan's efforts to universalize the paternal law in language, she nevertheless concedes that the semiotic is invariably subordinate to the Symbolic, that it assumes its specificity within the terms of a hierarchy immune to challenge. If the semiotic promotes the possibility of the subversion, displacement, or disruption of the paternal law, what meanings can those terms have if the Symbolic always reasserts its hegemony?

The criticism of Kristeva which follows takes issue with several steps in Kristeva's argument in favor of the semiotic as a source of effective subversion. First, it is unclear whether the primary relationship to the maternal body which both Kristeva and Lacan appear to accept is a viable construct and whether it is even a knowable experience according to either of their linguistic theories. The multiple drives that characterize the semiotic constitute a prediscursive libidinal economy which occasionally makes itself known in language, but which maintains an ontological status prior to language itself. Manifest in language, in poetic language in particular, this prediscursive libidinal economy becomes a locus of cultural subversion. A second problem emerges when Kristeva argues that this libidinal source of subversion cannot be maintained within the terms of culture, that its sustained presence within culture leads to psychosis and to the breakdown of cultural life itself. Kristeva thus alternately posits and denies the semiotic as an emancipatory ideal. Though she tells us that it is a dimension of language regularly repressed, she also concedes that it is a kind of language which never can be consistently maintained.

In order to assess her seemingly self-defeating theory, we need to ask how this libidinal multiplicity becomes manifest in language, and what conditions its temporary lifespan there? Moreover, Kristeva describes the maternal body as bearing a set of meanings that are prior to culture itself. She thereby safeguards the notion of culture as a paternal structure and delimits maternity as an essentially precultural reality. Her naturalistic descriptions of the maternal body effectively reify motherhood and preclude an analysis of its cultural construction and variability. In asking whether a prediscursive libidinal multiplicity is possible, we will also consider whether what Kristeva claims to discover in the prediscursive maternal body is itself a production of a given historical discourse, an *effect* of culture rather than its secret and primary cause.

Even if we accept Kristeva's theory of primary drives, it is unclear that the subversive effects of such drives can serve, via the semiotic, as anything more than a temporary and futile disruption of the hegemony of the paternal law. I will try to show how the failure of her political strategy follows in part from her largely uncritical appropriation of drive theory. Moreover, upon careful scrutiny of her descriptions of the semiotic function within language, it appears that Kristeva reinstates the paternal law at the level of the semiotic itself. In the end, it seems that Kristeva offers us a strategy of subversion that can never become a sustained political practice. In the final part of this section, I will suggest a way to reconceptualize the relation between drives, language, and patriarchal prerogative which might serve a more effective strategy of subversion.

Kristeva's description of the semiotic proceeds through a number of problematic steps. She assumes that drives have aims prior to their emergence into language, that language invariably represses or sublimates these drives, and that such drives are manifest only in those linguistic expressions which disobey, as it were, the univocal requirements of signification within the Symbolic domain. She claims further that the emergence of multiplicitous drives into language is evident in the

103

semiotic, that domain of linguistic meaning distinct from the Symbolic, which is the maternal body manifest in poetic speech.

As early as *Revolution in Poetic Language* (1974), Kristeva argues for a necessary causal relation between the heterogeneity of drives and the plurivocal possibilities of poetic language. Differing from Lacan, she maintains that poetic language is not predicated upon a repression of primary drives. On the contrary, poetic language, she claims, is the linguistic occasion on which drives break apart the usual, univocal terms of language and reveal an irrepressible heterogeneity of multiple sounds and meanings. Kristeva thereby contests Lacan's equation of the Symbolic with all linguistic meaning by asserting that poetic language has its own modality of meaning which does not conform to the requirements of univocal designation.

In this same work, she subscribes to a notion of free or uncathected energy which makes itself known in language through the poetic function. She claims, for instance, that "in the intermingling of drives in language . . . we shall see the economy of poetic language" and that in this economy, "the unitary subject can no longer find his [*sic*] place."[2] This poetic function is a rejective or divisive linguistic function which tends to fracture and multiply meanings; it enacts the heterogeneity of drives through the proliferation and destruction of univocal signification. Hence, the urge toward a highly differentiated or plurivocal set of meanings appears as the revenge of drives against the rule of the Symbolic, which, in turn, is predicated upon their repression. Kristeva defines the semiotic as the multiplicity of drives manifest in language. With their insistent energy and heterogeneity, these drives disrupt the signifying function. Thus, in this early work, she defines the semiotic as "the signifying function . . . connected to the modality [of] primary process."[3]

In the essays that comprise *Desire in Language* (1977), Kristeva ground her definition of the semiotic more fully in psychoanalytic terms. The primary drives that the Symbolic represses and the semiotic obliquely indicates are now understood as *maternal drives*, not only those drives belonging to the mother, but those which characterize the dependency of the infant's body (of either sex) on the mother. In other words, "the maternal body" designates a relation of continuity rather than a discrete subject or object of desire; indeed, it designates that *jouissance* which precedes desire and the subject/object dichotomy that desire presupposes. While the Symbolic is predicated upon the rejection of the mother, the semiotic, through rhythm, assonance, intonations, sound play, and repetition, re-presents or recovers the maternal body in poetic speech. Even the "first echolalias of infants" and the "glossalalias in psychotic discourse" are manifestations of the continuity of the mother-infant relation, a heterogeneous field of impulse prior to the separation/individuation of infant and mother, alike effected by the imposition of the incest taboo.[4] The separation of the mother and infant effected by the taboo is expressed linguistically as the severing of sound from sense. In Kristeva's words, "a phoneme, as distinctive element of meaning, belongs to language as Symbolic. But this same phoneme is involved in rhythmic, intonational repetitions; it thereby tends toward autonomy from meaning so as to maintain itself in a semiotic disposition near the instinctual drive's body."[5]

The semiotic is described by Kristeva as destroying or eroding the Symbolic; it is said to be "before" meaning, as when a child begins to vocalize, or "after" meaning, as when a psychotic no longer uses words to signify. If the Symbolic and the semiotic are understood as two modalities of language, and if the semiotic is understood to be generally repressed by the Symbolic, then language for Kristeva is understood as a system in which the Symbolic remains hegemonic except when the semiotic disrupts its signifying process through elision, repetition, mere sound, and the multiplication of meaning through indefinitely signifying images and metaphors. In its Symbolic mode, language rests upon a severance of the relation of maternal dependency, whereby it becomes abstract (abstracted from the materiality of language) and univocal; this is most apparent in quantitative or purely formal reasoning. In its semiotic mode, language is engaged in a poetic recovery of

105

the maternal body, that diffuse materiality that resists all discrete and univocal signification. Kristeva writes:

> In any poetic language, not only do the rhythmic constraints, for example, go so far as to violate certain grammatical rules of a national language ... but in recent texts, these semiotic constraints (rhythm, vocalic timbres in Symbolist work, but also graphic disposition on the page) are accompanied by nonrecoverable syntactic elisions; it is impossible to reconstitute the particular elided syntactic category (object or verb), which makes the meaning of the utterance decidable.[6]

For Kristeva, this undecidability is precisely the instinctual moment in language, its disruptive function. Poetic language thus suggests a dissolution of the coherent, signifying subject into the primary continuity which is the maternal body:

> Language as Symbolic function constitutes itself at the cost of repressing instinctual drive and continuous relation to the mother. On the contrary, the unsettled and questionable subject of poetic language (from whom the word is never uniquely sign) maintains itself at the cost of reactivating this repressed, instinctual, maternal element.[7]

Kristeva's references to the "subject" of poetic language are not wholly appropriate, for poetic language erodes and destroys the subject, where the subject is understood as a speaking being participating in the Symbolic. Following Lacan, she maintains that the prohibition against the incestuous union with the mother is the founding law of the subject, a foundation which severs or breaks the continuous relation of maternal dependency. In creating the subject, the prohibitive law creates the domain of the Symbolic or language as a system of univocally signifying signs. Hence, Kristeva concludes that "poetic language would be for its questionable subject-in-process the equivalent of incest."[8] The breaking of Symbolic language against its own founding law or, equivalently, the emergence of rupture into language from within its own interior instinctuality, is not merely the outburst of libidinal heterogeneity into language; it also signifies the somatic state of dependency on the maternal body prior to the individuation of the ego. Poetic language thus always indicates a return to the maternal terrain, where the maternal signifies both libidinal dependency and the heterogeneity of drives.

In "Motherhood According to Bellini," Kristeva suggests that, because the maternal body signifies the loss of coherent and discrete identity, poetic language verges on psychosis. And in the case of a woman's semiotic expressions in language, the return to the maternal signifies a prediscursive homosexuality that Kristeva also clearly associates with psychosis. Although Kristeva concedes that poetic language is sustained culturally through its participation in the Symbolic and, hence, in the norms of linguistic communicability, she fails to allow that homosexuality is capable of the same nonpsychotic social expression. The key to Kristeva's view of the psychotic nature of homosexuality is to be understood, I would suggest, in her acceptance of the structuralist assumption that heterosexuality is coextensive with the founding of the Symbolic. Hence, the cathexis of homosexual desire can be achieved, according to Kristeva, only through displacements that are sanctioned within the Symbolic, such as poetic language or the act of giving birth:

> By giving birth, the women enters into contact with her mother; she becomes, she is her own mother; they are the same continuity differentiating itself. She thus actualizes the homosexual facet of motherhood, through which a woman is simultaneously closer to her instinctual memory, more open to her psychosis, and consequently, more negatory of the social, symbolic bond.[9]

According to Kristeva, the act of giving birth does not successfully reestablish that continuous relation prior to individuation because the infant invariably suffers the prohibition on incest and is separated off as a discrete identity. In the case of the mother's separation from the girl-child, the result is melancholy for both, for the separation is never fully completed.

As opposed to grief or mourning, in which separation is recognized and the libido attached to the original object is successfully displaced onto a new substitute object, melancholy designates a failure to grieve in which the loss is simply internalized and, in that sense, *refused*. Instead of a negative attachment to the body, the maternal body is internalized as a negation, so that the girl's identity becomes itself a kind of loss, a characteristic privation or lack.

The alleged psychosis of homosexuality, then, consists in its thorough break with the paternal law and with the grounding of the female "ego," tenuous though it may be, in the melancholic response to separation from the maternal body. Hence, according to Kristeva, female homosexuality is the emergence of psychosis into culture:

> The homosexual-maternal facet is a whirl of words, a complete absence of meaning and seeing; it is feeling, displacement, rhythm, sound, flashes, and fantasied clinging to the maternal body as a screen against the plunge . . . for woman, a paradise lost but seemingly close at hand.[10]

For women, however, this homosexuality is manifest in poetic language which becomes, in fact, the only form of the semiotic, besides childbirth, which can be sustained within the terms of the Symbolic. For Kristeva, then, overt homosexuality cannot be a culturally sustainable activity, for it would constitute a breaking of the incest taboo in an unmediated way. And yet why is this the case?

Kristeva accepts the assumption that culture is equivalent to the Symbolic, that the Symbolic is fully subsumed under the "Law of the Father," and that the only modes of nonpsychotic activity are those which participate in the Symbolic to some extent. Her strategic task, then, is neither to replace the Symbolic with the semiotic nor to establish the semiotic as a rival cultural possibility, but rather to validate those experiences within the Symbolic that permit a manifestation of the borders which divide the Symbolic from the semiotic. Just as birth is understood to be a cathexis of instinctual drives for the purposes of a social teleology, so poetic production is conceived as the site in which the split between instinct and representation exists in culturally communicable form:

> The speaker reaches this limit, this requisite of sociality, only by virtue of a particular, discursive practice called "art." A woman also attains it (and in our society, *especially*) through the strange form of split symbolization (threshold of language and instinctual drive, of the "symbolic" and the "semiotic") of which the act of giving birth consists.[11]

Hence, for Kristeva, poetry and maternity represent privileged practices within paternally sanctioned culture which permit a nonpsychotic experience of that heterogeneity and dependency characteristic of the maternal terrain. These acts of *poesis* reveal an instinctual heterogeneity that subsequently exposes the repressed ground of the Symbolic, challenges the mastery of the univocal signifier, and diffuses the autonomy of the subject who postures as their necessary ground. The heterogeneity of drives operates culturally as a subversive strategy of displacement, one which dislodges the hegemony of the paternal law by releasing the repressed multiplicity interior to language itself. Precisely because that instinctual heterogeneity must be re-presented in and through the paternal law, it cannot defy the incest taboo altogether, but must remain within the most fragile regions of the Symbolic. Obedient, then, to syntactical requirements, the poetic-maternal practices of displacing the paternal law always remain tenuously tethered to that law. Hence, a full-scale refusal of the Symbolic is impossible, and a discourse of "emancipation," for Kristeva, is out of the question. At best, tactical subversions and displacements of the law challenge its self-grounding presumption. But, once again, Kristeva does not seriously challenge the structuralist assumption that the prohibitive paternal law is foundational to culture itself. Hence, the subversion of paternally sanctioned culture can not come from another version of culture, but only from within the repressed interior of culture itself, from the heterogeneity of drives that constitutes culture's concealed foundation.

This relation between heterogeneous drives and the paternal law produces an exceedingly problematic view of psychosis. On the one hand, it designates female homosexuality as a culturally unintelligible practice, inherently psychotic: on the other hand, it mandates maternity as a compulsory defense against libidinal chaos. Although Kristeva does not make either claim explicitly, both implications follow from her views on the law, language, and drives. Consider that for Kristeva poetic language breaks the incest taboo and, as such, verges always on psychosis. As a return to the maternal body and a concomitant de-individuation of the ego, poetic language becomes especially threatening when uttered by women. The poetic then contests not only the incest taboo, but the taboo against homosexuality as well. Poetic language is thus, for women, both displaced maternal dependency and, because that dependency is libidinal, displaced homosexuality.

For Kristeva, the unmediated cathexis of female homosexual desire leads unequivocally to psychosis. Hence, one can satisfy this drive only through a series of displacements: the incorporation of maternal identity—that is, by becoming a mother oneself—or through poetic language which manifests obliquely the heterogeneity of drives characteristic of maternal dependency. As the only socially sanctioned and, hence, nonpsychotic displacements for homosexual desire, both maternity and poetry constitute melancholic experiences for women appropriately acculturated into heterosexuality. The heterosexual poet-mother suffers interminably from the displacement of the homosexual cathexis. And yet, the consummation of this desire would lead to the psychotic unraveling of identity, according to Kristeva—the presumption being that, for women, heterosexuality and coherent selfhood are indissolubly linked.

How are we to understand this constitution of lesbian experience

110

as the site of an irretrievable self-loss? Kristeva clearly takes heterosexuality to be prerequisite to kinship and to culture. Consequently, she identifies lesbian experience as the psychotic alternative to the acceptance of paternally sanctioned laws. And yet why is lesbianism constituted as psychosis? From what cultural perspective is lesbianism constructed as a site of fusion, self-loss, and psychosis?

By projecting the lesbian as "Other" to culture, and characterizing lesbian speech as the psychotic "whirl-of-words," Kristeva constructs lesbian sexuality as intrinsically unintelligible. This tactical dismissal and reduction of lesbian experience performed in the name of the law positions Kristeva within the orbit of paternal-heterosexual privilege. The paternal law which protects her from this radical incoherence is precisely the mechanism that produces the construct of lesbianism as a site of irrationality. Significantly, this description of lesbian experience is effected from the outside and tells us more about the fantasies that a fearful heterosexual culture produces to defend against its own homosexual possibilities than about lesbian experience itself.

In claiming that lesbianism designates a loss of self, Kristeva appears to be delivering a psychoanalytic truth about the repression necessary for individuation. The fear of such a "regression" to homosexuality is, then, a fear of losing cultural sanction and privilege altogether. Although Kristeva claims that this loss designates a place *prior* to culture, there is no reason not to understand it as a new or unacknowledged cultural form. In other words, Kristeva prefers to explain lesbian experience as a regressive libidinal state prior to acculturation itself, rather than to take up the challenge that lesbianism offers to her restricted view of paternally sanctioned cultural laws. Is the fear encoded in the construction of the lesbian as psychotic the result of a developmentally necessitated repression, or is it, rather, the fear of losing cultural legitimacy and, hence, being cast, not outside or prior to culture, but outside cultural *legitimacy,* still within culture, but culturally "out-lawed"?

Kristeva describes both the maternal body and lesbian experience

111

from a position of sanctioned heterosexuality that fails to acknowledge its own fear of losing that sanction. Her reification of the paternal law not only repudiates female homosexuality, but denies the varied meanings and possibilities of motherhood as a cultural practice. But *cultural* subversion is not really Kristeva's concern, for subversion, when it appears, emerges from beneath the surface of culture only inevitably to return there. Although the semiotic is a possibility of language that escapes the paternal law, it remains inevitably within or, indeed, beneath the territory of that law. Hence, poetic language and the pleasures of maternity constitute local displacements of the paternal law, temporary subversions which finally submit to that against which they initially rebel. By relegating the source of subversion to a site outside of culture itself, Kristeva appears to foreclose the possibility of subversion as an effective or realizable cultural practice. Pleasure beyond the paternal law can be imagined only together with its inevitable impossibility.

Kristeva's theory of thwarted subversion is premised on her problematic view of the relation among drives, language, and the law. Her postulation of a subversive multiplicity of drives raises a number of epistemological and political questions. In the first place, if these drives are manifest only in language or cultural forms already determined as Symbolic, then how is it that we can verify their pre-Symbolic ontological status? Kristeva argues that poetic language gives us access to these drives in their fundamental multiplicity, but this answer is not fully satisfactory. Since poetic language is said to depend upon the prior existence of these multiplicitous drives, we cannot, then, in circular fashion, justify the postulated existence of these drives through recourse to poetic language. If drives must first be repressed for language to exist, and if we can attribute meaning only to that which is representable in language, then to attribute meaning to drives prior to their emergence into language is impossible. Similarly, to attribute a causality to drives which facilitates their transformation into language and by which language itself is to be explained cannot reasonably be done within the confines of language itself. In other words, we know these drives as "causes" only in and through their effects, and, as such, we have no reason for not identifying drives with their effects. It follows that either (a) drives and their representations are coextensive or (b) representations preexist the drives themselves.

This last alterative is, I would argue, an important one to consider, for how do we know that the instinctual object of Kristeva's discourse is not a construction of the discourse itself? And what grounds do we have for positing this object, this multiplicitous field, as prior to signification? If poetic language must participate in the Symbolic in order to be culturally communicable, and if Kristeva's own theoretical texts are emblematic of the Symbolic, then where are we to find a convincing "outside" to this domain? Her postulation of a prediscursive corporeal multiplicity becomes all the more problematic when we discover that maternal drives are considered part of a "biological destiny" and are themselves manifestations of "a non-symbolic, nonpaternal causality." [12] This pre-Symbolic, nonpaternal causality is, for Kristeva, a semiotic, *maternal* causality, or, more specifically, a teleological conception of maternal instincts:

> Material compulsion, spasm of a memory belonging to the species that either binds together or splits apart to perpetuate itself, series of markers with no other significance than the eternal return of the life-death biological cycle. How can we verbalize this prelinguistic, unrepresentable memory? Heraclitus' flux, Epicurus' atoms, the whirling dust of cabalic, Arab and Indian mystics, and the stippled drawings of psychedelics—all seem better metaphors than the theory of Being, the logos, and its laws. [13]

Here, the repressed maternal body is not only the locus of multiple drives, but the bearer of a biological teleology as well, one which, it seems, makes itself evident in the early stages of Western philosophy, in non-Western religious beliefs and practices, in aesthetic representations produced by psychotic or near-psychotic states, and even in avant-garde artistic practices. But why are we to assume that these

113

various cultural expressions manifest the selfsame principle of maternal heterogeneity? Kristeva simply subordinates each of these cultural moments to the same principle. Consequently, the semiotic represents any cultural effort to displace the logos (which, curiously, she *contrasts* with Heraclitus' flux), where the logos represents the univocal signifier, the law of identity. Her opposition between the semiotic and the Symbolic reduces here to a metaphysical quarrel between the principle of multiplicity that escapes the charge of non-contradiction and a principle of identity based on the suppression of that multiplicity. Oddly, that very principle of multiplicity that Kristeva everywhere defends operates in much the same manner as a principle of identity. Note the way in which all manner of things "primitive" and "Oriental" are summarily subordinated to the principle of the maternal body. Surely, her description warrants not only the charge of Orientalism, but raises the very significant question of whether, ironically, multiplicity has become a univocal signifier.

Her ascription of a teleological aim to maternal drives prior to their constitution in language or culture raises a number of questions about Kristeva's political program. Although she clearly sees subversive and disruptive potential in those semiotic expressions that challenge the hegemony of the paternal law, it is less clear in what precisely this subversion consists. If the law is understood to rest on a constructed ground, beneath which lurks the repressed maternal terrain, what concrete cultural options emerge within the terms of culture as a consequence of this revelation? Ostensibly, the multiplicity associated with the maternal libidinal economy has the force to disperse the univocity of the paternal signifier and seemingly to create the possibility of other cultural expressions no longer tightly constrained by the law of non-contradiction. But is this disruptive activity the opening of a field of significations, or is it the manifestation of a biological archaism which operates according to a natural and "prepaternal" causality? If Kristeva believed the former were the case (and she does not), then she would be interested in a displacement of the paternal law in favor of a proliferating field of cultural possibilities. But instead, she prescribes a return to a principle of maternal heterogeneity which proves to be a closed concept, indeed, a heterogeneity confined by a teleology both unilinear and univocal.

Kristeva understands the desire to give birth as a species-desire, part of a collective and archaic female libidinal drive that constitutes an ever-recurring metaphysical reality. Here Kristeva reifies maternity and then promotes this reification as the disruptive potential of the semiotic. As a result, the paternal law, understood as the ground of univocal signification, is displaced by an equally univocal signifier, the principle of the maternal body which remains self-identical in its teleology regardless of its "multiplicitous" manifestations.

Insofar as Kristeva conceptualizes this maternal instinct as having an ontological status prior to the paternal law, she fails to consider the way in which that very law might well be the *cause* of the very desire it is said to *repress*. Rather than the manifestation of a prepaternal causality, these desires might attest to maternity as a social practice required and recapitulated by the exigencies of kinship. Kristeva accepts Lévi-Strauss's analysis of the exchange of women as prerequisite for the consolidation of kinship bonds. She understands this exchange, however, as the cultural moment in which the maternal body is repressed, rather than as a mechanism for the compulsory cultural construction of the female body *as* a maternal body. Indeed, we might understand the exchange of women as imposing a compulsory obligation on women's bodies to reproduce. According to Gayle Rubin's reading of Lévi-Strauss, kinship effects a "sculpting of . . . sexuality" such that the desire to give birth is the result of social practices which require and produce such desires in order to effect their reproductive ends.[14]

What grounds, then, does Kristeva have for imputing a maternal teleology to the female body prior to its emergence into culture? To pose the question in this way is already to question the distinction between the Symbolic and the semiotic on which her conception of the maternal body is premised. The maternal body in its originary

115

signification is considered by Kristeva to be prior to signification itself; hence, it becomes impossible within her framework to consider the maternal itself as a signification, open to cultural variability. Her argument makes clear that maternal drives constitute those primary processes that language invariably represses or sublimates. But perhaps her argument could be recast within an even more encompassing framework: What cultural configuration of language, indeed, of *discourse,* generates the trope of a pre-discursive libidinal multiplicity, and for what purposes?

By restricting the paternal law to a prohibitive or repressive function, Kristeva fails to understand the paternal mechanisms by which affectivity itself is generated. The law that is said to repress the semiotic may well be the governing principle of the semiotic itself, with the result that what passes as "maternal instinct" may well be a culturally constructed desire which is interpreted through a naturalistic vocabulary. And if that desire is constructed according to a law of kinship which requires the heterosexual production and reproduction of desire, then the vocabulary of naturalistic affect effectively renders that "paternal law" invisible. What for Kristeva is a pre-paternal causality would then appear as a *paternal* causality under the guise of a natural or distinctively maternal causality.

Significantly, the figuration of the maternal body and the teleology of its instincts as a self-identical and insistent metaphysical principle—an archaism of a collective, sex-specific biological constitution—bases itself on a univocal conception of the female sex. And this sex, conceived as both origin and causality, poses as a principle of pure generativity. Indeed, for Kristeva, it is equated with *poesis* itself, that activity of making upheld in Plato's *Symposium* as an act of birth and poetic conception at once.[15] But is female generativity truly an uncaused cause, and does it begin the narrative that takes all of humanity under the force of the incest taboo and into language? Does the pre-paternal causality whereof Kristeva speaks signify a primary female economy of pleasure and meaning? Can we reverse the very

order of this causality and understand this semiotic economy as a production of a prior discourse?

In the final chapter of Foucault's first volume of *The History of Sexuality,*
he cautions against using the category of sex as a "fictitious unity . . .
[and] causal principle" and argues that the fictitious category of sex
facilitates a reversal of causal relations such that "sex" is understood to
cause the structure and meaning of desire:

> the notion of 'sex' made it possible to group together, in an artificial
> unity, anatomical elements, biological functions, conducts, sensa-
> tions, and pleasures, and it enabled one to make use of this fictitious
> unity as a causal principle, an omnipresent meaning: sex was thus
> able to function as a unique signifier and as a universal signified.[16]

For Foucault, the body is not "sexed" in any significant sense prior to
its determination within a discourse through which it becomes invested with an "idea" of natural or essential sex. The body gains meaning
within discourse only in the context of power relations. Sexuality is an
historically specific organization of power, discourse, bodies, and
affectivity. As such, sexuality is understood by Foucault to produce
"sex" as an artificial concept which effectively extends and disguises
the power relations responsible for its genesis.

Foucault's framework suggests a way to solve some of the epistemological and political difficulties that follow from Kristeva's view of
the female body. We can understand Kristeva's assertion of a "prepaternal causality" as fundamentally inverted. Whereas Kristeva posits a
maternal body prior to discourse that exerts its own causal force in the
structure of drives, Foucault would doubtless argue that the discursive
production of the maternal body as prediscursive is a tactic in the self-
amplification and concealment of those specific power relations by
which the trope of the maternal body is produced. In these terms, the
maternal body would no longer be understood as the hidden ground of
all signification, the tacit cause of all culture. It would be understood,

rather, as an effect or consequence of a system of sexuality in which the female body is required to assume maternity as the essence of its self and the law of its desire.

If we accept Foucault's framework, we are compelled to redescribe the maternal libidinal economy as a product of an historically specific organization of sexuality. Moreover, the discourse of sexuality, itself suffused by power relations, becomes the true ground of the trope of the prediscursive maternal body. Kristeva's formulation suffers a thoroughgoing reversal: The Symbolic and the semiotic are no longer interpreted as those dimensions of language which follow upon the repression or manifestation of the maternal libidinal economy. This very economy is understood instead as a reification that both extends and conceals the institution of motherhood as compulsory for women. Indeed, when the desires that maintain the institution of motherhood are transvaluated as pre-paternal and pre-cultural drives, then the institution gains a permanent legitimation in the invariant structures of the female body. Indeed, the clearly paternal law that sanctions and requires the female body to be characterized primarily in terms of its reproductive function is inscribed on that body as the law of its natural necessity. Kristeva, safeguarding that law of a biologically necessitated maternity as a subversive operation that pre-exists the paternal law itself, aids in the systematic production of its invisibility and, consequently, the illusion of its inevitability.

Because Kristeva restricts herself to an exclusively *prohibitive* conception of the paternal law, she is unable to account for the ways in which the paternal law *generates* certain desires in the form of natural drives. The female body that she seeks to express is itself a construct produced by the very law it is supposed to undermine. In no way do these criticisms of Kristeva's conception of the paternal law necessarily invalidate her general position that culture or the Symbolic is predicated upon a repudiation of women's bodies. I want to suggest, however, that any theory that asserts that signification is predicated upon the denial or repression of a female principle ought to consider

118

whether that femaleness is really external to the cultural norms by which it is repressed. In other words, on my reading, the repression of the feminine does not require that the agency of repression and the object of repression be ontologically distinct. Indeed, repression may be understood to produce the object that it comes to deny. That production may well be an elaboration of the agency of repression itself. As Foucault makes clear, the culturally contradictory enterprise of the mechanism of repression is prohibitive and generative at once and makes the problematic of "liberation" especially acute. The female body that is freed from the shackles of the paternal law may well prove to be yet another incarnation of that law, posing as subversive but operating in the service of that law's self-amplification and proliferation. In order to avoid the emancipation of the oppressor in the name of the oppressed, it is necessary to take into account the full complexity and subtlety of the law and to cure ourselves of the illusion of a true body beyond the law. If subversion is possible, it will be a subversion from within the terms of the law, through the possibilities that emerge when the law turns against itself and spawns unexpected permutations of itself. The culturally constructed body will then be liberated, neither to its "natural" past, nor to its original pleasures, but to an open future of cultural possibilities.

II. FOUCAULT, HERCULINE, AND THE POLITICS OF SEXUAL DISCONTINUITY

Foucault's genealogical critique has provided a way to criticize those Lacanian and neo-Lacanian theories that cast culturally marginal forms of sexuality as culturally unintelligible. Writing within the terms of a disillusionment with the notion of a liberatory Eros, Foucault understands sexuality as saturated with power and offers a critical view of theories that lay claim to a sexuality before or after the law. When we consider, however, those textual occasions on which Foucault criticizes the categories of sex and the power regime of sexuality, it is clear that his own theory maintains an unacknowledged emancipatory ideal that proves increasingly difficult to maintain, even within the strictures of his own critical apparatus.

Foucault's theory of sexuality offered in *The History of Sexuality, Volume I* is in some ways contradicted by his short but significant introduction to the journals he published of Herculine Barbin, a nineteenth-century French hermaphrodite. Herculine was assigned the sex of "female" at birth. In h/er early twenties, after a series of confessions to doctors and priests, s/he was legally compelled to change h/er sex to "male." The journals that Foucault claims to have found are published in this collection, along with the medical and legal documents that discuss the basis on which the designation of h/er "true" sex was decided. A satiric short story by the German writer, Oscar Panizza, is also included. Foucault supplies an introduction to the English translation of the text in which he questions whether the notion of a true sex is necessary. At first, this question appears to be continuous with the critical genealogy of the category of "sex" he offers toward the conclusion of the first volume of *The History of Sexuality.*[17] However, the journals and their introduction offer an occasion to consider Foucault's reading of Herculine against his theory of sexuality in *The History of Sexuality, Volume I.* Although he argues in *The History of Sexuality* that sexuality is coextensive with power, he fails to recognize the concrete relations of power that both construct and condemn Herculine's sexuality. Indeed, he appears to romanticize h/er world of pleasures as the "happy limbo of a non-identity" (xiii), a world that exceeds the categories of sex and of identity. The reemergence of a discourse on sexual difference and the categories of sex within Herculine's own autobiographical writings will lead to an alternative reading of Herculine against Foucault's romanticized appropriation and refusal of her text.

In the first volume of *The History of Sexuality,* Foucault argues that the univocal construct of "sex" (one is one's sex and, therefore, not the other) is (a) produced in the service of the social regulation and control of sexuality and (b) conceals and artificially unifies a variety of disparate and unrelated sexual functions and then (c) postures within discourse as a *cause,* an interior essence which both produces and renders intelligible all manner of sensation, pleasure, and desire as sex-specific. In other words, bodily pleasures are not merely causally reducible to this ostensibly sex-specific essence, but they become readily interpretable as manifestations or signs of this "sex."[18]

In opposition to this false construction of "sex" as both univocal and causal, Foucault engages a reverse-discourse which treats "sex" as an *effect* rather than an origin. In the place of "sex" as the original and continuous cause and signification of bodily pleasures, he proposes "sexuality" as an open and complex historical system of discourse and power that produces the misnomer of "sex" as part of a strategy to conceal and, hence, to perpetuate power-relations. One way in which power is both perpetuated and concealed is through the establishment of an external or arbitrary relation between power, conceived as repression or domination, and sex, conceived as a brave but thwarted energy waiting for release or authentic self-expression. The use of this juridical model presumes that the relation between power and sexuality is not only ontologically distinct, but that power always and only works to subdue or liberate a sex which is fundamentally intact, self-sufficient, and other than power itself. When "sex" is essentialized in this way, it becomes ontologically immunized from power relations and from its own historicity. As a result, the analysis of sexuality is collapsed into the analysis of "sex," and any inquiry into the historical production of the category of "sex" itself is precluded by this inverted and falsifying causality. According to Foucault, "sex" must not only be recontextualized within the terms of *sexuality,* but juridical power must be reconceived as a construction produced by a generative power which, in turn, conceals the mechanism of its own productivity:

the notion of sex brought about a fundamental reversal; it made it possible to invert the representation of the relationships of power to sexuality, causing the latter to appear, *not in its essential and positive relation to power,* but as being rooted in a specific and irreducible urgency which power tries as best it can to dominate. (154)

Foucault explicitly takes a stand against emancipatory or liberationist models of sexuality in *The History of Sexuality* because they subscribe to a juridical model that does not acknowledge the historical production of "sex" as a category, that is, as a mystifying "effect" of power relations. His ostensible problem with feminism seems also to emerge here: Where feminist analysis takes the category of sex and, thus, according to him, the binary restriction on gender, as its point of departure, Foucault understands his own project to be an inquiry into how the category of "sex" and sexual difference are constructed within discourse as necessary features of bodily identity. The juridical model of law which structures the feminist emancipatory model presumes, in his view, that the subject of emancipation, "the sexed body" in some sense, is not itself in need of a critical deconstruction. As Foucault remarks about some humanist efforts at prison reform, the criminal subject who gets emancipated may be even more deeply shackled than the humanist originally thought. To be sexed, for Foucault, is to be subjected to a set of social regulations, to have the law that directs those regulations reside both as the formative principle of one's sex, gender, pleasures, and desires and as the hermeneutic principle of self-interpretation. The category of sex is thus inevitably regulative, and any analysis which makes that category presuppositional uncritically extends and further legitimates that regulative strategy as a power/knowledge regime.

In editing and publishing the journals of Herculine Barbin, Foucault is clearly trying to show how an hermaphroditic or inter-sexed body implicitly exposes and refutes the regulative strategies of sexual categorization. Because he thinks that "sex" unifies bodily functions and meanings that have no necessary relationship with one another, he predicts that the disappearance of "sex" results in a happy dispersal of these various functions, meanings, organs, somatic and

physiological processes as well as in the proliferation of pleasures outside of the framework of intelligibility enforced by univocal sexes
within a binary relation. The sexual world in which Herculine resides,
according to Foucault, is one in which bodily pleasures do not immediately signify "sex" as their primary cause and ultimate meaning; it is a
world, he claims, in which "grins hung about without the cat" (xiii).
Indeed, these are pleasures that clearly transcend the regulation
imposed upon them, and here we see Foucault's sentimental indul-
gence in the very emancipatory discourse his analysis in *The History of
Sexuality* was meant to displace. According to this Foucaultian model of
emancipatory sexual politics, the overthrow of "sex" results in the
release of a primary sexual multiplicity, a notion not so far afield from
the psychoanalytic postulation of primary polymorphousness or
Marcuse's notion of an original and creative bisexual Eros subsequently repressed by an instrumentalist culture.

The significant difference between Foucault's position in the first volume of *The History of Sexuality* and in his introduction to *Herculine
Barbin* is already to be found as an unresolved tension within the *History
of Sexuality* itself (he refers there to "bucolic" and "innocent" pleasures
of intergenerational sexual exchange that exist prior to the imposition
of various regulative strategies [31]). On the one hand, Foucault wants
to argue that there is no "sex" in itself which is not produced by complex interactions of discourse and power, and yet there does seem to
be a "multiplicity of pleasures" *in itself* which is not the effect of any
specific discourse/power exchange. In other words, Foucault invokes a
trope of prediscursive libidinal multiplicity that effectively presupposes a sexuality "before the law," indeed, a sexuality waiting for emancipation from the shackles of "sex." On the other hand, Foucault
officially insists that sexuality and power are coextensive and that we
must not think that by saying yes to sex we say no to power. In his anti-
juridical and anti-emancipatory mode, the "official" Foucault argues
that sexuality is always situated within matrices of power, that it is

always produced or constructed within specific historical practices, both discursive and institutional, and that recourse to a sexuality before the law is an illusory and complicitous conceit of emancipatory sexual politics.

The journals of Herculine provide the opportunity to read Foucault against himself, or, perhaps more appropriately, to expose the constitutive contradiction of this kind of anti-emancipatory call for sexual freedom. Herculine, called Alexina throughout the text, narrates a story about h/er tragic plight as one who lives a life of unjust victimization, deceit, longing, and inevitable dissatisfaction. From the time s/he was a young girl, s/he reports, s/he was different from the other girls. This difference is a cause for alternating states of anxiety and self-importance through the story, but it is there as tacit knowledge before the law becomes an explicit actor in the story. Although Herculine does not report directly on h/er anatomy in the journals, the medical reports that Foucault publishes along with Herculine's own text suggest that Herculine might reasonably be said to have what is described as either a small penis or an enlarged clitoris, that where one might expect to find a vagina one finds a "cul-de-sac," as the doctors put it, and, further, that she doesn't appear to have identifiably female breasts. There seems also to be some capacity for ejaculation that is not fully accounted for within the medical documents. Herculine never refers to anatomy as such, but relates h/er predicament in terms of a natural mistake, a metaphysical homelessness, a state of insatiable desire, and a radical solitariness that, before h/er suicide, is transformed into a full-blown rage, first directed toward men, but finally toward the world as such.

Herculine relates in elliptical terms h/er relations with the girls at school, the "mothers" at the convent, and finally h/er most passionate attachment with Sara who becomes h/er lover. Plagued first with guilt and then with some unspecified genital ailment, Herculine exposes h/er secret to a doctor and then a priest, a set of confessional acts that effectively force h/er separation from Sara. Authorities confer and

effect h/er legal transformation into a man whereupon s/he is legally
obligated to dress in men's clothing and to exercise the various rights of
men in society. Written in a sentimental and melodramatic tone, the
journals report a sense of perpetual crisis that culminates in suicide.
One could argue that prior to the legal transformation of Alexina into a
man, s/he was free to enjoy those pleasures that are effectively free of
the juridical and regulatory pressures of the category of "sex." Indeed,
Foucault appears to think that the journals provide insight into precisely
that unregulated field of pleasures prior to the imposition of the law of
univocal sex. His reading, however, constitutes a radical misreading of
the way in which those pleasures are always already embedded in the
pervasive but inarticulate law and, indeed, generated by the very law
they are said to defy.

The temptation to romanticize Herculine's sexuality as the utopian
play of pleasures prior to the imposition and restrictions of "sex" surely ought to be refused. It still remains possible, however, to ask the
alternative Foucaultian question: What social practices and conventions produce sexuality in this form? In pursuing the question, we
have, I think, the opportunity to understand something about (a) the
productive capacity of power—that is, the way in which regulative
strategies produce the subjects they come to subjugate; and (b) the
specific mechanism by which power produces sexuality in the context
of this autobiographical narrative. The question of sexual difference
reemerges in a new light when we dispense with the metaphysical
reification of multiplicitous sexuality and inquire in the case of
Herculine into the concrete narrative structures and political and cultural conventions that produce and regulate the tender kisses, the diffuse pleasures, and the thwarted and transgressive thrills of
Herculine's sexual world.

Among the various matrices of power that produce sexuality
between Herculine and h/er partners are, clearly, the conventions of
female homosexuality both encouraged and condemned by the convent and its supporting religious ideology. One thing about Herculine

we know is that s/he reads, and reads a good deal, that h/er nineteenth-century French education involved schooling in the classics as well as French Romanticism, and that h/er own narrative takes place within an established set of literary conventions. Indeed, these conventions produce and interpret for us this sexuality that both Foucault and Herculine take to be outside of all convention. Romantic and sentimental narratives of impossible loves seem also to produce all manner of desire and suffering in this text, and so do Christian legends about ill-fated saints, Greek myths about suicidal androgynes, and, obviously, the Christ figure itself. Whether "before" the law as a multiplicitous sexuality or "outside" the law as an unnatural transgression, those positionings are invariably "inside" a discourse which produces sexuality and then conceals that production through a configuring of a courageous and rebellious sexuality "outside" of the text itself.

The effort to explain Herculine's sexual relations with young girls through recourse to the masculine component of h/er biological doubleness is, of course, the constant temptation of the text. If Herculine desires a girl, then perhaps there is evidence in hormonal or chromosomal structures or in the anatomical presence of the imperforate penis to suggest a more discrete, masculine sex that subsequently generates heterosexual capacity and desire. The pleasures, the desires, the acts—do they not in some sense emanate from the biological body, and is there not some way of understanding that emanation as both causally necessitated by that body and expressive of its sex-specificity?

Perhaps because Herculine's body is hermaphroditic, the struggle to separate conceptually the description of h/er primary sexual characteristics from h/er gender identity (h/er sense of h/er own gender which, by the way, is ever-shifting and far from clear) and the directionality and objects of h/er desire is especially difficult. S/he herself presumes at various points that h/er body is the *cause* of h/er gender confusion and h/er transgressive pleasures, as if they were both result and manifestation of an essence which somehow falls outside the natural/metaphysical order of things. But rather than understand h/er

126

anomalous body as the cause of h/er desire, h/er trouble, h/er affairs and confession, we might read this body, here fully textualized, as a sign of an irresolvable ambivalence produced by the juridical discourse on univocal sex. In the place of univocity, we fail to discover multiplicity, as Foucault would have us do; instead, we confront a fatal ambivalence, produced by the prohibitive law, which for all its effects of happy dispersal nevertheless culminates in Herculine's suicide.

If one follows Herculine's narrative self-exposition, itself a kind of confessional production of the self, it seems that h/er sexual disposition is one of ambivalence from the outset, that h/er sexuality recapitulates the ambivalent structure of its production, construed in part as the institutional injunction to pursue the love of the various "sisters" and "mothers" of the extended convent family and the absolute prohibition against carrying that love too far. Foucault inadvertently suggests that Herculine's "happy limbo of a non-identity" was made possible by an historically specific formation of sexuality, namely, "her sequestered existence among the almost exclusive company of women." This "strange happiness," as he describes it, was at once "obligatory and forbidden" within the confines of convent conventions. His clear suggestion here is that this homosexual environment, structured as it is by an eroticized taboo, was one in which this "happy limbo of a non-identity" is subtly promoted. Foucault then swiftly retracts the suggestion of Herculine as participating in a practice of female homosexual conventions, insisting that "non-identity" rather than a variety of female identities is at play. For Herculine to occupy the discursive position of "the female homosexual" would be for Foucault to engage the category of sex—precisely what Foucault wants Herculine's narrative to persuade us to reject.

But perhaps Foucault does want to have it both ways; indeed, he wants implicitly to suggest that nonidentity is what is produced in homosexual contexts—namely, that homosexuality is instrumental to the overthrow of the category of sex. Note in Foucault's following description of Herculine's pleasures how the category of sex is at once invoked and refused: The school and the convent "foster the tender pleasures that sexual nonidentity discovers and provokes when it goes astray in the midst of all those bodies that are similar to one another" (xiv). Here Foucault assumes that the likenesses of these bodies condition the happy limbo of their nonidentity, a difficult formulation to accept both logically and historically, but also as an adequate description of Herculine. Is it the awareness of their likeness that conditions the sexual play of the young women in the convent, or is it, rather, the eroticized presence of the law forbidding homosexuality that produces these transgressive pleasures in the compulsory mode of a confessional? Herculine maintains h/er own discourse of sexual difference even within this ostensibly homosexual context: s/he notes and enjoys h/er difference from the young women s/he desires, and yet this difference is not a simple reproduction of the heterosexual matrix for desire. S/he knows that her position in that exchange is transgressive, that she is a "usurper" of a masculine prerogative, as s/he puts it, and that s/he contests that privilege even as s/he replicates it.

The language of usurpation suggests a participation in the very categories from which s/he feels inevitably distanced, suggesting also the denaturalized and fluid possibilities of such categories once they are no longer linked causally or expressively to the presumed fixity of sex. Herculine's anatomy does not fall outside the categories of sex, but confuses and redistributes the constitutive elements of those categories; indeed, the free play of attributes has the effect of exposing the illusory character of sex as an abiding substantive substrate to which these various attributes are presumed to adhere. Moreover, Herculine's sexuality constitutes a set of gender transgressions which challenge the very distinction between heterosexual and lesbian erotic exchange, underscoring the points of their ambiguous convergence and redistribution.

But it seems we are compelled to ask, is there not, even at the level of a discursively constituted sexual ambiguity, some questions of "sex" and, indeed, of its relation to "power" that set limits on the free play of sexual categories? In other words, how free is that play, whether conceived as a prediscursive libidinal multiplicity or as a discursively constituted multiplicity? Foucault's original objection to the category of sex is that it imposes the artifice of unity and univocity on a set of ontologically disparate sexual functions and elements. In an almost Rousseauian move, Foucault constructs the binary of an artificial cultural law that reduces and distorts what we might well understand as a *natural* heterogeneity. Herculine h/erself refers to h/er sexuality as "this incessant struggle of nature against reason" (103). A cursory examination of these disparate "elements," however, suggests their thorough medicalization as "functions," "sensations," even "drives." Hence, the heterogeneity to which Foucault appeals is itself constituted by the very medical discourse that he positions as the repressive juridical law. But what is this heterogeneity that Foucault seems to prize, and what purpose does it serve?

If Foucault contends that sexual nonidentity is promoted in homosexual contexts, he would seem to identify heterosexual contexts as precisely those in which identity is constituted. We know already that he understands the category of sex and of identity generally to be the effect and instrument of a regulatory sexual regime, but it is less clear whether that regulation is reproductive or heterosexual, or something else. Does that regulation of sexuality produce male and female identities within a symmetrical binary relation? If homosexuality produces sexual nonidentity, then homosexuality itself no longer relies on identities being *like* one another; indeed, homosexuality could no longer be described as such. But if homosexuality is meant to designate the place of an *unnameable* libidinal heterogeneity, perhaps we can ask whether this is, instead, a love that either cannot or dare not speak its name? In other words, Foucault, who gave only one interview on homosexuality and has always resisted the confessional moment in his own work, nevertheless presents Herculine's confession to us in an unabashedly didactic mode. Is this a displaced confession that presumes a continuity or parallel between his life and hers?

129

On the cover of the French edition, he remarks that Plutarch understood illustrious persons to constitute *parallel* lives which in some sense travel infinite lines that eventually meet in eternity. He remarks that there are some lives that veer off the track of infinity and threaten to disappear into an obscurity that can never be recovered—lives that do not follow the "straight" path, as it were, into an eternal community of greatness, but deviate and threaten to become fully irrecoverable. "That would be the inverse of Plutarch," he writes, "lives at parallel points that nothing can bring back together" (my translation). Here the textual reference is most clearly to the separation of Herculine, the adopted male name (though with a curiously feminine ending), and Alexina, the name that designated Herculine in the female mode. But it is also a reference to Herculine and Sara, h/er lover, who are quite literally separated and whose paths quite obviously diverge. But perhaps Herculine is in some sense also parallel to Foucault, parallel precisely in the sense in which divergent lifelines, which are in no sense "straight," might well be. Indeed, perhaps Herculine and Foucault are parallel, not in any literal sense, but in their very contestation of the literal as such, especially as it applies to the categories of sex.

Foucault's suggestion in the preface that there are bodies which are in some sense "similar" to each other disregards the hermaphroditic distinctness of Herculine's body, as well as h/er own presentation of h/erself as very much unlike the women s/he desires. Indeed, after some manner of sexual exchange, Herculine engages the language of appropriation and triumph, avowing Sara as her eternal property when she remarks, "From that moment on, Sara belonged to me ... !!!" (51). So why would Foucault resist the very text that he wants to use in order to make such a claim? In the one interview Foucault gave on homosexuality, James O'Higgins, the interviewer, remarks that "there is a growing tendency in American intellectual circles, particularly among radical feminists, to distinguish between male and female homosexuality," a position, he argues, that claims that very different things happen physically in the two sorts of encounters and that lesbians tend to prefer monogamy and the like while gay men generally do not. Foucault responds by laughing, suggested by the bracketed "[Laughs]," and he says, "All I can do is explode with laughter."[19] This explosive laughter, we may remember, also followed Foucault's reading of Borges, reported in the preface to *The Order of Things (Les mots et les choses)*:

> This book first arose out of a passage in Borges, out of the laughter that shattered, as I read the passage, all the familiar landmarks of my thought ... breaking up all the ordered surfaces and all the planes with which we are accustomed to tame the wild profusion of existing things, and continuing long afterwards to disturb and threaten with collapse our age-old distinction between the Same and the Other.[20]

The passage is, of course, from the Chinese encyclopedia which confounds the Aristotelian distinction between universal categories and particular instances. But there is also the "shattering laughter" of Pierre Rivière whose murderous destruction of his family, or, perhaps, for Foucault, of *the* family, seems quite literally to negate the categories of kinship and, by extension, of sex.[21] And there is, of course, Bataille's now famous laughter which, Derrida tells us in *Writing and Difference,* designates that excess that escapes the conceptual mastery of Hegel's dialectic.[22] Foucault, then, seems to laugh precisely because the question instates the very binary that he seeks to displace, that dreary binary of Same and Other that has plagued not only the legacy of dialectics, but the dialectic of sex as well. But then there is, of course, the laugh of Medusa, which, Hélène Cixous tells us, shatters the placid surface constituted by the petrifying gaze and which exposes the dialectic of Same and Other as taking place through the axis of sexual difference.[23] In a gesture that resonates self-consciously with the tale of Medusa, Herculine h/erself writes of "the cold fixity of my gaze [that] seems to freeze" (105) those who encounter it.

But it is, of course, Irigaray who exposes this dialectic of Same and Other as a false binary, the illusion of a symmetrical difference which

consolidates the metaphysical economy of phallogocentrism, the economy of the same. In her view, the Other as well as the Same are marked
as masculine; the Other is but the negative elaboration of the masculine subject with the result that the female sex is unrepresentable—
that is, it is the sex which, within this signifying economy, is not one.
But it is not one also in the sense that it eludes the univocal signification characteristic of the Symbolic, and because it is not a substantive
identity, but always and only an undetermined relation of difference to
the economy which renders it absent. It is not "one" in the sense that it
is multiple and diffuse in its pleasures and its signifying mode. Indeed,
perhaps Herculine's apparently multiplicitous pleasures would qualify
for the mark of the feminine in its polyvalence and in its refusal to submit to the reductive efforts of univocal signification.

But let us not forget Herculine's relation to the laugh which seems
to appear twice, first in the fear of being laughed *at* (23) and later as a
laugh of scorn that s/he directs against the doctor, for whom s/he
loses respect after he fails to tell the appropriate authorities of the natural irregularity that has been revealed to him (71). For Herculine,
then, laughter appears to designate either humiliation or scorn, two
positions unambiguously related to a damning law, subjected to it
either as its instrument or object. Herculine does not fall outside the
jurisdiction of that law; even h/er exile is understood on the model of
punishment. On the very first page, s/he reports that h/er "place was
not marked out [*pas marquée*] in this world that shunned me." And s/he
articulates the early sense of abjection that is later enacted first as a
devoted daughter or lover to be likened to a "dog" or a "slave" and then
finally in a full and fatal form as s/he is expelled and expels h/erself
from the domain of all human beings. From this presuicidal isolation,
s/he claims to soar above both sexes, but h/er anger is most fully
directed against men, whose "title" s/he sought to usurp in h/er inti-
macy with Sara and whom s/he now indicts without restraint as those
who somehow forbid h/er the possibility of love.

At the beginning of the narrative, s/he offers two one-sentence paragraphs "parallel" to one another which suggest a melancholic incorporation of the lost father, a postponement of the anger of abandonment through the structural instatement of that negativity into h/er identity and desire. Before s/he tells us that s/he h/erself was abandoned by h/er mother quickly and without advance notice, s/he tells us that for reasons unstated s/he spent a few years in a house for abandoned and orphaned children. S/he refers to the "poor creatures, deprived from their cradle of a mother's love." In the next sentence s/he refers to this institution as a "refuge [*asile*] of suffering and affliction," and in the following sentence refers to h/er father "whom a sudden death tore away . . . from the tender affection of my mother" (4). Although h/er own abandonment is twice deflected here through the pity for others who are suddenly rendered motherless, s/he establishes an identification through that deflection, one that later reappears as the joint plight of father and daughter cut off from the maternal caress. The deflections of desire are semantically compounded, as it were, as Herculine proceeds to fall in love with "mother" after "mother" and then falls in love with various mothers' "daughters," which scandalizes all manner of mother. Indeed, s/he vacillates between being the object of everyone's adoration and excitement and an object of scorn and abandonment, the split consequence of a melancholic structure left to feed on itself without intervention. If melancholy involves self-recrimination, as Freud argues, and if that recrimination is a kind of negative narcissism (attending to the self, even if only in the mode of berating that self), then Herculine can be understood to be constantly falling into the opposition between negative and positive narcissism, at once avowing h/erself as the most abandoned and neglected creature on earth but also as the one who casts a spell of enchantment on everyone who comes near h/er, indeed, one who is better for all women than any "man" (107).

S/he refers to the hospital for orphaned children as that early "refuge of suffering," an abode that s/he figuratively reencounters at the close of the narrative as the "refuge of the tomb." Just as that early refuge provides a magical communion and identification with the phantom father, so the tomb of death is already occupied by the very father whom s/he hopes death will let h/er meet: "The sight of the tomb reconciles me to life," she writes. "It makes me feel an indefinable tenderness for the one whose bones are lying there beneath my feet [*là à mes pieds*]" (109). But this love, formulated as a kind of solidarity against the abandoning mother, is itself in no way purified of the anger of abandonment: The father "beneath [h/er] feet" is earlier enlarged to become the totality of men over whom s/he soars, and whom s/he claims to dominate (107), and toward whom s/he directs h/er laugh of disdain. Earlier s/he remarks about the doctor who discovered h/er anomalous condition, "I wished he were a hundred feet underground!" (69).

Herculine's ambivalence here implies the limits of Foucault's theory of the "happy limbo of a non-identity." Almost prefiguring the place Herculine will assume for Foucault, s/he wonders whether s/he is not "the plaything of an impossible dream" (79). Herculine's sexual disposition is one of ambivalence from the outset, and, as argued earlier, h/er sexuality recapitulates the ambivalent structure of its production, construed in part as the institutional injunction to pursue the love of the various "sisters" and "mothers" of the extended convent family and the absolute prohibition against carrying that love too far. H/er sexuality is not outside the law, but is the ambivalent production of the law, one in which the very notion of *prohibition* spans the psychoanalytic and institutional terrains. H/er confessions, as well as h/er desires, are subjection and defiance at once. In other words, the love prohibited by death or abandonment, or both, is a love that takes prohibition to be its condition and its aim.

After submitting to the law, Herculine becomes a juridically sanctioned subject as a "man," and yet the gender category proves less fluid than h/er own references to Ovid's *Metamorphoses* suggest. H/er heteroglossic discourse challenges the viability of the notion of a "person" who might be said to preexist gender or exchange one gender for the other. If s/he is not actively condemned by others, s/he condemns h/erself (even calls h/erself a "judge" [106]), revealing that the juridical law in effect is much greater than the empirical law that effects h/er gender conversion. Indeed, Herculine can never embody that law precisely because s/he cannot provide the occasion by which that law naturalizes itself in the symbolic structures of anatomy. In other words, the law is not simply a cultural imposition on an otherwise natural heterogeneity; the law requires conformity to its own notion of "nature" and gains its legitimacy through the binary and asymmetrical naturalization of bodies in which the Phallus, though clearly not identical with the penis, nevertheless deploys the penis as its naturalized instrument and sign.

Herculine's pleasures and desires are in no way the bucolic innocence that thrives and proliferates prior to the imposition of a juridical law. Neither does s/he fully fall outside the signifying economy of masculinity. S/he is "outside" the law, but the law maintains this "outside" within itself. In effect, s/he embodies the law, not as an entitled subject, but as an enacted testimony to the law's uncanny capacity to produce only those rebellions that it can guarantee will—out of fidelity—defeat themselves and those subjects who, utterly subjected, have no choice but to reiterate the law of their genesis.

Concluding Unscientific Postscript

Within *The History of Sexuality, Volume I,* Foucault appears to locate the quest for identity within the context of juridical forms of power that become fully articulate with the advent of the sexual sciences, including psychoanalysis, toward the end of the nineteenth century. Although Foucault revised his historiography of sex at the outset of *The Use of Pleasure* (*L'Usage des plaisirs*) and sought to discover the repressive/generative rules of subject-formation in early Greek and Roman texts, his philosophical project to expose the regulatory production of identity-effects remained constant. A contemporary example of this quest for identity can be found in recent developments in cell biology, an exam-

135

ple that inadvertently confirms the continuing applicability of a Foucaultian critique.

One place to interrogate the univocity of sex is the recent controversy over the master gene that researchers at MIT in late 1987 claim to have discovered as the secret and certain determinant of sex. With the use of highly sophisticated technological means, the master gene, which constitutes a specific DNA sequence on the Y chromosome, was discovered by Dr. David Page and his colleagues and named "TDF" or testis-determining factor. In the publication of his findings in *Cell* (No. 51), Dr. Page claimed to have discovered "the binary switch upon which hinges all sexually dimorphic characteristics."[24] Let us then consider the claims of this discovery and see why the unsettling questions regarding the decidability of sex continue to be asked.

According to Page's article, "The Sex-Determining Region of the Human Y Chromosome Encodes a Finger Protein," samples of DNA were taken from a highly unusual group of people, some of whom had XX chromosomes, but had been medically designated as males, and some of whom had XY chromosomal constitution, but had been medically designated as female. He does not tell us exactly on what basis they had been designated contrary to the chromosomal findings, but we are left to presume that obvious primary and secondary characteristics suggested that those were, indeed, the appropriate designations. Page and his coworkers made the following hypothesis: There must be some stretch of DNA, which cannot be seen under the usual microscopic conditions, that determines the male sex, and this stretch of DNA must have been moved somehow from the Y chromosome, its usual location, to some other chromosome, where one would not expect to find it. Only if we could presume (a) this undetectable DNA sequence and (b) prove its translocatability, could we understand why it is that an XX male had no detectable Y chromosome, but was, in fact, still male. Similarly, we could explain the curious presence of the Y chromosome on females precisely because that stretch of DNA had somehow been misplaced.

Although the pool that Page and his researchers used to come up with this finding was limited, the speculation on which they base their research, in part, is that a good ten percent of the population has chromosomal variations that do not fit neatly into the XX-female and XY-male set of categories. Hence, the discovery of the "master-gene" is considered to be a more certain basis for understanding sex-determination and, hence, sex-difference, than previous chromosomal criteria could provide.

Unfortunately for Page, there was one persistent problem that haunted the claims made on behalf of the discovery of the DNA sequence. Exactly the same stretch of DNA said to determine male-ness was, in fact, found to be present on the X chromosomes of females. Page first responded to this curious discovery by claiming that perhaps it was not the *presence* of the gene sequence in males versus its *absence* in females that was determining, but that it was *active* in males and *passive* in females (Aristotle lives!). But this suggestion remains hypothetical and, according to Anne Fausto-Sterling, Page and his coworkers failed to mention in that *Cell* article that the individuals from whom the gene samples were taken were far from unambiguous in their anatomical and reproductive constitutions. I quote from her article, "Life in the XY Corral":

> the four XX males whom they studied were all sterile (no sperm production), had small testes which totally lacked germ cells, i.e., precursor cells for sperms. They also had high hormone levels and low testosterone levels. Presumably they were classified as males because of their external genitalia and the presence of testes. . . . Similarly . . . both of the XY females' external genitalia were normal, [but] their ovaries lacked germ cells. (328)

Clearly these are cases in which the component parts of sex do not add up to the recognizable coherence or unity that is usually designated by the category of sex. This incoherence troubles Page's argument as well, for it is unclear why we should agree at the outset that these *are*

XX-males and XY-females, when it is precisely the designation of male and female that is under question and that is implicitly already decided by the recourse to external genitalia. Indeed, if external genitalia were sufficient as a criterion by which to determine or assign sex, then the experimental research into the master gene would hardly be necessary at all.

But consider a different kind of problem with the way in which that particular hypothesis is formulated, tested, and validated. Notice that Page and his coworkers conflate sex-determination with male-determination, and with testis-determination. Geneticists Eva Eicher and Linda L. Washburn in the *Annual Review of Genetics* suggest that ovary-determination is never considered in the literature on sex-determination and that femaleness is always conceptualized in terms of the absence of the male-determining factor or of the passive presence of that factor. As absent or passive, it is definitionally disqualified as an object of study. Eicher and Washburn suggest, however, that it *is* active and that a cultural prejudice, indeed, a set of gendered assumptions about sex, and about what might make such an inquiry valuable, skew and limit the research into sex-determination. Fausto-Sterling quotes Eicher and Washburn:

> Some investigators have overemphasized the hypothesis that the Y chromosome is involved in testis-determination by presenting the induction of testicular tissue as an active, (gene-directed, dominant) event while presenting the induction of ovarian tissue as a passive (automatic) event. Certainly, the induction of ovarian tissue is as much an active, genetically directed developmental process as the induction of testicular tissue, or for that matter, the induction of any cellular differentiation process. Almost nothing has been written about genes involved in the induction of ovarian tissue from the undifferentiated gonad. (325)

In related fashion, the entire field of embryology has come under criticism for its focus on the central role of the nucleus in cell differen-

138

tiation. Feminist critics of the field of molecular cell biology have argued against its nucleocentric assumptions. As opposed to a research orientation that seeks to establish the nucleus of a fully differentiated cell as the master or director of the development of a complete and well-formed new organism, a research program is suggested that would reconceive the nucleus as something which gains its meaning and control only within its cellular context. According to Fausto-Sterling, "the question to ask is not how a cell nucleus changes during differentiation, but, rather, how the dynamic nuclear-cytoplasmic interactions alter during differentation" (323–24).

The structure of Page's inquiry fits squarely within the general trends of molecular cell biology. The framework suggests a refusal from the outset to consider that these individuals implicitly challenge the descriptive force of the available categories of sex; the question he pursues is that of how the "binary switch" gets started, not whether the description of bodies in terms of binary sex is adequate to the task at hand. Moreover, the concentration on the "master gene" suggests that femaleness ought to be understood as the presence or absence of maleness or, at best, the presence of a passivity that, in men, would invariably be active. This claim is, of course, made within the research context in which active ovarian contributions to sex differentiation have never been strongly considered. The conclusion here is not that valid and demonstrable claims cannot be made about sex-determination, but rather that cultural assumptions regarding the relative status of men and women and the binary relation of gender itself frame and focus the research into sex-determination. The task of distinguishing sex from gender becomes all the more difficult once we understand that gendered meanings frame the hypothesis and the reasoning of those biomedical inquiries that seek to establish "sex" for us as it is prior to the cultural meanings that it acquires. Indeed, the task is even more complicated when we realize that the language of biology participates in other kinds of languages and reproduces that cultural sedimentation in the objects it purports to discover and neutrally describe.

139

Is it not a purely cultural convention to which Page and others refer when they decide that an anatomically ambiguous XX individual is male, a convention that takes genitalia to be the definitive "sign" of sex? One might argue that the discontinuities in these instances cannot be resolved through recourse to a single determinant and that sex, as a category that comprises a variety of elements, functions, and chromosomal and hormonal dimensions, no longer operates within the binary framework that we take for granted. The point here is not to seek recourse to the exceptions, the bizarre, in order merely to relativize the claims made in behalf of normal sexual life. As Freud suggests in *Three Essays on the Theory of Sexuality,* however, it is the exception, the strange, that gives us the clue to how the mundane and taken-for-granted world of sexual meanings is constituted. Only from a self-consciously denaturalized position can we see how the appearance of naturalness is itself constituted. The presuppositions that we make about sexed bodies, about them being one or the other, about the meanings that are said to inhere in them or to follow from being sexed in such a way are suddenly and significantly upset by those examples that fail to comply with the categories that naturalize and stabilize that field of bodies for us within the terms of cultural conventions. Hence, the strange, the incoherent, that which falls "outside," gives us a way of understanding the taken-for-granted world of sexual categorization as a constructed one, indeed, as one that might well be constructed differently.

Although we may not immediately agree with the analysis that Foucault supplies—namely, that the category of sex is constructed in the service of a system of regulatory and reproductive sexuality—it is interesting to note that Page designates the external genitalia, those anatomical parts essential to the symbolization of reproductive sexuality, as the unambiguous and *a priori* determinants of sex assignment. One might well argue that Page's inquiry is beset by two discourses that, in this instance, conflict: the cultural discourse that takes external genitalia to be the sure signs of sex, and does that in the service of reproductive interests, and the discourse that seeks to establish the male principle as active and monocausal, if not autogenetic. The desire to determine sex once and for all, and to determine it as one sex rather than the other, thus seems to issue from the social organization of sexual reproduction through the construction of the clear and unequivocal identities and positions of sexed bodies with respect to each other.

Because within the framework of reproductive sexuality the male body is usually figured as the active agent, the problem with Page's inquiry is, in a sense, to reconcile the discourse of reproduction with the discourse of masculine activity, two discourses that usually work together culturally, but in this instance have come apart. Interesting, then, is Page's willingness to settle on the active DNA sequence as the last word, in effect giving the principle of masculine activity priority over the discourse of reproduction.

This priority, however, would constitute only an appearance, according to the theory of Monique Wittig. The category of sex belongs to a system of compulsory heterosexuality that clearly operates through a system of compulsory sexual reproduction. In Wittig's view, to which we now turn, "masculine" and "feminine," "male" and "female" exist *only* within the heterosexual matrix; indeed, they are the naturalized terms that keep that matrix concealed and, hence, protected from a radical critique.

III. MONIQUE WITTIG: BODILY DISINTEGRATION AND FICTIVE SEX

> *Language casts sheaves of reality upon the social body.*
> —MONIQUE WITTIG

Simone de Beauvoir wrote in *The Second Sex* that "one is not born a woman, but rather *becomes* one." The phrase is odd, even nonsensical, for how can one become a woman if one wasn't a woman all along? And who is this "one" who does the becoming? Is there some human who becomes its gender at some point in time? Is it fair to assume that this human was not its gender before it became its gender? How does one "become" a gender? What is the moment or mechanism of gender

141

construction? And, perhaps most pertinently, when does this mechanism arrive on the cultural scene to transform the human subject into a gendered subject?

Are there ever humans who are not, as it were, always already gendered? The mark of gender appears to "qualify" bodies as human bodies; the moment in which an infant becomes humanized is when the question, "is it a boy or girl?" is answered. Those bodily figures who do not fit into either gender fall outside the human, indeed, constitute the domain of the dehumanized and the abject against which the human itself is constituted. If gender is always there, delimiting in advance what qualifies as the human, how can we speak of a human who becomes its gender, as if gender were a postscript or a cultural afterthought?

Beauvoir, of course, meant merely to suggest that the category of women is a variable cultural accomplishment, a set of meanings that are taken on or taken up within a cultural field, and that no one is born with a gender—gender is always acquired. On the other hand, Beauvoir was willing to affirm that one is born with a sex, as a sex, sexed, and that being sexed and being human are coextensive and simultaneous; sex is an analytic attribute of the human; there is no human who is not sexed; sex qualifies the human as a necessary attribute. But sex does not cause gender, and gender cannot be understood to reflect or express sex; indeed, for Beauvoir, sex is immutably factic, but gender acquired, and whereas sex cannot be changed—or so she thought—gender is the variable cultural construction of sex, the myriad and open possibilities of cultural meaning occasioned by a sexed body.

Beauvoir's theory implied seemingly radical consequences, ones that she herself did not entertain. For instance, if sex and gender are radically distinct, then it does not follow that to be a given sex is to become a given gender; in other words, "woman" need not be the cultural construction of the female body, and "man" need not interpret male bodies. This radical formulation of the sex/gender distinction suggests that sexed bodies can be the occasion for a number of different genders, and further, that gender itself need not be restricted to the usual two. If sex does not limit gender, then perhaps there are genders, ways of culturally interpreting the sexed body, that are in no way restricted by the apparent duality of sex. Consider the further consequence that if gender is something that one becomes—but can never be—then gender is itself a kind of becoming or activity, and that gender ought not to be conceived as a noun or a substantial thing or a static cultural marker, but rather as an incessant and repeated action of some sort. If gender is not tied to sex, either causally or expressively, then gender is a kind of action that can potentially proliferate beyond the binary limits imposed by the apparent binary of sex. Indeed, gender would be a kind of cultural/corporeal action that requires a new vocabulary that institutes and proliferates present participles of various kinds, resignifiable and expansive categories that resist both the binary and substantializing grammatical restrictions on gender. But how would such a project become culturally conceivable and avoid the fate of an impossible and vain utopian project?

"One is not born a woman." Monique Wittig echoed that phrase in an article by the same name, published in *Feminist Issues* (1:1). But what sort of echo and re-presentation of Beauvoir does Monique Wittig offer? Two of her claims both recall Beauvoir and set Wittig apart from her: one, that the category of sex is neither invariant nor natural, but is a specifically political use of the category of nature that serves the purposes of reproductive sexuality. In other words, there is no reason to divide up human bodies into male and female sexes except that such a division suits the economic needs of heterosexuality and lends a naturalistic gloss to the institution of heterosexuality. Hence, for Wittig, there is no distinction between sex and gender; the category of "sex" is itself a *gendered* category, fully politically invested, naturalized but not natural. The second rather counter-intuitive claim that Wittig makes is the following: a lesbian is not a woman. A woman, she argues, only exists as a term that stabilizes and consolidates a binary and oppositional relation to a man; that relation, she argues, is heterosexuality. A

143

lesbian, she claims, in refusing heterosexuality is no longer defined in terms of that oppositional relation. Indeed, a lesbian, she maintains, transcends the binary opposition between woman and man; a lesbian is neither a woman nor a man. But further, a lesbian has no sex; she is beyond the categories of sex. Through the lesbian refusal of those categories, the lesbian exposes (pronouns are a problem here) the contingent cultural constitution of those categories and the tacit yet abiding presumption of the heterosexual matrix. Hence, for Wittig, we might say, one is not born a woman, one becomes one; but further, one is not born female, one *becomes female*; but even more radically, one can, if one chooses, become neither female nor male, woman nor man. Indeed, the lesbian appears to be a third gender or, as I shall show, a category that radically problematizes both sex and gender as stable political categories of description.

Wittig argues that the linguistic discrimination of "sex" secures the political and cultural operation of compulsory heterosexuality. This *relation* of heterosexuality, she argues, is neither reciprocal nor binary in the usual sense; "sex" is always already female, and there is only one sex, the feminine. To be male is not to be "sexed"; to be "sexed" is always a way of becoming particular and relative, and males within this system participate in the form of the universal person. For Wittig, then, the "female sex" does not imply some other sex, as in a "male sex"; the "female sex" implies only itself, enmeshed, as it were, in sex, trapped in what Beauvoir called the circle of immanence. Because "sex" is a political and cultural interpretation of the body, there is no sex/gender distinction along conventional lines; gender is built into sex, and sex proves to have been gender from the start. Wittig argues that within this set of compulsory social relations, women become ontologically suffused with sex; they *are* their sex, and, conversely, sex is necessarily feminine.

Wittig understands "sex" to be discursively produced and circulated by a system of significations oppressive to women, gays, and lesbians. She refuses to take part in this signifying system or to believe in the viability of taking up a reformist or subversive position within the system; to invoke a part of it is to invoke and confirm the entirety of it. As a result, the political task she formulates is to overthrow the entire discourse on sex, indeed, to overthrow the very grammar that institutes "gender"—or "fictive sex"—as an essential attribute of humans and objects alike (especially pronounced in French).[25] Through her theory and fiction she calls for a radical reorganization of the description of bodies and sexualities without recourse to sex and, consequently, without recourse to the pronominal differentiations that regulate and distribute rights of speech within the matrix of gender.

Wittig understands discursive categories like "sex" as abstractions forcibly imposed upon the social field, ones that produce a second-order or reified "reality." Although it appears that individuals have a "direct perception" of sex, taken as an objective datum of experience, Wittig argues that such an object has been violently shaped into such a datum and that the history and mechanism of that violent shaping no longer appears with that object.[26] Hence, "sex" is the reality-effect of a violent process that is concealed by that very effect. All that appears is "sex," and so "sex" is perceived to be the totality of what is, uncaused, but only because the cause is nowhere to be seen. Wittig realizes that her position is counterintuitive, but the political cultivation of intuition is precisely what she wants to elucidate, expose, and challenge:

> Sex is taken as an "immediate given," "a sensible given," "physical features," belonging to a natural order. But what we believe to be a physical and direct perception is only a sophisticated and mythic construction, an "imaginary formation," which reinterprets physical features (in themselves as neutral as others but marked by a social system), through the network of relationships in which they are perceived.[27]

"Physical features" appear to be in some sense *there* on the far side of language, unmarked by a social system. It is unclear, however, that these features could be named in a way that would not reproduce the reductive operation of the categories of sex. These numerous features gain social meaning and unification through their articulation within the category of sex. In other words, "sex" imposes an artificial unity on an otherwise discontinuous set of attributes. As both *discursive* and *perceptual,* "sex" denotes an historically contingent epistemic regime, a language that forms perception by forcibly shaping the interrelationships through which physical bodies are perceived.

Is there a "physical" body prior to the perceptually perceived body? An impossible question to decide. Not only is the gathering of attributes under the category of sex suspect, but so is the very discrimination of the "features" themselves. That penis, vagina, breasts, and so forth, are *named* sexual parts is both a restriction of the erogenous body to those parts and a fragmentation of the body as a whole. Indeed, the "unity" imposed upon the body by the category of sex is a "disunity," a fragmentation and compartmentalization, and a reduction of erotogeneity. No wonder, then, that Wittig textually enacts the "overthrow" of the category of sex through a destruction and fragmentation of the sexed body in *The Lesbian Body.* As "sex" fragments the body, so the lesbian overthrow of "sex" targets as models of domination those sexually differentiated norms of bodily integrity that dictate what "unifies" and renders coherent the body as a sexed body. In her theory and fiction, Wittig shows that the "integrity" and "unity" of the body, often thought to be positive ideals, serve the purposes of fragmentation, restriction, and domination.

Language gains the power to create "the socially real" through the locutionary acts of speaking subjects. There appear to be two levels of reality, two orders of ontology, in Wittig's theory. Socially constituted ontology emerges from a more fundamental ontology that appears to be pre-social and pre-discursive. Whereas "sex" belongs to a discursively constituted reality (second-order), there is a pre-social ontology that accounts for the constitution of the discursive itself. She clearly refuses the structuralist assumption of a set of universal signifying structures prior to the speaking subject that orchestrate the formation of that subject and his or her speech. In her view, there are historically contingent structures characterized as heterosexual and compulsory that distribute the rights of full and authoritative speech to males and deny them to females. But this socially constituted asymmetry disguises and violates a pre-social ontology of unified and equal persons.

The task for women, Wittig argues, is to assume the position of the authoritative, speaking subject—which is in some sense their ontologically grounded "right"—and to overthrow both the category of sex and the system of compulsory heterosexuality that is its origin. Language, for Wittig, is a set of acts, repeated over time, that produce reality-effects that are eventually misperceived as "facts." Collectively considered, the repeated practice of naming sexual difference has created this appearance of natural division. The "naming" of sex is an act of domination and compulsion, an institutionalized performative that both creates and legislates social reality by requiring the discursive/perceptual construction of bodies in accord with principles of sexual difference. Hence, Wittig concludes, "we are compelled in our bodies and our minds to correspond, feature by feature, with the idea of nature that has been established for us . . . 'men' and 'women' are political categories, and not natural facts."[28]

"Sex," the category, compels "sex," the social configuration of bodies, through what Wittig calls a coerced contract. Hence, the category of "sex" is a name that enslaves. Language "casts sheaves of reality upon the social body," but these sheaves are not easily discarded. She continues: "stamping it and violently shaping it."[29] Wittig argues that the "straight mind," evident in the discourses of the human sciences, "oppress all of us, lesbians, women, and homosexual men" because they "take for granted that what founds society, any society, is heterosexuality."[30] Discourse becomes oppressive when it requires that the speaking subject, in order to speak, participate in the very terms of that oppression—that is, take for granted the speaking subject's own impossibility or unintelligibility. This presumptive heterosexuality, she argues, functions within discourse to communicate a threat:

147

"'you-will-be-straight-or-you-will-not-be.'"[31] Women, lesbians, and gay men, she argues, cannot assume the position of the speaking subject within the linguistic system of compulsory heterosexuality. To speak within the system is to be deprived of the possibility of speech; hence, to speak at all in that context is a performative contradiction, the linguistic assertion of a self that cannot "be" within the language that asserts it.

The power Wittig accords to this "system" of language is enormous. Concepts, categories, and abstractions, she argues, can effect a physical and material violence against the bodies they claim to organize and interpret: "There is nothing abstract about the power that sciences and theories have to act materially and actually upon our bodies and minds, even if the discourse that produces it is abstract. It is one of the forms of domination, its very expression, as Marx said. I would say, rather, one of its exercises. All of the oppressed know this power and have had to deal with it."[32] The power of language to work on bodies is both the cause of sexual oppression and the way beyond that oppression. Language works neither magically nor inexorably: "there is a plasticity of the real to language: language has a plastic action upon the real."[33] Language assumes and alters its power to act upon the real through locutionary acts, which, repeated, become entrenched practices and, ultimately, institutions. The asymmetrical structure of language that identifies the subject who speaks for and as the universal with the male and identifies the female speaker as "particular" and "interested" is in no sense intrinsic to particular languages or to language itself. These asymmetrical positions cannot be understood to follow from the "nature" of men or women, for, as Beauvoir established, no such "nature" exists: "One must understand that men are not born with a faculty for the universal and that women are not reduced at birth to the particular. The universal has been, and is continually, at every moment, appropriated by men. It does not happen, it must be done. It is an act, a criminal act, perpetrated by one class against another. It is an act carried out at the level of concepts, philosophy, politics."[34]

Although Irigaray argues that "the subject is always already masculine," Wittig disputes the notion that "the subject" is exclusively masculine territory. The very plasticity of language, for her, resists the fixing of the subject position as masculine. Indeed, the presumption of an absolute speaking subject is, for Wittig, the political goal for "women," which, if achieved, will effectively dissolve the category of "women" altogether. A woman cannot use the first person "I" because as a woman, the speaker is "particular" (relative, interested, perspectival), and the invocation of the "I" presumes the capacity to speak for and as the universal human: "a relative subject is inconceivable, a relative subject could not speak at all."[35] Relying on the assumption that all speaking presupposes and implicitly invokes the entirety of language, Wittig describes the speaking subject as one who, in the act of saying "I," "reappropriates language as a whole, proceeding from oneself alone, with the power to use all language." This absolute grounding of the speaking "I" assumes god-like dimensions within Wittig's discussion. This privilege to speak "I" establishes a sovereign self, a center of absolute plenitude and power; speaking establishes "the supreme act of subjectivity." This coming into subjectivity is the effective overthrow of sex and, hence, the feminine: "no woman can say I without being for herself a total subject—that is, ungendered, universal, whole."[36]

Wittig continues with a startling speculation on the nature of language and "being" that situates her own political project within the traditional discourse of ontotheology. In her view, the primary ontology of language gives every person the same opportunity to establish subjectivity. The practical task that women face in trying to establish subjectivity through speech depends on their collective ability to cast off the reifications of sex imposed on them which deform them as partial or relative beings. Since this discarding follows upon the exercise of a full invocation of "I," women *speak* their way out of their gender. The social reifications of sex can be understood to mask or distort a prior ontological reality, that reality being the equal opportunity of all persons, prior to the marking by sex, to exercise language in the assertion

149

of subjectivity. In speaking, the "I" assumes the totality of language and, hence, speaks potentially from all positions—that is, in a universal mode. "Gender . . . works upon this ontological fact to annul it," she writes, assuming the primary principle of equal access to the universal to qualify as that "ontological fact."[37] This principle of equal access, however, is itself grounded in an ontological presumption of the unity of speaking beings in a Being that is prior to sexed being. Gender, she argues, "tries to accomplish the division of Being," but "Being as being is not divided."[38] Here the coherent assertion of the "I" presupposes not only the totality of language, but the unity of being.

If nowhere else quite so plainly, Wittig places herself here within the traditional discourse of the philosophical pursuit of presence, Being, radical and uninterrupted plenitude. In distinction from a Derridean position that would understand all signification to rely on an operational *différance,* Wittig argues that speaking requires and invokes a seamless identity of all things. This foundationalist fiction gives her a point of departure by which to criticize existing social institutions. The critical question remains, however, what contingent social relations does that presumption of being, authority, and universal subjecthood serve? Why value the usurpation of that authoritarian notion of the subject? Why not pursue the decentering of the subject and its universalizing epistemic strategies? Although Wittig criticizes "the straight mind" for universalizing its point of view, it appears that she not only universalizes "the" straight mind, but fails to consider the totalitarian consequences of such a theory of sovereign speech acts.

Politically, the division of being—a violence against the field of ontological plenitude, in her view—into the distinction between the universal and the particular conditions a relation of subjection. Domination must be understood as the denial of a prior and primary unity of all persons in a prelinguistic being. Domination occurs through a language which, in its plastic social action, creates a second-order, artificial ontology, an illusion of difference, disparity, and, consequently, hierarchy that *becomes* social reality.

Paradoxically, Wittig nowhere entertains an Aristophanic myth about the original unity of genders, for gender is a divisive principle, a tool of subjection, one that resists the very notion of unity. Significantly, her novels follow a narrative strategy of *dis*integration, suggesting that the binary formulation of sex needs to fragment and proliferate to the point where the binary itself is revealed as contingent. The free play of attributes or "physical features" is never an absolute destruction, for the ontological field distorted by gender is one of continuous plenitude. Wittig criticizes "the straight mind" for being unable to liberate itself from the thought of "difference." In temporary alliance with Deleuze and Guattari, Wittig opposes psychoanalysis as a science predicated on an economy of "lack" and "negation." In "Paradigm," an early essay, Wittig considers that the overthrow of the system of binary sex might initiate a cultural field of *many* sexes. In that essay she refers to *Anti-Oedipus*: "For us there are, not one or two sexes, but many (cf. Guattari/Deleuze), as many sexes as there are individuals."[39] The limitless proliferation of sexes, however, logically entails the negation of sex as such. If the number of sexes corresponds to the number of existing individuals, sex would no longer have any general application as a term: one's sex would be a radically singular property and would no longer be able to operate as a useful or descriptive generalization.

The metaphors of destruction, overthrow, and violence that work in Wittig's theory and fiction have a difficult ontological status. Although linguistic categories shape reality in a "violent" way, creating social fictions in the name of the real, there appears to be a truer reality, an ontological field of unity against which these social fictions are measured. Wittig refuses the distinction between an "abstract" concept and a "material" reality, arguing that concepts are formed and circulated within the materiality of language and that that language works in a *material* way to construct the social world.[40] On the other hand, these "constructions" are understood as distortions and reifications to be judged against a prior ontological field of radical unity and plenitude.

Constructs are thus "real" to the extent that they are fictive phenomena that gain power within discourse. These constructs are disempowered, however, through locutionary acts that implicitly seek recourse to the universality of language and the unity of Being. Wittig argues that "it is quite possible for a work of literature to operate as a war machine," even "a perfect war machine."[41] The main strategy of this war is for women, lesbians, and gay men—all of whom have been particularized through an identification with "sex"—to preempt the position of the speaking subject and its invocation of the universal point of view.

The question of how a particular and relative subject can speak his or her way out of the category of sex directs Wittig's various considerations of Djuna Barnes,[42] Marcel Proust,[43] and Natalie Sarraute.[44] The literary text as war machine is, in each instance, directed against the hierarchical division of gender, the splitting of universal and particular in the name of a recovery of a prior and essential unity of those terms. To universalize the point of view of women is simultaneously to destroy the category of women and to establish the possibility of a new humanism. Destruction is thus always restoration—that is, the destruction of a set of categories that introduce artificial divisions into an otherwise unified ontology.

Literary works, however, maintain a privileged access to this primary field of ontological abundance. The split between form and content corresponds to the artificial philosophical distinction between abstract, universal thought and concrete, material reality. Just as Wittig invokes Bakhtin to establish concepts as material realities, so she invokes literary language more generally to reestablish the unity of language as indissoluble form and content: "through literature . . . words come back to us whole again"[45]; "language exists as a paradise made of visible, audible, palpable, palatable words."[46] Above all, literary works offer Wittig the occasion to experiment with pronouns that within systems of compulsory meaning conflate the masculine with the universal and invariably particularize the feminine. In *Les Guérillères*,[47] she seeks to eliminate any he-they (*il-ils*) conjunctions, indeed, any "he" (*il*), and to offer *elles* as standing for the general, the universal. "The goal of this approach," she writes, "is not to feminize the world but to make the categories of sex obsolete in language."[48]

In a self-consciously defiant imperialist strategy, Wittig argues that only by taking up the universal and absolute point of view, effectively lesbianizing the entire world, can the compulsory order of heterosexuality be destroyed. The *j/e* of *The Lesbian Body* is supposed to establish the lesbian, not as a split subject, but as the sovereign subject who can wage war linguistically against a "world" that has constituted a semantic and syntactic assault against the lesbian. Her point is not to call attention to the presence of rights of "women" or "lesbians" as individuals, but to counter the globalizing heterosexist episteme by a reverse discourse of equal reach and power. The point is not to assume the position of the speaking subject in order to be a recognized individual within a set of reciprocal linguistic relations; rather, the speaking subject becomes more than the individual, becomes an absolute perspective that imposes its categories on the entire linguistic field, known as "the world." Only a war strategy that rivals the proportions of compulsory heterosexuality, Wittig argues, will operate effectively to challenge the latter's epistemic hegemony.

In its ideal sense, speaking is, for Wittig, a potent act, an assertion of sovereignty that simultaneously implies a relationship of equality with other speaking subjects.[49] This ideal or primary "contract" of language operates at an implicit level. Language has a dual possibility: It can be used to assert a true and inclusive universality of persons, or it can institute a hierarchy in which only some persons are eligible to speak and others, by virtue of their exclusion from the universal point of view, cannot "speak" without simultaneously deauthorizing that speech. Prior to this asymmetrical relation to speech, however, is an ideal social contract, one in which every first-person speech act presupposes and affirms an absolute reciprocity among speaking subjects—Wittig's version of the ideal speech situation. Distorting and concealing that ideal reciprocity, however, is the *heterosexual contract,*

153

the focus of Wittig's most recent theoretical work,[50] although present in her theoretical essays all along.[51]

Unspoken but always operative, the heterosexual contract cannot be reduced to any of its empirical appearances. Wittig writes:

> I confront a nonexistent object, a fetish, an ideological form which cannot be grasped in reality, except through its effects, whose existence lies in the mind of people, but in a way that affects their whole life, the way they act, the way they move, the way they think. So we are dealing with an object both imaginary and real.[52]

As in Lacan, the idealization of heterosexuality appears even within Wittig's own formulation to exercise a control over the bodies of practicing heterosexuals that is finally impossible, indeed, that is bound to falter on its own impossibility. Wittig appears to believe that only the radical departure from heterosexual contexts—namely becoming lesbian or gay—can bring about the downfall of this heterosexual regime. But this political consequence follows only if one understands all "participation" in heterosexuality to be a repetition and consolidation of heterosexual oppression. The possibilities of resignifying heterosexuality itself are refused precisely because heterosexuality is understood as a total system that requires a thoroughgoing displacement. The political options that follow from such a totalizing view of heterosexist power are (a) radical conformity or (b) radical revolution.

Assuming the systemic integrity of heterosexuality is extremely problematic both for Wittig's understanding of heterosexual practice and for her conception of homosexuality and lesbianism. As radically "outside" the heterosexual matrix, homosexuality is conceived as radically unconditioned by heterosexual norms. This purification of homosexuality, a kind of lesbian modernism, is currently contested by numerous lesbian and gay discourses that understand lesbian and gay culture as embedded in the larger structures of heterosexuality even as they are positioned in subversive or resignificatory relationships to heterosexual cultural configurations. Wittig's view refuses the possibility, it seems, of a volitional or optional heterosexuality; yet, even if heterosexuality is presented as obligatory or presumptive, it does not follow that all heterosexual acts are radically determined. Further, Wittig's radical disjunction between straight and gay replicates the kind of disjunctive binarism that she herself characterizes as the divisive philosophical gesture of the straight mind.

My own conviction is that the radical disjunction posited by Wittig between heterosexuality and homosexuality is simply not true, that there are structures of psychic homosexuality within heterosexual relations, and structures of psychic heterosexuality within gay and lesbian sexuality and relationships. Further, there are other power/discourse centers that construct and structure both gay and straight sexuality; heterosexuality is not the only compulsory display of power that informs sexuality. The ideal of a coherent heterosexuality that Wittig describes as the norm and standard of the heterosexual contract is an impossible ideal, a "fetish," as she herself points out. A psychoanalytic elaboration might contend that this impossibility is exposed in virtue of the complexity and resistance of an unconscious sexuality that is not always already heterosexual. In this sense, heterosexuality offers normative sexual positions that are intrinsically impossible to embody, and the persistent failure to identify fully and without incoherence with these positions reveals heterosexuality itself not only as a compulsory law, but as an inevitable comedy. Indeed, I would offer this insight into heterosexuality as both a compulsory system and an intrinsic comedy, a constant parody of itself, as an alternative gay/lesbian perspective.

Clearly, the norm of compulsory heterosexuality does operate with the force and violence that Wittig describes, but my own position is that this is not the *only* way that it operates. For Wittig, the strategies for political resistance to normative heterosexuality are fairly direct. Only the array of embodied persons who are not engaged in a heterosexual relationship within the confines of the family which takes reproduction to be the end or telos of sexuality are, in effect, actively contesting the categories of sex or, at least, not in compliance with the

155

normative presuppositions and purposes of that set of categories. To be lesbian or gay is, for Wittig, no longer to know one's sex, to be engaged in a confusion and proliferation of categories that make sex an impossible category of identity. As emancipatory as this sounds, Wittig's proposal overrides those discourses within gay and lesbian culture that proliferate specifically gay sexual identities by appropriating and redeploying the categories of sex. The terms *queens, butches, femmes, girls,* even the parodic reappropriation of *dyke, queer,* and *fag* redeploy and destabilize the categories of sex and the originally derogatory categories for homosexual identity. All of these terms might be understood as symptomatic of "the straight mind," modes of identifying with the oppressor's version of the identity of the oppressed. On the other hand, *lesbian* has surely been partially reclaimed from it historical meanings, and parodic categories serve the purposes of denaturalizing sex itself. When the neighborhood gay restaurant closes for vacation, the owners put out a sign, explaining that "she's overworked and needs a rest." This very gay appropriation of the feminine works to multiply possible sites of application of the term, to reveal the arbitrary relation between the signifier and the signified, and to destabilize and mobilize the sign. Is this a colonizing "appropriation" of the feminine? My sense is no. That accusation assumes that the feminine belongs to women, an assumption surely suspect.

Within lesbian contexts, the "identification" with masculinity that appears as butch identity is not a simple assimilation of lesbianism back into the terms of heterosexuality. As one lesbian femme explained, she likes her boys to be girls, meaning that "being a girl" contextualizes and resignifies "masculinity" in a butch identity. As a result, that masculinity, if that it can be called, is always brought into relief against a culturally intelligible "female body." It is precisely this dissonant juxtaposition and the sexual tension that its transgression generates that constitute the object of desire. In other words, the object [and clearly, there is not just one] of lesbian-femme desire is neither some decontextualized female body nor a discrete yet superimposed masculine identity, but the destabilization of both terms as they come into erotic interplay. Similarly, some heterosexual or bisexual women may well prefer that the relation of "figure" to "ground" work in the opposite direction—that is, they may prefer that their girls be boys. In that case, the perception of "feminine" identity would be juxtaposed on the "male body" as ground, but both terms would, through the juxtaposition, lose their internal stability and distinctness from each other. Clearly, this way of thinking about gendered exchanges of desire admits of much greater complexity, for the play of masculine and feminine, as well as the inversion of ground to figure can constitute a highly complex and structured production of desire. Significantly, both the sexed body as "ground" and the butch or femme identity as "figure" can shift, invert, and create erotic havoc of various sorts. Neither can lay claim to "the real," although either can qualify as an object of belief, depending on the dynamic of the sexual exchange. The idea that butch and femme are in some sense "replicas" or "copies" of heterosexual exchange underestimates the erotic significance of these identities as internally dissonant and complex in their resignification of the hegemonic categories by which they are enabled. Lesbian femmes may recall the heterosexual scene, as it were, but also displace it at the same time. In both butch and femme identities, the very notion of an original or natural identity is put into question; indeed, it is precisely that question as it is embodied in these identities that becomes one source of their erotic significance.

Although Wittig does not discuss the meaning of butch/femme identities, her notion of fictive sex suggests a similar dissimulation of a natural or original notion of gendered coherence assumed to exist among sexed bodies, gender identities, and sexualities. Implicit in Wittig's description of sex as a fictive category is the notion that the various components of "sex" may well disaggregate. In such a breakdown of bodily coherence, the category of sex could no longer operate descriptively in any given cultural domain. If the category of "sex" is established through repeated *acts,* then conversely, the social action of bodies within the cultural field can withdraw the very power of reality that they themselves invested in the category.

For power to be withdrawn, power itself would have to be understood as the retractable operation of volition; indeed, the heterosexual contract would be understood to be sustained through a series of choices, just as the social contract in Locke or Rousseau is understood to presuppose the rational choice or deliberate will of those it is said to govern. If power is not reduced to volition, however, and the classical liberal and existential model of freedom is refused, then power-relations can be understood, as I think they ought to be, as constraining and constituting the very possibilities of volition. Hence, power can be neither withdrawn nor refused, but only redeployed. Indeed, in my view, the normative focus for gay and lesbian practice ought to be on the subversive and parodic redeployment of power rather than on the impossible fantasy of its full-scale transcendence.

Whereas Wittig clearly envisions lesbianism to be a full-scale refusal of heterosexuality, I would argue that even that refusal constitutes an engagement and, ultimately, a radical dependence on the very terms that lesbianism purports to transcend. If sexuality and power are coextensive, and if lesbian sexuality is no more and no less constructed than other modes of sexuality, then there is no promise of limitless pleasure after the shackles of the category of sex have been thrown off. The structuring presence of heterosexual constructs within gay and lesbian sexuality does not mean that those constructs *determine* gay and lesbian sexuality nor that gay and lesbian sexuality are derivable or reducible to those constructs. Indeed, consider the disempowering and denaturalizing effects of a specifically gay deployment of heterosexual constructs. The presence of these norms not only constitute a site of power that cannot be refused, but they can and do become the site of parodic contest and display that robs compulsory heterosexuality of its claims to naturalness and originality. Wittig calls for a position beyond sex that returns her theory to a problematic humanism based in a problematic metaphysics of presence. And yet, her literary works

158

appear to enact a different kind of political strategy than the one for which she explicitly calls in her theoretical essays. In *The Lesbian Body* and in *Les Guérillères,* the narrative strategy through which political transformation is articulated makes use of redeployment and transvaluation time and again both to make use of originally oppressive terms and to deprive them of their legitimating functions.

Although Wittig herself is a "materialist," the term has a specific meaning within her theoretical framework. She wants to overcome the split between materiality and representation that characterizes "straight" thinking. Materialism implies neither a reduction of ideas to matter nor the view of theory as a reflection of its economic base, strictly conceived. Wittig's materialism takes social institutions and practices, in particular, the institution of heterosexuality, as the basis of critical analysis. In "The Straight Mind" and "On the Social Contract,"[53] she understands the institution of heterosexuality as the founding basis of the male-dominated social orders. "Nature" and the domain of materiality are ideas, ideological constructs, produced by these social institutions to support the political interests of the heterosexual contract. In this sense, Wittig is a classic idealist for whom nature is understood as a mental representation. A language of compulsory meanings produces this representation of nature to further the political strategy of sexual domination and to rationalize the institution of compulsory heterosexuality.

Unlike Beauvoir, Wittig sees nature not as a resistant materiality, a medium, surface, or an object; it is an "idea" generated and sustained for the purposes of social control. The very elasticity of the ostensible materiality of the body is shown in *The Lesbian Body* as language figures and refigures the parts of the body into radically new social configurations of form (and antiform). Like those mundane and scientific languages that circulate the idea of "nature" and so produce the naturalized conception of discretely sexed bodies, Wittig's own language enacts an alternative disfiguring and refiguring of bodies. Her aim is to expose the idea of a natural body as a construction and to offer a deconstructive/reconstructive set of strategies for configuring

159

bodies to contest the power of heterosexuality. The very shape and form of bodies, their unifying principle, their composite parts, are always figured by a language imbued with political interests. For Wittig, the political challenge is to seize *language* as the means of representation *and* production, to treat it as an instrument that invariably constructs the field of bodies and that ought to be used to deconstruct and reconstruct bodies outside the oppressive categories of sex.

If the multiplication of gender possibilities expose and disrupt the binary reifications of gender, what is the nature of such a subversive enactment? How can such an enactment constitute a subversion? In *The Lesbian Body,* the act of love-making literally tears the bodies of its partners apart. As *lesbian* sexuality, this set of acts outside of the reproductive matrix produces the body itself as an incoherent center of attributes, gestures, and desires. And in Wittig's *Les Guérillères,* the same kind of disintegrating effect, even violence, emerges in the struggle between the "women" and their oppressors. In that context, Wittig clearly distances herself from those who would defend the notion of a "specifically feminine" pleasure, writing, or identity; she all but mocks those who would hold up the "circle" as their emblem. For Wittig, the task is not to prefer the feminine side of the binary to the masculine, but to displace the binary as such through a specifically lesbian disintegration of its constitutive categories.

The disintegration appears literal in the fictional text, as does the violent struggle in *Les Guérillères.* Wittig's texts have been criticized for this use of violence and force—notions that on the surface seem antithetical to feminist aims. But note that Wittig's narrative strategy is not to identify the feminine through a strategy of differentiation or exclusion from the masculine. Such a strategy consolidates hierarchy and binarisms through a transvaluation of values by which women now represent the domain of positive value. In contrast to a strategy that consolidates women's identity through an exclusionary process of differentiation, Wittig offers a strategy of reappropriation and subversive redeployment of precisely those "values" that originally appeared to belong to the masculine domain. One might well object that Wittig has assimilated masculine values or, indeed, that she is "male-identified," but the very notion of "identification" reemerges in the context of this literary production as immeasurably more complex than the uncritical use of that term suggests. The violence and struggle in her text is, significantly, recontextualized, no longer sustaining the same meanings that it has in oppressive contexts. It is neither a simple "turning of the tables" in which women now wage violence against men, nor a simple *internalization* of masculine norms such that women now wage violence against themselves. The violence of the text has the identity and coherence of the category of sex as its target, a lifeless construct, a construct out to deaden the body. Because that category is the naturalized construct that makes the institution of normative heterosexuality seem inevitable, Wittig's textual violence is enacted against that institution, and not primarily for its heterosexuality, but for its compulsoriness.

Note as well that the category of sex and the naturalized institution of heterosexuality are *constructs,* socially instituted and socially regulated fantasies or "fetishes," not *natural* categories, but *political* ones (categories that prove that recourse to the "natural" in such contexts is always political). Hence, the body which is torn apart, the wars waged among women, are *textual* violences, the deconstruction of constructs that are always already a kind of violence against the body's possibilities.

But here we might ask: What is left when the body rendered coherent through the category of sex is *dis*aggregated, rendered chaotic? Can this body be re-membered, be put back together again? Are there possibilities of agency that do not require the coherent reassembling of this construct? Wittig's text not only deconstructs sex and offers a way to disintegrate the false unity designated by sex, but enacts as well a kind of diffuse corporeal agency generated from a number of different centers of power. Indeed, the source of personal and political agency comes not from within the individual, but in and through the complex cultural exchanges among bodies in which identity itself is ever-shifting, indeed, where identity itself is constructed, disintegrated, and

recirculated only within the context of a dynamic field of cultural relations. To *be* a woman is, then, for Wittig as well as for Beauvoir, to
become a woman, but because this process is in no sense fixed, it is possible to become a being whom neither *man* nor *woman* truly describes.
This is not the figure of the androgyne nor some hypothetical "third
gender," nor is it a *transcendence* of the binary. Instead, it is an internal
subversion in which the binary is both presupposed and proliferated to
the point where it no longer makes sense. The force of Wittig's fiction,
its linguistic challenge, is to offer an experience beyond the categories
of identity, an erotic struggle to create new categories from the ruins of
the old, new ways of being a body within the cultural field, and whole
new languages of description.

In response to Beauvoir's notion "one is not born a woman, but,
rather, becomes one," Wittig claims that instead of becoming a woman,
one (anyone?) can become a lesbian. By refusing the category of
women, Wittig's lesbian-feminism appears to cut off any kind of solidarity with heterosexual women and implicitly to assume that lesbianism is the logically or politically necessary consequence of feminism.
This kind of separatist prescriptivism is surely no longer viable. But
even if it were politically desirable, what criteria would be used to
decide the question of sexual "identity"?

If to become a lesbian is an *act,* a leave-taking of heterosexuality, a
self-naming that contests the compulsory meanings of heterosexuality's *women* and *men,* what is to keep the name of lesbian from becoming
an equally compulsory category? What qualifies as a lesbian? Does anyone know? If a lesbian refutes the radical disjunction between heterosexual and homosexual economies that Wittig promotes, is that lesbian
no longer a lesbian? And if it is an "act" that founds the identity as a performative accomplishment of sexuality, are there certain kinds of acts
that qualify over others as foundational? Can one do the act with a
"straight mind"? Can one understand lesbian sexuality not only as a
contestation of the category of "sex," of "women," of "natural bodies,"
but also of "lesbian"?

Interestingly, Wittig suggests a necessary relationship between the homosexual point of view and that of figurative language, as if to be a homosexual is to contest the compulsory syntax and semantics that construct "the real." Excluded from the real, the homosexual point of view, if there is one, might well understand the real as constituted through a set of exclusions, margins that do not appear, absences that do not figure. What a tragic mistake, then, to construct a gay/lesbian identity through the same exclusionary means, as if the excluded were not, precisely through its exclusion, always presupposed and, indeed, *required* for the construction of that identity. Such an exclusion, paradoxically, institutes precisely the relation of radical dependency it seeks to overcome: Lesbianism would then *require* heterosexuality. Lesbianism that defines itself in radical exclusion from heterosexuality deprives itself of the capacity to resignify the very heterosexual constructs by which it is partially and inevitably constituted. As a result, that lesbian strategy would consolidate compulsory heterosexuality in its oppressive forms.

The more insidious and effective strategy it seems is a thoroughgoing appropriation and redeployment of the categories of identity themselves, not merely to contest "sex," but to articulate the convergence of multiple sexual discourses at the site of "identity" in order to render that category, in whatever form, permanently problematic.

IV. BODILY INSCRIPTIONS, PERFORMATIVE SUBVERSIONS

> *"Garbo 'got in drag' whenever she took some heavy glamour part, when-*
> *ever she melted in or out of a man's arms, whenever she simply let that*
> *heavenly-flexed neck . . . bear the weight of her thrown-back head. . . .*
> *How resplendent seems the art of acting! It is all* impersonation,
> *whether the sex underneath is true or not."*
> —PARKER TYLER, "THE GARBO IMAGE" QUOTED
> IN ESTHER NEWTON, *Mother Camp*

Categories of true sex, discrete gender, and specific sexuality have constituted the stable point of reference for a great deal of feminist theory and politics. These constructs of identity serve as the points of epistemic departure from which theory emerges and politics itself is shaped. In the case of feminism, politics is ostensibly shaped to express the interests, the perspectives, of "women." But is there a political shape to "women," as it were, that precedes and prefigures the political elaboration of their interests and epistemic point of view? How is that identity shaped, and is it a political shaping that takes the very morphology and boundary of the sexed body as the ground, surface, or site of cultural inscription? What circumscribes that site as "the female body"? Is "the body" or "the sexed body" the firm foundation on which gender and systems of compulsory sexuality operate? Or is "the body" itself shaped by political forces with strategic interests in keeping that body bounded and constituted by the markers of sex?

The sex/gender distinction and the category of sex itself appear to presuppose a generalization of "the body" that preexists the acquisition of its sexed significance. This "body" often appears to be a passive medium that is signified by an inscription from a cultural source figured as "external" to that body. Any theory of the culturally construct-ed body, however, ought to question "the body" as a construct of suspect generality when it is figured as passive and prior to discourse. There are Christian and Cartesian precedents to such views which, prior to the emergence of vitalistic biologies in the nineteenth century, understand "the body" as so much inert matter, signifying nothing or, more specifically, signifying a profane void, the fallen state: deception, sin, the premonitional metaphorics of hell and the eternal feminine. There are many occasions in both Sartre's and Beauvoir's work where "the body" is figured as a mute facticity, anticipating some meaning that can be attributed only by a transcendent consciousness, understood in Cartesian terms as radically immaterial. But what establishes this dual-ism for us? What separates off "the body" as indifferent to signification, and signification itself as the act of a radically disembodied conscious-ness or, rather, the act that radically disembodies that consciousness? To what extent is that Cartesian dualism presupposed in phenomenology adapted to the structuralist frame in which mind/body is redescribed as culture/nature? With respect to gender discourse, to what extent do these problematic dualisms still operate within the very descriptions that are supposed to lead us out of that binarism and its implicit hierarchy? How are the contours of the body clearly marked as the taken-for-granted ground or surface upon which gender significations are inscribed, a mere facticity devoid of value, prior to significance?

Wittig suggests that a culturally specific epistemic *a priori* establishes the naturalness of "sex." But by what enigmatic means has "the body" been accepted as a *prima facie* given that admits of no genealogy? Even within Foucault's essay on the very theme of genealogy, the body is figured as a surface and the scene of a cultural inscription: "the body is the inscribed surface of events."[54] The task of genealogy, he claims, is "to expose a body totally imprinted by history." His sentence continues, however, by referring to the goal of "history"—here clearly understood on the model of Freud's "civilization"—as the "destruction of the body" (148). Forces and impulses with multiple directionalities are precisely that which history both destroys and preserves through the *Entstehung* (historical event) of inscription. As "a volume in perpetual disintegration" (148), the body is always under siege, suffering destruction by the very terms of history. And history is the creation of values and meanings by a signifying practice that requires the subjection of the body. This corporeal destruction is necessary to produce the speaking subject and its significations. This is a body, described through the language of surface and force, weakened through a "single drama" of domination, inscription, and creation (150). This is not the *modus vivendi* of one kind of history rather than another, but is, for Foucault, "history" (148) in its essential and repressive gesture.

Although Foucault writes, "Nothing in man [*sic*]—not even his body—is sufficiently stable to serve as the basis for self-recognition or for understanding other men [*sic*]" (153), he nevertheless points to the constancy of cultural inscription as a "single drama" that acts on the body. If the creation of values, that historical mode of signification,

165

requires the destruction of the body, much as the instrument of torture in Kafka's "In the Penal Colony" destroys the body on which it writes, then there must be a body prior to that inscription, stable and self-identical, subject to that sacrificial destruction. In a sense, for Foucault, as for Nietzsche, cultural values emerge as the result of an inscription on the body, understood as a medium, indeed, a blank page; in order for this inscription to signify, however, that medium must itself be destroyed—that is, fully transvaluated into a sublimated domain of values. Within the metaphorics of this notion of cultural values is the figure of history as a relentless writing instrument, and the body as the medium which must be destroyed and transfigured in order for "culture" to emerge.

By maintaining a body prior to its cultural inscription, Foucault appears to assume a materiality prior to signification and form. Because this distinction operates as essential to the task of genealogy as he defines it, the distinction itself is precluded as an object of genealogical investigation. Occasionally in his analysis of Herculine, Foucault subscribes to a prediscursive multiplicity of bodily forces that break through the surface of the body to disrupt the regulating practices of cultural coherence imposed upon that body by a power regime, understood as a vicissitude of "history." If the presumption of some kind of precategorial source of disruption is refused, is it still possible to give a genealogical account of the demarcation of the body as such as a signifying practice? This demarcation is not initiated by a reified history or by a subject. This marking is the result of a diffuse and active structuring of the social field. This signifying practice effects a social space for and of the body within certain regulatory grids of intelligibility.

Mary Douglas's *Purity and Danger* suggests that the very contours of "the body" are established through markings that seek to establish specific codes of cultural coherence. Any discourse that establishes the boundaries of the body serves the purpose of instating and naturalizing certain taboos regarding the appropriate limits, postures, and modes of exchange that define what it is that constitutes bodies:

166

ideas about separating, purifying, demarcating and punishing transgressions have as their main function to impose system on an inherently untidy experience. It is only by exaggerating the difference
between within and without, above and below, male and female, with
and against, that a semblance of order is created.[55]

Although Douglas clearly subscribes to a structuralist distinction
between an inherently unruly nature and an order imposed by cultural
means, the "untidiness" to which she refers can be redescribed as a
region of *cultural* unruliness and disorder. Assuming the inevitably
binary structure of the nature/culture distinction, Douglas cannot
point toward an alternative configuration of culture in which such distinctions become malleable or proliferate beyond the binary frame.
Her analysis, however, provides a possible point of departure for
understanding the relationship by which social taboos institute and
maintain the boundaries of the body as such. Her analysis suggests that
what constitutes the limit of the body is never merely material, but
that the surface, the skin, is systemically signified by taboos and anticipated transgressions; indeed, the boundaries of the body become,
within her analysis, the limits of the social *per se*. A poststructuralist
appropriation of her view might well understand the boundaries of the
body as the limits of the socially *hegemonic*. In a variety of cultures, she
maintains, there are

pollution powers which inhere in the structure of ideas itself and
which punish a symbolic breaking of that which should be joined or
joining of that which should be separate. It follows from this that pollution is a type of danger which is not likely to occur except where
the lines of structure, cosmic or social, are clearly defined.

A polluting person is always in the wrong. He [*sic*] has developed
some wrong condition or simply crossed over some line which
should not have been crossed and this displacement unleashes danger
for someone.[56]

In a sense, Simon Watney has identified the contemporary construction of "the polluting person" as the person with AIDS in his *Policing Desire: AIDS, Pornography, and the Media.*[57] Not only is the illness figured as the "gay disease," but throughout the media's hysterical and homophobic response to the illness there is a tactical construction of a continuity between the polluted status of the homosexual by virtue of the boundary-trespass that is homosexuality and the disease as a specific modality of homosexual pollution. That the disease is transmitted through the exchange of bodily fluids suggests within the sensationalist graphics of homophobic signifying systems the dangers that permeable bodily boundaries present to the social order as such. Douglas remarks that "the body is a model that can stand for any bounded system. Its boundaries can represent any boundaries which are threatened or precarious."[58] And she asks a question which one might have expected to read in Foucault: "Why should bodily margins be thought to be specifically invested with power and danger?"[59]

Douglas suggests that all social systems are vulnerable at their margins, and that all margins are accordingly considered dangerous. If the body is synecdochal for the social system *per se* or a site in which open systems converge, then any kind of unregulated permeability constitutes a site of pollution and endangerment. Since anal and oral sex among men clearly establishes certain kinds of bodily permeabilities unsanctioned by the hegemonic order, male homosexuality would, within such a hegemonic point of view, constitute a site of danger and pollution, prior to and regardless of the cultural presence of AIDS. Similarly, the "polluted" status of lesbians, regardless of their low-risk status with respect to AIDS, brings into relief the dangers of their bodily exchanges. Significantly, being "outside" the hegemonic order does not signify being "in" a state of filthy and untidy nature. Paradoxically, homosexuality is almost always conceived within the homophobic signifying economy as *both* uncivilized and unnatural.

The construction of stable bodily contours relies upon fixed sites of corporeal permeability and impermeability. Those sexual practices in both homosexual and heterosexual contexts that open surfaces and orifices to erotic signification or close down others effectively rein-scribe the boundaries of the body along new cultural lines. Anal sex among men is an example, as is the radical re-membering of the body in Wittig's *The Lesbian Body*. Douglas alludes to "a kind of sex pollution which expresses a desire to keep the body (physical and social) intact,"[60] suggesting that the naturalized notion of "the" body is itself a consequence of taboos that render that body discrete by virtue of its stable boundaries. Further, the rites of passage that govern various bodily orifices presuppose a heterosexual construction of gendered exchange, positions, and erotic possibilities. The deregulation of such exchanges accordingly disrupts the very boundaries that determine what it is to be a body at all. Indeed, the critical inquiry that traces the regulatory practices within which bodily contours are constructed constitutes precisely the genealogy of "the body" in its discreteness that might further radicalize Foucault's theory.[61]

Significantly, Kristeva's discussion of abjection in *Powers of Horror* begins to suggest the uses of this structuralist notion of a boundary-constituting taboo for the purposes of constructing a discrete subject through exclusion.[62] The "abject" designates that which has been expelled from the body, discharged as excrement, literally rendered "Other." This appears as an expulsion of alien elements, but the alien is effectively established through this expulsion. The construction of the "not-me" as the abject establishes the boundaries of the body which are also the first contours of the subject. Kristeva writes:

> *nausea* makes me balk at that milk cream, separates me from the
> mother and father who proffer it. "I" want none of that element, sign
> of their desire; "I" do not want to listen, "I" do not assimilate it, "I"
> expel it. But since the food is not an "other" for "me," who am only in

their desire, I expel *myself*, I spit *myself* out, I abject *myself* within the same motion through which "I" claim to establish myself.[63]

The boundary of the body as well as the distinction between internal and external is established through the ejection and transvaluation of something originally part of identity into a defiling otherness. As Iris Young has suggested in her use of Kristeva to understand sexism, homophobia, and racism, the repudiation of bodies for their sex, sexuality, and/or color is an "expulsion" followed by a "repulsion" that founds and consolidates culturally hegemonic identities along sex/race/sexuality axes of differentiation.[64] Young's appropriation of Kristeva shows how the operation of repulsion can consolidate "identities" founded on the instituting of the "Other" or a set of Others through exclusion and domination. What constitutes through division the "inner" and "outer" worlds of the subject is a border and boundary tenuously maintained for the purposes of social regulation and control. The boundary between the inner and outer is confounded by those excremental passages in which the inner effectively becomes outer, and this excreting function becomes, as it were, the model by which other forms of identity-differentiation are accomplished. In effect, this is the mode by which Others become shit. For inner and outer worlds to remain utterly distinct, the entire surface of the body would have to achieve an impossible impermeability. This sealing of its surfaces would constitute the seamless boundary of the subject; but this enclosure would invariably be exploded by precisely that excremental filth that it fears.

Regardless of the compelling metaphors of the spatial distinctions of inner and outer, they remain linguistic terms that facilitate and articulate a set of fantasies, feared and desired. "Inner" and "outer" make sense only with reference to a mediating boundary that strives for stability. And this stability, this coherence, is determined in large part by cultural orders that sanction the subject and compel its differentiation from the abject. Hence, "inner" and "outer" constitute a binary distinction that stabilizes and consolidates the coherent subject. When that subject is challenged, the meaning and necessity of the terms are subject to displacement. If the "inner world" no longer designates a topos, then the internal fixity of the self and, indeed, the internal locale of gender identity, become similarly suspect. The critical question is not *how* did that identity become *internalized*? as if internalization were a process or a mechanism that might be descriptively reconstructed. Rather, the question is: From what strategic position in public discourse and for what reasons has the trope of interiority and the disjunctive binary of inner/outer taken hold? In what language is "inner space" figured? What kind of figuration is it, and through what figure of the body is it signified? How does a body figure on its surface the very invisibility of its hidden depth?

From Interiority to Gender Performatives

In *Discipline and Punish* Foucault challenges the language of internalization as it operates in the service of the disciplinary regime of the subjection and subjectivation of criminals.[65] Although Foucault objected to what he understood to be the psychoanalytic belief in the "inner" truth of sex in *The History of Sexuality,* he turns to a criticism of the doctrine of internalization for separate purposes in the context of his history of criminology. In a sense, *Discipline and Punish* can be read as Foucault's effort to rewrite Nietzsche's doctrine of internalization in *On the Genealogy of Morals* on the model of *inscription.* In the context of prisoners, Foucault writes, the strategy has been not to enforce a repression of their desires, but to compel their bodies to signify the prohibitive law as their very essence, style, and necessity. That law is not literally internalized, but incorporated, with the consequence that bodies are produced which signify that law on and through the body; there the law is manifest as the essence of their selves, the meaning of their soul, their conscience, the law of their desire. In effect, the law is at once fully manifest and fully latent, for it never appears as external to the bodies it subjects and subjectivates. Foucault writes:

171

It would be wrong to say that the soul is an illusion, or an ideological effect. On the contrary, it exists, it has a reality, it is produced permanently *around, on, within,* the body by the functioning of a power that is exercised on those that are punished. (my emphasis)[66]

The figure of the interior soul understood as "within" the body is signified through its inscription *on* the body, even though its primary mode of signification is through its very absence, its potent invisibility. The effect of a structuring inner space is produced through the signification of a body as a vital and sacred enclosure. The soul is precisely what the body lacks; hence, the body presents itself as a signifying lack. That lack which *is* the body signifies the soul as that which cannot show. In this sense, then, the soul is a surface signification that contests and displaces the inner/outer distinction itself, a figure of interior psychic space inscribed *on* the body as a social signification that perpetually renounces itself as such. In Foucault's terms, the soul is not imprisoned by or within the body, as some Christian imagery would suggest, but "the soul is the prison of the body."[67]

The redescription of intrapsychic processes in terms of the surface politics of the body implies a corollary redescription of gender as the disciplinary production of the figures of fantasy through the play of presence and absence on the body's surface, the construction of the gendered body through a series of exclusions and denials, signifying absences. But what determines the manifest and latent text of the body politic? What is the prohibitive law that generates the corporeal stylization of gender, the fantasied and fantastic figuration of the body? We have already considered the incest taboo and the prior taboo against homosexuality as the generative moments of gender identity, the prohibitions that produce identity along the culturally intelligible grids of an idealized and compulsory heterosexuality. That disciplinary production of gender effects a false stabilization of gender in the interests of the heterosexual construction and regulation of sexuality within the reproductive domain. The construction of coherence conceals the gender discontinuities that run rampant within heterosexual, bisexual, and gay and lesbian contexts in which gender does not necessarily follow from sex, and desire, or sexuality generally, does not seem to follow from gender—indeed, where none of these dimensions of significant corporeality express or reflect one another. When the disorganization and disaggregation of the field of bodies disrupt the regulatory fiction of heterosexual coherence, it seems that the expressive model loses its descriptive force. That regulatory ideal is then exposed as a norm and a fiction that disguises itself as a developmental law regulating the sexual field that it purports to describe.

According to the understanding of identification as an enacted fantasy or incorporation, however, it is clear that coherence is desired, wished for, idealized, and that this idealization is an effect of a corporeal signification. In other words, acts, gestures, and desire produce the effect of an internal core or substance, but produce this *on the surface* of the body, through the play of signifying absences that suggest, but never reveal, the organizing principle of identity as a cause. Such acts, gestures, enactments, generally construed, are *performative* in the sense that the essence or identity that they otherwise purport to express are *fabrications* manufactured and sustained through corporeal signs and other discursive means. That the gendered body is performative suggests that it has no ontological status apart from the various acts which constitute its reality. This also suggests that if that reality is fabricated as an interior essence, that very interiority is an effect and function of a decidedly public and social discourse, the public regulation of fantasy through the surface politics of the body, the gender border control that differentiates inner from outer, and so institutes the "integrity" of the subject. In other words, acts and gestures, articulated and enacted desires create the illusion of an interior and organizing gender core, an illusion discursively maintained for the purposes of the regulation of sexuality within the obligatory frame of reproductive heterosexuality. If the "cause" of desire, gesture, and act can be localized within the "self" of the actor, then the political regulations and disciplinary

173

practices which produce that ostensibly coherent gender are effectively displaced from view. The displacement of a political and discursive origin of gender identity onto a psychological "core" precludes an analysis of the political constitution of the gendered subject and its fabricated notions about the ineffable interiority of its sex or of its true identity.

If the inner truth of gender is a fabrication and if a true gender is a fantasy instituted and inscribed on the surface of bodies, then it seems that genders can be neither true nor false, but are only produced as the truth effects of a discourse of primary and stable identity. In *Mother Camp: Female Impersonators in America,* anthropologist Esther Newton suggests that the structure of impersonation reveals one of the key fabricating mechanisms through which the social construction of gender takes place.[68] I would suggest as well that drag fully subverts the distinction between inner and outer psychic space and effectively mocks both the expressive model of gender and the notion of a true gender identity. Newton writes:

> At its most complex, [drag] is a double inversion that says, "appearance is an illusion." Drag says [Newton's curious personification] "my 'outside' appearance is feminine, but my essence 'inside' [the body] is masculine." At the same time it symbolizes the opposite inversion; "my appearance 'outside' [my body, my gender] is masculine but my essence 'inside' [myself] is feminine."[69]

Both claims to truth contradict one another and so displace the entire enactment of gender significations from the discourse of truth and falsity.

The notion of an original or primary gender identity is often parodied within the cultural practices of drag, cross-dressing, and the sexual stylization of butch/femme identities. Within feminist theory, such parodic identities have been understood to be either degrading to women, in the case of drag and cross-dressing, or an uncritical appropriation of sex-role stereotyping from within the practice of heterosexuality, especially in the case of butch/femme lesbian identities. But the relation between the "imitation" and the "original" is, I think, more complicated than that critique generally allows. Moreover, it gives us a clue to the way in which the relationship between primary identification—that is, the original meanings accorded to gender—and subsequent gender experience might be reframed/The performance of drag plays upon the distinction between the anatomy of the performer and the gender that is being performed. But we are actually in the presence of three contingent dimensions of significant corporeality: anatomical sex, gender identity, and gender performance. If the anatomy of the performer is already distinct from the gender of the performer, and both of those are distinct from the gender of the performance, then the performance suggests a dissonance not only between sex and performance, but sex and gender, and gender and performance. As much as drag creates a unified picture of "woman" (what its critics often oppose), it also reveals the distinctness of those aspects of gendered experience which are falsely naturalized as a unity through the regulatory fiction of heterosexual coherence. *In imitating gender, drag implicitly reveals the imitative structure of gender itself—as well as its contingency.* Indeed, part of the pleasure, the giddiness of the performance is in the recognition of a radical contingency in the relation between sex and gender in the face of cultural configurations of causal unities that are regularly assumed to be natural and necessary. In the place of the law of heterosexual coherence, we see sex and gender denaturalized by means of a performance which avows their distinctness and dramatizes the cultural mechanism of their fabricated unity.

The notion of gender parody defended here does not assume that there is an original which such parodic identities imitate. Indeed, the parody is *of* the very notion of an original; just as the psychoanalytic notion of gender identification is constituted by a fantasy of a fantasy, the transfiguration of an Other who is always already a "figure" in that double sense, so gender parody reveals that the original identity after which gender fashions itself is an imitation without an origin. To be more precise, it is a production which, in effect—that is, in its effect—postures as an imitation. This perpetual displacement constitutes a fluidity of identities that suggests an openness to resignification and recontextualization; parodic proliferation deprives hegemonic culture and its critics of the claim to naturalized or essentialist gender identities. Although the gender meanings taken up in these parodic styles are clearly part of hegemonic, misogynist culture, they are nevertheless denaturalized and mobilized through their parodic recontextualization. As imitations which effectively displace the meaning of the original, they imitate the myth of originality itself. In the place of an original identification which serves as a determining cause, gender identity might be reconceived as a personal/cultural history of received meanings subject to a set of imitative practices which refer laterally to other imitations and which, jointly, construct the illusion of a primary and interior gendered self or parody the mechanism of that construction.

According to Fredric Jameson's "Postmodernism and Consumer Society," the imitation that mocks the notion of an original is characteristic of pastiche rather than parody:

> Pastiche is, like parody, the imitation of a peculiar or unique style, the wearing of a stylistic mask, speech in a dead language: but it is a neutral practice of mimicry, without parody's ulterior motive, without the satirical impulse, without laughter, without that still latent feeling that there exists something *normal* compared to which what is being imitated is rather comic. Pastiche is blank parody, parody that has lost it humor.[70]

The loss of the sense of "the normal," however, can be its own occasion for laughter, especially when "the normal," "the original" is revealed to be a copy, and an inevitably failed one, an ideal that no one *can* embody. In this sense, laughter emerges in the realization that all along the original was derived.

Parody by itself is not subversive, and there must be a way to understand what makes certain kinds of parodic repetitions effectively disruptive, truly troubling, and which repetitions become domesticated and recirculated as instruments of cultural hegemony. A typology of actions would clearly not suffice, for parodic displacement, indeed, parodic laughter, depends on a context and reception in which subversive confusions can be fostered. What performance where will invert the inner/outer distinction and compel a radical rethinking of the psychological presuppositions of gender identity and sexuality? What performance where will compel a reconsideration of the *place* and stability of the masculine and the feminine? And what kind of gender performance will enact and reveal the performativity of gender itself in a way that destabilizes the naturalized categories of identity and desire.

If the body is not a "being," but a variable boundary, a surface whose permeability is politically regulated, a signifying practice within a cultural field of gender hierarchy and compulsory heterosexuality, then what language is left for understanding this corporeal enactment, gender, that constitutes its "interior" signification on its surface? Sartre would perhaps have called this act "a style of being," Foucault, "a stylistics of existence." And in my earlier reading of Beauvoir, I suggest that gendered bodies are so many "styles of the flesh." These styles all never fully self-styled, for styles have a history, and those histories condition and limit the possibilities. Consider gender, for instance, as *a corporeal style,* an "act," as it were, which is both intentional and performative, where "*performative*" suggests a dramatic and contingent construction of meaning.

Wittig understands gender as the workings of "sex," where "sex" is an obligatory injunction for the body to become a cultural sign, to materialize itself in obedience to a historically delimited possibility, and to do this, not once or twice, but as a sustained and repeated corporeal project. The notion of a "project," however, suggests the originating force of a radical will, and because gender is a project which has cultural survival as its end, the term *strategy* better suggests the situation of

177

duress under which gender performance always and variously occurs. Hence, as a strategy of survival within compulsory systems, gender is a performance with clearly punitive consequences. Discrete genders are part of what "humanizes" individuals within contemporary culture; indeed, we regularly punish those who fail to do their gender right. Because there is neither an "essence" that gender expresses or external-izes nor an objective ideal to which gender aspires, and because gender is not a fact, the various acts of gender create the idea of gender, and without those acts, there would be no gender at all. Gender is, thus, a construction that regularly conceals its genesis; the tacit collective agreement to perform, produce, and sustain discrete and polar genders as cultural fictions is obscured by the credibility of those productions— and the punishments that attend not agreeing to believe in them; the construction "compels" our belief in its necessity and naturalness. The historical possibilities materialized through various corporeal styles are nothing other than those punitively regulated cultural fictions alter-nately embodied and deflected under duress.

Consider that a sedimentation of gender norms produces the peculiar phenomenon of a "natural sex" or a "real woman" or any num-ber of prevalent and compelling social fictions, and that this is a sedi-mentation that over time has produced a set of corporeal styles which, in reified form, appear as the natural configuration of bodies into sexes existing in a binary relation to one another. If these styles are enacted, and if they produce the coherent gendered subjects who pose as their originators, what kind of performance might reveal this ostensible "cause" to be an "effect"?

In what senses, then, is gender an act? As in other ritual social dra-mas, the action of gender requires a performance that is *repeated*. This repetition is at once a reenactment and reexperiencing of a set of meanings already socially established; and it is the mundane and ritual-ized form of their legitimation.[71] Although there are individual bodies that enact these significations by becoming stylized into gendered modes, this "action" is a public action. There are temporal and collec-

178

tive dimensions to these actions, and their public character is not inconsequential; indeed, the performance is effected with the strategic aim of maintaining gender within its binary frame—an aim that cannot be attributed to a subject, but, rather, must be understood to found and consolidate the subject.

Gender ought not to be construed as a stable identity or locus of agency from which various acts follow; rather, gender is an identity tenuously constituted in time, instituted in an exterior space through a *stylized repetition of acts.* The effect of gender is produced through the stylization of the body and, hence, must be understood as the mundane way in which bodily gestures, movements, and styles of various kinds constitute the illusion of an abiding gendered self. This formulation moves the conception of gender off the ground of a substantial model of identity to one that requires a conception of gender as a constituted *social temporality.* Significantly, if gender is instituted through acts which are internally discontinuous, then the *appearance of substance* is precisely that, a constructed identity, a performative accomplishment which the mundane social audience, including the actors themselves, come to believe and to perform in the mode of belief. Gender is also a norm that can never be fully internalized; "the internal" is a surface signification, and gender norms are finally phantasmatic, impossible to embody. If the ground of gender identity is the stylized repetition of acts through time and not a seemingly seamless identity, then the spatial metaphor of a "ground" will be displaced and revealed as a stylized configuration, indeed, a gendered corporealization of time. The abiding gendered self will then be shown to be structured by repeated acts that seek to approximate the ideal of a substantial ground of identity, but which, in their occasional *dis*continuity, reveal the temporal and contingent groundlessness of this "ground." The possibilities of gender transformation are to be found precisely in the arbitrary relation between such acts, in the possibility of a failure to repeat, a de-formity, or a parodic repetition that exposes the phantasmatic effect of abiding identity as a politically tenuous construction.

179

If gender attributes, however, are not expressive but performative, then these attributes effectively constitute the identity they are said to express or reveal. The distinction between expression and performativeness is crucial. If gender attributes and acts, the various ways in which a body shows or produces its cultural signification, are performative, then there is no preexisting identity by which an act or attribute might be measured; there would be no true or false, real or distorted acts of gender, and the postulation of a true gender identity would be revealed as a regulatory fiction. That gender reality is created through sustained social performances means that the very notions of an essential sex and a true or abiding masculinity or femininity are also constituted as part of the strategy that conceals gender's performative character and the performative possibilities for proliferating gender configurations outside the restricting frames of masculinist domination and compulsory heterosexuality.

Genders can be neither true nor false, neither real nor apparent, neither original nor derived. As credible bearers of those attributes, however, genders can also be rendered thoroughly and radically *incredible*.

Conclusion:
From Parody to Politics

I began with the speculative question of whether feminist politics could do without a "subject" in the category of women. At stake is not whether it still makes sense, strategically or transitionally, to refer to women in order to make representational claims in their behalf. The feminist "we" is always and only a phantasmatic construction, one that has its purposes, but which denies the internal complexity and indeterminacy of the term and constitutes itself only through the exclusion of some part of the constituency that it simultaneously seeks to represent. The tenuous or phantasmatic status of the "we," however, is not cause for despair or, at least, it is not *only* cause for despair. The radical instability of the category sets into question the *foundational* restrictions on feminist political theorizing and opens up other configurations, not only of genders and bodies, but of politics itself.

The foundationalist reasoning of identity politics tends to assume that an identity must first be in place in order for political interests to be elaborated and, subsequently, political action to be taken. My argument is that there need not be a "doer behind the deed," but that the "doer" is variably constructed in and through the deed. This is not a return to an existential theory of the self as constituted through its acts, for the existential theory maintains a prediscursive structure for both the self and its acts. It is precisely the discursively variable construction of each in and through the other that has interested me here.

181

The question of locating "agency" is usually associated with the viability of the "subject," where the "subject" is understood to have some stable existence prior to the cultural field that it negotiates. Or, if the subject is culturally constructed, it is nevertheless vested with an agency, usually figured as the capacity for reflexive mediation, that remains intact regardless of its cultural embeddedness. On such a model, "culture" and "discourse" *mire* the subject, but do not constitute that subject. This move to qualify and enmire the preexisting subject has appeared necessary to establish a point of agency that is not fully *determined* by that culture and discourse. And yet, this kind of reasoning falsely presumes (a) agency can only be established through recourse to a prediscursive "I," even if that "I" is found in the midst of a discursive convergence, and (b) that to be *constituted* by discourse is to be *determined* by discourse, where determination forecloses the possibility of agency.

Even within the theories that maintain a highly qualified or situated subject, the subject still encounters its discursively constituted environment in an oppositional epistemological frame. The culturally enmired subject negotiates its constructions, even when those constructions are the very predicates of its own identity. In Beauvoir, for example, there is an "I" that does its gender, that becomes its gender, but that "I," invariably associated with its gender, is nevertheless a point of agency never fully identifiable with its gender. That *cogito* is never fully *of* the cultural world that it negotiates, no matter the narrowness of the ontological distance that separates that subject from its cultural predicates. The theories of feminist identity that elaborate predicates of color, sexuality, ethnicity, class, and able-bodiedness invariably close with an embarrassed "etc." at the end of the list. Through this horizontal trajectory of adjectives, these positions strive to encompass a situated subject, but invariably fail to be complete. This failure, however, is instructive: what political impetus is to be derived from the exasperated "etc." that so often occurs at the end of such lines? This is a sign of exhaustion as well as of the illimitable process of signification itself. It is the *supplément*, the excess that necessarily accompanies any effort to

182

posit identity once and for all. This illimitable *et cetera,* however, offers itself as a new departure for feminist political theorizing.

If identity is asserted through a process of signification, if identity is always already signified, and yet continues to signify as it circulates within various interlocking discourses, then the question of agency is not to be answered through recourse to an "I" that preexists signification. In other words, the enabling conditions for an assertion of "I" are provided by the structure of signification, the rules that regulate the legitimate and illegitimate invocation of that pronoun, the practices that establish the terms of intelligibility by which that pronoun can circulate. Language is not an *exterior medium or instrument* into which I pour a self and from which I glean a reflection of that self. The Hegelian model of self-recognition that has been appropriated by Marx, Lukacs, and a variety of contemporary liberatory discourses presupposes a potential adequation between the "I" that confronts its world, including its language, as an object, and the "I" that finds itself as an object in that world. But the subject/object dichotomy, which here belongs to the tradition of Western epistemology, conditions the very problematic of identity that it seeks to solve.

What discursive tradition establishes the "I" and its "Other" in an epistemological confrontation that subsequently decides where and how questions of knowability and agency are to be determined? What kinds of agency are foreclosed through the positing of an epistemological subject precisely because the rules and practices that govern the invocation of that subject and regulate its agency in advance are ruled out as sites of analysis and critical intervention? That the epistemological point of departure is in no sense inevitable is naively and pervasively confirmed by the mundane operations of ordinary language—widely documented within anthropology—that regard the subject/object dichotomy as a strange and contingent, if not violent, philosophical imposition. The language of appropriation, instrumentality, and distanciation germane to the epistemological mode also belong to a strategy of domination that pits the "I" against an "Other" and, once that separation is effected, creates an artificial set of questions about the knowability and recoverability of that Other.

As part of the epistemological inheritance of contemporary political discourses of identity, this binary opposition is a strategic move within a given set of signifying practices, one that establishes the "I" in and through this opposition and which reifies that opposition as a necessity, concealing the discursive apparatus by which the binary itself is constituted. The shift from an *epistemological* account of identity to one which locates the problematic within practices of *signification* permits an analysis that takes the epistemological mode itself as one possible and contingent signifying practice. Further, the question of *agency* is reformulated as a question of how signification and resignification work. In other words, what is signified as an identity is not signified at a given point in time after which it is simply there as an inert piece of entitative language. Clearly, identities *can* appear as so many inert substantives; indeed, epistemological models tend to take this appearance as their point of theoretical departure. However, the substantive "I" only appears as such through a signifying practice that seeks to conceal its own workings and to naturalize its effects. Further, to qualify as a substantive identity is an arduous task, for such appearances are rule-generated identities, ones which rely on the consistent and repeated invocation of rules that condition and restrict culturally intelligible practices of identity. Indeed, to understand identity as a *practice,* and as a signifying practice, is to understand culturally intelligible subjects as the resulting effects of a rule-bound discourse that inserts itself in the pervasive and mundane signifying acts of linguistic life. Abstractly considered, language refers to an open system of signs by which intelligibility is insistently created and contested. As historically specific organizations of language, discourses present themselves in the plural, coexisting within temporal frames, and instituting unpredictable and inadvertent convergences from which specific modalities of discursive possibilities are engendered.

As a process, signification harbors within itself what the epistemological discourse refers to as "agency." The rules that govern intelligible identity, i.e., that enable and restrict the intelligible assertion of an "I," rules that are partially structured along matrices of gender hierarchy and compulsory heterosexuality, operate through *repetition*. Indeed, when the subject is said to be constituted, that means simply that the subject is a consequence of certain rule-governed discourses that govern the intelligible invocation of identity. The subject is not *determined* by the rules through which it is generated because signification is *not a founding act, but rather a regulated process of repetition* that both conceals itself and enforces its rules precisely through the production of substantializing effects. In a sense, all signification takes place within the orbit of the compulsion to repeat; "agency," then, is to be located within the possibility of a variation on that repetition. If the rules governing signification not only restrict, but enable the assertion of alternative domains of cultural intelligibility, i.e., new possibilities for gender that contest the rigid codes of hierarchical binarisms, then it is only *within* the practices of repetitive signifying that a subversion of identity becomes possible. The injunction *to be* a given gender produces necessary failures, a variety of incoherent configurations that in their multiplicity exceed and defy the injunction by which they are generated. Further, the very injunction to be a given gender takes place through discursive routes: to be a good mother, to be a heterosexually desirable object, to be a fit worker, in sum, to signify a multiplicity of guarantees in response to a variety of different demands all at once. The coexistence or convergence of such discursive injunctions produces the possibility of a complex reconfiguration and redeployment; it is not a transcendental subject who enables action in the midst of such a convergence. There is no self that is prior to the convergence or who maintains "integrity" prior to its entrance into this conflicted cultural field. There is only a taking up of the tools where they lie, where the very "taking up" is enabled by the tool lying there.

What constitutes a subversive repetition within signifying practices of gender? I have argued ("I" deploy the grammar that governs the genre of the philosophical conclusion, but note that it is the grammar itself that deploys and enables this "I," even as the "I" that insists itself here repeats, redeploys, and—as the critics will determine—contests the philosophical grammar by which it is both enabled and restricted) that, for instance, within the sex/gender distinction, sex poses as "the real" and the "factic," the material or corporeal ground upon which gender operates as an act of cultural *inscription*. And yet gender is not written on the body as the torturing instrument of writing in Kafka's "In the Penal Colony" inscribes itself unintelligibly on the flesh of the accused. The question is not: what meaning does that inscription carry within it, but what cultural apparatus arranges this meeting between instrument and body, what interventions into this ritualistic repetition are possible? The "real" and the "sexually factic" are phantasmatic constructions—illusions of substance—that bodies are compelled to approximate, but never can. What, then, enables the exposure of the rift between the phantasmatic and the real whereby the real admits itself as phantasmatic? Does this offer the possibility for a repetition that is not fully constrained by the injunction to reconsolidate naturalized identities? Just as bodily surfaces are enacted *as* the natural, so these surfaces can become the site of a dissonant and denaturalized performance that reveals the performative status of the natural itself.

Practices of parody can serve to reengage and reconsolidate the very distinction between a privileged and naturalized gender configuration and one that appears as derived, phantasmatic, and mimetic—a failed copy, as it were. And surely parody has been used to further a politics of despair, one which affirms a seemingly inevitable exclusion of marginal genders from the territory of the natural and the real. And yet this failure to become "real" and to embody "the natural" is, I would argue, a constitutive failure of all gender enactments for the very reason that these ontological locales are fundamentally uninhabitable. Hence, there is a subversive laughter in the pastiche-effect of parodic practices in which the original, the authentic, and the real are themselves constituted as effects. The loss of gender norms would have the effect of proliferating gender configurations, destabilizing substantive identity, and depriving the naturalizing narratives of compulsory heterosexuality of their central protagonists: "man" and "woman." The parodic repetition of gender exposes as well the illusion of gender identity as an intractable depth and inner substance. As the effects of a subtle and politically enforced performativity, gender is an "act," as it were, that is open to splittings, self-parody, self-criticism, and those hyperbolic exhibitions of "the natural" that, in their very exaggeration, reveal its fundamentally phantasmatic status.

I have tried to suggest that the identity categories often presumed to be foundational to feminist politics, that is, deemed necessary in order to mobilize feminism as an identity politics, simultaneously work to limit and constrain in advance the very cultural possibilities that feminism is supposed to open up. The tacit constraints that produce culturally intelligible "sex" ought to be understood as generative political structures rather than naturalized foundations. Paradoxically, the reconceptualization of identity as an *effect,* that is, as *produced* or *generated,* opens up possibilities of "agency" that are insidiously foreclosed by positions that take identity categories as foundational and fixed. For an identity to be an effect means that it is neither fatally determined nor fully artificial and arbitrary. That the *constituted* status of identity is misconstrued along these two conflicting lines suggests the ways in which the feminist discourse on cultural construction remains trapped within the unnecessary binarism of free will and determinism. Construction is not opposed to agency; it is the necessary scene of agency, the very terms in which agency is articulated and becomes culturally intelligible. The critical task for feminism is not to establish a point of view outside of constructed identities; that conceit is the construction of an epistemological model that would disavow its own cultural location and, hence, promote itself as a global subject, a position that deploys precisely the imperialist strategies that feminism ought to criticize. The critical task is, rather, to locate strategies of subversive repetition enabled by those constructions, to affirm the local possibilities of intervention through participating in precisely those practices of repetition that constitute identity and, therefore, present the immanent possibility of contesting them.

This theoretical inquiry has attempted to locate the political in the very signifying practices that establish, regulate, and deregulate identity. This effort, however, can only be accomplished through the introduction of a set of questions that extend the very notion of the political. How to disrupt the foundations that cover over alternative cultural configurations of gender? How to destabilize and render in their phantasmatic dimension the "premises" of identity politics?

This task has required a critical genealogy of the naturalization of sex and of bodies in general. It has also demanded a reconsideration of the figure of the body as mute, prior to culture, awaiting signification, a figure that cross-checks with the figure of the feminine, awaiting the inscription-as-incision of the masculine signifier for entrance into language and culture. From a political analysis of compulsory heterosexuality, it has been necessary to question the construction of sex as binary, as a hierarchical binary. From the point of view of gender as enacted, questions have emerged over the fixity of gender identity as an interior depth that is said to be externalized in various forms of "expression." The implicit construction of the primary heterosexual construction of desire is shown to persist even as it appears in the mode of primary bisexuality. Strategies of exclusion and hierarchy are also shown to persist in the formulation of the sex/gender distinction and its recourse to "sex" as the prediscursive as well as the priority of sexuality to culture and, in particular, the cultural construction of sexuality as the prediscursive. Finally, the epistemological paradigm that presumes the priority of the doer to the deed establishes a global and globalizing subject who disavows its own locality as well as the conditions for local intervention.

If taken as the grounds of feminist theory or politics, these "effects" of gender hierarchy and compulsory heterosexuality are not only misdescribed as foundations, but the signifying practices that enable this metaleptic misdescription remain outside the purview of a feminist critique of gender relations. To enter into the repetitive practices of this terrain of signification is not a choice, for the "I" that might enter is always already inside: there is no possibility of agency or reality outside of the discursive practices that give those terms the intelligibility that they have. The task is not whether to repeat, but how to repeat or, indeed, to repeat and, through a radical proliferation of gender, *to displace* the very gender norms that enable the repetition itself. There is no ontology of gender on which we might construct a politics, for gender ontologies always operate within established political contexts as normative injunctions, determining what qualifies as intelligible sex, invoking and consolidating the reproductive constraints on sexuality, setting the prescriptive requirements whereby sexed or gendered bodies come into cultural intelligibility. Ontology is, thus, not a foundation, but a normative injunction that operates insidiously by installing itself into political discourse as its necessary ground.

The deconstruction of identity is not the deconstruction of politics; rather, it establishes as political the very terms through which identity is articulated. This kind of critique brings into question the foundationalist frame in which feminism as an identity politics has been articulated. The internal paradox of this foundationalism is that it presumes, fixes, and constrains the very "subjects" that it hopes to represent and liberate. The task here is not to celebrate each and every new possibility *qua* possibility, but to redescribe those possibilities that *already* exist, but which exist within cultural domains designated as culturally unintelligible and impossible. If identities were no longer fixed as the premises of a political syllogism, and politics no longer understood as a set of practices derived from the alleged interests that belong to a set of ready-made subjects, a new configuration of politics

189

would surely emerge from the ruins of the old. Cultural configurations of sex and gender might then proliferate or, rather, their present proliferation might then become articulable within the discourses that establish intelligible cultural life, confounding the very binarism of sex, and exposing its fundamental unnaturalness. What other local strategies for engaging the "unnatural" might lead to the denaturalization of gender as such?

Notes

PREFACE (1999)

1. At this printing, there are French publishers considering the translation of this work, but only because Didier Eribon and others have inserted the arguments of the text into current French political debates on the legal ratification of same-sex partnerships.

2. I have written two brief pieces on this issue: "Afterword" for *Butch\Femme: Inside Lesbian Gender*, ed. Sally Munt (London: Cassell, 1998), and another Afterword for "Transgender in Latin America: Persons, Practices and Meanings," a special issue of the journal *Sexualities*, Vol. 5, No. 3, 1998.

3. Catharine MacKinnon, *Feminism Unmodified: Discourses on Life and Law* (Cambridge: Harvard University Press, 1987), pp. 6–7.

4. Unfortunately, *Gender Trouble* preceded the publication of Eve Kosofsky Sedgwick's monumental *Epistemology of the Closet* (Berkeley and Los Angeles: University of California Press, 1991) by some months, and my arguments here were not able to benefit from her nuanced discussion of gender and sexuality in the first chapter of that book.

5. Jonathan Goldberg persuaded me of this point.

6. For a more or less complete bibliography of my publications and citations of my work, see the excellent work of Eddie Yeghiayan at the University of California at Irvine Library: http://sun3.lib.uci.edu/~scctr/ Wellek/index.html.

7. I am especially indebted to Biddy Martin, Eve Sedgwick, Slavoj Žižek, Wendy Brown, Saidiya Hartman, Mandy Merck, Lynne Layton, Timothy Kaufmann-Osborne, Jessica Benjamin, Seyla Benhabib, Nancy Fraser,

191

Diana Fuss, Jay Presser, Lisa Duggan, and Elizabeth Grosz for their insightful criticisms of the theory of performativity.

8. This notion of the ritual dimension of performativity is allied with the notion of the habitus in Pierre Bourdieu's work, something which I only came to realize after the fact of writing this text. For my belated effort to account for this resonance, see the final chapter of *Excitable Speech: A Politics of the Performative* (New York: Routledge, 1997).

9. Jacqueline Rose usefully pointed out to me the disjunction between the earlier and later parts of this text. The earlier parts interrogate the melancholy construction of gender, but the later seem to forget the psychoanalytic beginnings. Perhaps this accounts for some of the "mania" of the final chapter, a state defined by Freud as part of the disavowal of loss that is melancholia. *Gender Trouble* in its closing pages seems to forget or disavow the loss it has just articulated.

10. See *Bodies that Matter* (New York: Routledge, 1993) as well as an able and interesting critique that relates some of the questions raised there to contemporary science studies by Karen Barad, "Getting Real: Technoscientific Practices and the Materialization of Reality," *differences*, Vol. 5, No. 2, pp. 87–126.

11. Saidiya Hartman, Lisa Lowe, and Dorinne Kondo are scholars whose work has influenced my own. Much of the current scholarship on "passing" has also taken up this question. My own essay on Nella Larsen's "Passing" in *Bodies That Matter* sought to address the question in a preliminary way. Of course, Homi Bhabha's work on the mimetic splitting of the postcolonial subject is close to my own in several ways: not only the appropriation of the colonial "voice" by the colonized, but the split condition of identification are crucial to a notion of performativity that emphasizes the way minority identities are produced and riven at the same time under conditions of domination.

12. The work of Kobena Mercer, Kendall Thomas, and Hortense Spillers has been extremely useful to my post-*Gender Trouble* thinking on this subject. I also hope to publish an essay on Frantz Fanon soon engaging questions of mimesis and hyperbole in his *Black Skins, White Masks*. I am grateful to Greg Thomas, who has recently completed his dissertation in rhetoric at Berkeley, on racialized sexualities in the U.S., for provoking and enriching my understanding of this crucial intersection.

13. I have offered reflections on universality in subsequent writings, most prominently in chapter 2 of *Excitable Speech*.

14. See the important publications of the Intersex Society of North America (including the publications of Cheryl Chase) which has, more than any other organization, brought to public attention the severe and violent gender policing done to infants and children born with gender anomalous bodies. For more information, contact them at http://www.isna.org.

15. I thank Wendy Brown, Joan W. Scott, Alexandra Chasin, Frances Bartkowski, Janet Halley, Michel Feher, Homi Bhabha, Drucilla Cornell, Denise Riley, Elizabeth Weed, Kaja Silverman, Ann Pellegrini, William Connolly, Gayatri Chakravorty Spivak, Ernesto Laclau, Eduardo Cadava, Florence Dore, David Kazanjian, David Eng, and Dina Al-kassim for their support and friendship during the Spring of 1999 when this preface was written.

1. SUBJECTS OF SEX/GENDER/DESIRE

1. See Michel Foucault, "Right of Death and Power over Life," in *The History of Sexuality, Volume I, An Introduction,* trans. Robert Hurley (New York: Vintage, 1980), originally published as *Histoire de la sexualité 1: La volonté de savoir* (Paris: Gallimard, 1978). In that final chapter, Foucault discusses the relation between the juridical and productive law. His notion of the productivity of the law is clearly derived from Nietzsche, although not identical with Nietzsche's will-to-power. The use of Foucault's notion of productive power is not meant as a simple-minded "application" of Foucault to gender issues. As I show in chapter 3, section ii, "Foucault, Herculine, and the Politics of Sexual Discontinuity," the consideration of sexual difference within the terms of Foucault's own work reveals central contradictions in his theory. His view of the body also comes under criticism in the final chapter.

2. References throughout this work to a subject before the law are extrapolations of Derrida's reading of Kafka's parable "Before the Law," in *Kafka and the Contemporary Critical Performance: Centenary Readings,* ed. Alan Udoff (Bloomington: Indiana University Press, 1987).

3. See Denise Riley, *Am I That Name?: Feminism and the Category of 'Women' in History* (New York: Macmillan, 1988).

4. See Sandra Harding, "The Instability of the Analytical Categories of Feminist Theory," in *Sex and Scientific Inquiry,* eds. Sandra Harding and Jean F. O'Barr (Chicago: University of Chicago Press, 1987), pp. 283–302.

5. I am reminded of the ambiguity inherent in Nancy Cott's title, *The Grounding of Modern Feminism* (New Haven: Yale University Press, 1987). She argues that the early twentieth-century U.S. feminist movement sought to "ground" itself in a program that eventually "grounded" that movement. Her historical thesis implicitly raises the question of whether uncritically accepted foundations operate like the "return of the repressed"; based on exclusionary practices, the stable political identities that found political movements may invariably become threatened by the very instability that the foundationalist move creates.

6. I use the term *heterosexual matrix* throughout the text to designate that grid of cultural intelligibility through which bodies, genders, and desires are naturalized. I am drawing from Monique Wittig's notion of the "heterosexual contract" and, to a lesser extent, on Adrienne Rich's notion of "compulsory heterosexuality" to characterize a hegemonic discursive/epistemic model of gender intelligibility that assumes that for bodies to cohere and make sense there must be a stable sex expressed through a stable gender (masculine expresses male, feminine expresses female) that is oppositionally and hierarchically defined through the compulsory practice of heterosexuality.

7. For a discussion of the sex/gender distinction in structuralist anthropology and feminist appropriations and criticisms of that formulation, see chapter 2, section i, "Structuralism's Critical Exchange."

8. For an interesting study of the *berdache* and multiple-gender arrangements in Native American cultures, see Walter L. Williams, *The Spirit and the Flesh: Sexual Diversity in American Indian Culture* (Boston: Beacon Press, 1988). See also, Sherry B. Ortner and Harriet Whitehead, eds., *Sexual Meanings: The Cultural Construction of Sexuality* (New York: Cambridge University Press, 1981). For a politically sensitive and provocative analysis of the *berdache,* transsexuals, and the contingency of gender dichotomies, see Suzanne J. Kessler and Wendy McKenna, *Gender: An Ethnomethodological Approach* (Chicago: University of Chicago Press, 1978).

9. A great deal of feminist research has been conducted within the fields of biology and the history of science that assess the political interests inherent in the various discriminatory procedures that establish the scientific basis for sex. See Ruth Hubbard and Marian Lowe, eds., *Genes and Gender,* vols. 1 and 2 (New York: Gordian Press, 1978, 1979); the two issues on feminism and science of *Hypatia: A Journal of Feminist Philosophy,* Vol. 2, No. 3, Fall 1987, and Vol. 3, No. 1, Spring 1988, and especially The Biology and Gender Study Group, "The Importance of Feminist Critique for Contemporary Cell Biology" in this last issue (Spring 1988); Sandra Harding, *The Science Question in Feminism* (Ithaca: Cornell University Press, 1986); Evelyn Fox Keller, *Reflections on Gender and Science* (New Haven: Yale University Press, 1984); Donna Haraway, "In the Beginning was the Word: The Genesis of Biological Theory," *Signs: Journal of Women in Culture and Society,* Vol. 6, No. 3, 1981; Donna Haraway, *Primate Visions* (New York: Routledge, 1989); Sandra Harding and Jean F. O'Barr, *Sex and Scientific Inquiry* (Chicago: University of Chicago Press, 1987); Anne Fausto-Sterling, *Myths of Gender: Biological Theories About Women and Men* (New York: Norton, 1979).

10. Clearly Foucault's *History of Sexuality* offers one way to rethink the history of "sex" within a given modern Eurocentric context. For a more detailed consideration, see Thomas Laqueur and Catherine Gallagher, eds., *The Making of the Modern Body: Sexuality and Society in the 19th Century* (Berkeley: University of California Press, 1987), originally published as an issue of *Representations,* No. 14, Spring 1986.

11. See my "Variations on Sex and Gender: Beauvoir, Wittig, Foucault," in *Feminism as Critique,* eds. Seyla Benhabib and Drucilla Cornell (Basil Blackwell, dist. by University of Minnesota Press, 1987).

12. Simone de Beauvoir, *The Second Sex,* trans. E. M. Parshley (New York: Vintage, 1973), p. 301.

13. Ibid., p. 38.

14. See my "Sex and Gender in Beauvoir's *Second Sex*" *Yale French Studies, Simone de Beauvoir: Witness to a Century,* No. 72, Winter 1986.

15. Note the extent to which phenomenological theories such as Sartre's, Merleau-Ponty's, and Beauvoir's tend to use the term *embodiment.* Drawn as it is from theological contexts, the term tends to figure "the" body as a

mode of incarnation and, hence, to preserve the external and dualistic relationship between a signifying immateriality and the materiality of the body itself.

16. See Luce Irigaray, *This Sex Which Is Not One,* trans. Catherine Porter with Carolyn Burke (Ithaca: Cornell University Press, 1985), originally published as *Ce sexe qui n'en est pas un* (Paris: Éditions de Minuit, 1977).

17. See Joan Scott, "Gender as a Useful Category of Historical Analysis," in *Gender and the Politics of History* (New York: Columbia University Press, 1988), pp. 28–52, repr. from *American Historical Review,* Vol. 91, No. 5, 1986.

18. Beauvoir, *The Second Sex,* p. xxvi.

19. See my "Sex and Gender in Beauvoir's *Second Sex.*"

20. The normative ideal of the body as both a "situation" and an "instrumentality" is embraced by both Beauvoir with respect to gender and Frantz Fanon with respect to race. Fanon concludes his analysis of colonization through recourse to the body as an instrument of freedom, where freedom is, in Cartesian fashion, equated with a consciousness capable of doubt: "O my body, make of me always a man who questions!" (Frantz Fanon, *Black Skin, White Masks* [New York: Grove Press, 1967] p. 323, originally published as *Peau noire, masques blancs* [Paris: Éditions de Seuil, 1952]).

21. The radical ontological disjunction in Sartre between consciousness and the body is part of the Cartesian inheritance of his philosophy. Significantly, it is Descartes' distinction that Hegel implicitly interrogates at the outset of the "Master-Slave" section of *The Phenomenology of Spirit.* Beauvoir's analysis of the masculine Subject and the feminine Other is clearly situated in Hegel's dialectic and in the Sartrian reformulation of that dialectic in the section on sadism and masochism in *Being and Nothingness.* Critical of the very possibility of a "synthesis" of consciousness and the body, Sartre effectively returns to the Cartesian problematic that Hegel sought to overcome. Beauvoir insists that the body can be the instrument and situation of freedom and that sex can be the occasion for a gender that is not a reification, but a modality of freedom. At first this appears to be a synthesis of body and consciousness, where consciousness is understood as the condition of freedom. The question that

remains, however, is whether this synthesis requires and maintains the ontological distinction between body and mind of which it is composed and, by association, the hierarchy of mind over body and of masculine over feminine.

22. See Elizabeth V. Spelman, "Woman as Body: Ancient and Contemporary Views," *Feminist Studies,* Vol. 8, No. 1, Spring 1982.

23. Gayatri Spivak most pointedly elaborates this particular kind of binary explanation as a colonizing act of marginalization. In a critique of the "self-presence of the cognizing supra-historical self," which is characteristic of the epistemic imperialism of the philosophical cogito, she locates politics in the production of knowledge that creates and censors the margins that constitute, through exclusion, the contingent intelligibility of that subject's given knowledge-regime: "I call 'politics as such' the prohibition of marginality that is implicit in the production of any explanation. From that point of view, the choice of particular binary oppositions . . . is no mere intellectual strategy. It is, in each case, the condition of the possibility for centralization (with appropriate apologies) and, correspondingly, marginalization" (Gayatri Chakravorty Spivak, "Explanation and Culture: Marginalia," in *In Other Worlds: Essays in Cultural Politics* [New York: Routledge, 1987], p. 113).

24. See the argument against "ranking oppressions" in Cherríe Moraga, "La Güera," in *This Bridge Called My Back: Writings of Radical Women of Color,* eds. Gloria Anzaldúa and Cherríe Moraga (New York: Kitchen Table, Women of Color Press, 1982).

25. For a fuller elaboration of the unrepresentability of women in phallogocentric discourse, see Luce Irigaray, "Any Theory of the 'Subject' Has Always Been Appropriated by the Masculine," in *Speculum of the Other Woman,* trans. Gillian C. Gill (Ithaca: Cornell University Press, 1985). Irigaray appears to revise this argument in her discussion of "the feminine gender" in *Sexes et parentés* (see chapter 2, n. 10).

26. Monique Wittig, "One is Not Born a Woman," *Feminist Issues,* Vol. 1, No. 2, Winter 1981, p. 53. Also in *The Straight Mind and Other Essays,* pp. 9–20, see chapter 3, n. 49.

27. The notion of the "Symbolic" is discussed at some length in Section Two of this text. It is to be understood as an ideal and universal set of

cultural laws that govern kinship and signification and, within the terms of psychoanalytic structuralism, govern the production of sexual difference. Based on the notion of an idealized "paternal law," the Symbolic is reformulated by Irigaray as a dominant and hegemonic discourse of phallogocentrism. Some French feminists propose an alternative language to one governed by the Phallus or the paternal law, and so wage a critique against the Symbolic. Kristeva proposes the "semiotic" as a specifically maternal dimension of language, and both Irigaray and Hélène Cixous have been associated with *écriture feminine*. Wittig, however, has always resisted that movement, claiming that language in its structure is neither misogynist nor feminist, but an *instrument* to be deployed for developed political purposes. Clearly her belief in a "cognitive subject" that exists prior to language facilitates her understanding of language as an instrument, rather than as a field of significations that preexist and structure subject-formation itself.

28. Monique Wittig, "The Point of View: Universal or Particular?" *Feminist Issues*, Vol. 3, No. 2, Fall 1983, p. 64. Also in *The Straight Mind and Other Essays*, pp. 59–67, see chapter 3, n. 49.

29. "One must assume both a particular *and* a universal point of view, at least to be part of literature" (Monique Wittig, "The Trojan Horse," *Feminist Issues*, Vol. 4, No. 2, Fall 1984, p. 68. Also see chapter 3, n. 41).

30. The journal, *Questions Feministes*, available in English translation as *Feminist Issues*, generally defended a "materialist" point of view which took practices, institution, and the constructed status of language to be the "material grounds" of the oppression of women. Wittig was part of the original editorial staff. Along with Monique Plaza, Wittig argued that sexual difference was essentialist in that it derived the meaning of women's social function from their biological facticity, but also because it subscribed to the primary signification of women's bodies as maternal and, hence, gave ideological strength to the hegemony of reproductive sexuality.

31. Michel Haar, "Nietzsche and Metaphysical Language," *The New Nietzsche: Contemporary Styles of Interpretation,* ed. David Allison (New York: Delta, 1977), pp. 17–18.

32. Monique Wittig, "The Mark of Gender," *Feminist Issues*, Vol. 5, No. 2, Fall 1985, p. 4. Also see chapter 3, n. 25.

33. Ibid., p. 3.

34. Aretha's song, originally written by Carole King, also contests the naturalization of gender. "Like a natural woman" is a phrase that suggests that "naturalness" is only accomplished through analogy or metaphor. In other words, "You make me feel like a metaphor of the natural," and without "you," some denaturalized ground would be revealed. For a further discussion of Aretha's claim in light of Simone de Beauvoir's contention that "one is not born, but rather becomes a woman," see my "Beauvoir's Philosophical Contribution," in eds. Ann Garry and Marilyn Pearsall, *Women, Knowledge, and Reality* (Boston: Unwin Hyman, 1989): 2nd ed. (NewYork: Routledge, 1996).

35. Michel Foucault, ed., *Herculine Barbin, Being the Recently Discovered Memoirs of a Nineteenth-Century Hermaphrodite,* trans. Richard McDougall (New York: Colophon, 1980), originally published as *Herculine Barbin, dite Alexina B. presenté par Michel Foucault* (Paris: Gallimard, 1978). The French version lacks the introduction supplied by Foucault with the English translation.

36. See chapter 2, section ii.

37. Foucault, ed., *Herculine Barbin,* p. x.

38. Robert Stoller, *Presentations of Gender* (New Haven: Yale University Press, 1985), pp. 11–14.

39. Friedrich Nietzsche, *On the Genealogy of Morals,* trans. Walter Kaufmann (NewYork: Vintage, 1969), p. 45.

40. Wittig, "One is Not Born a Woman," p. 48. Wittig credits both the notion of the "mark" of gender and the "imaginary formation" of natural groups to Colette Guillaumin whose work on the mark of race provides an analogy for Wittig's analysis of gender in "Race et nature: Système des marques, idée de group naturel et rapport sociaux," *Pluriel,* Vol. 11, 1977. The "Myth of Woman" is a chapter of Beauvoir's *The Second Sex.*

41. Monique Wittig, "Paradigm," in *Homosexualities and French Literature: Cultural Contexts / Critical Texts,* eds. Elaine Marks and George Stambolian (Ithaca: Cornell University Press, 1979), p. 114.

42. Clearly, Wittig does not understand syntax to be the linguistic elaboration or reproduction of a kinship system paternally organized. Her refusal of structuralism at this level allows her to understand language as gender-

neutral. Irigaray's *Parler n'est jamais neutre* (Paris: Éditions de Minuit, 1985) criticizes precisely the kind of humanist position, here characteristic of Wittig, that claims the political and gender neutrality of language.

43. Monique Wittig, "The Point of View: Universal or Particular?" p. 63.

44. Monique Wittig, "The Straight Mind," *Feminist Issues,* Vol. 1, No. 1, Summer 1980, p. 108. Also see chapter 3, n. 30.

45. Monique Wittig, *The Lesbian Body,* trans. Peter Owen (New York: Avon, 1976), originally published as *Le corps lesbien* (Paris: Éditions de Minuit, 1973).

46. I am grateful to Wendy Owen for this phrase.

47. Of course, Freud himself distinguished between "the sexual" and "the genital," providing the very distinction that Wittig uses against him. See, for instance, "The Development of the Sexual Function" in Freud, *Outline of a Theory of Psychoanalysis,* trans. James Strachey (New York: Norton, 1979).

48. A more comprehensive analysis of the Lacanian position is provided in various parts of chapter 2 of this text.

49. Jacqueline Rose, *Sexuality in the Field of Vision* (London: Verso, 1987).

50. Jane Gallop, *Reading Lacan* (Ithaca: Cornell University Press, 1985); *The Daughter's Seduction: Feminism and Psychoanalysis* (Ithaca: Cornell University Press, 1982).

51. "What distinguishes psychoanalysis from sociological accounts of gender (hence for me the fundamental impasse of Nancy Chodorow's work) is that whereas for the latter, the internalisation of norms is assumed roughly to work, the basic premise and indeed starting point of psychoanalysis is that it does not. The unconscious constantly reveals the 'failure' of identity" (Jacqueline Rose, *Sexuality in the Field of Vision,* p. 90).

52. It is, perhaps, no wonder that the singular structuralist notion of "the Law" clearly resonates with the prohibitive law of the Old Testament. The "paternal law" thus comes under a post-structuralist critique through the understandable route of a French reappropriation of Nietzsche. Nietzsche faults the Judeo-Christian "slave-morality" for conceiving the law in both singular and prohibitive terms. The will-to-power, on the other hand, designates both the productive and multiple possibilities of the law, effectively exposing the notion of "the Law" in its singularity as a fictive and repressive notion.

53. See Gayle Rubin, "Thinking Sex: Notes for a Radical Theory of the Politics of Sexuality," in *Pleasure and Danger,* ed. Carole S. Vance (Boston: Routledge and Kegan Paul, 1984), pp. 267–319. Also in *Pleasure and Danger,* see Carole S. Vance, "Pleasure and Danger: Towards a Politics of Sexuality," pp. 1–28; Alice Echols, "The Taming of the Id: Feminist Sexual Politics, 1968–83," pp. 50–72; Amber Hollibaugh, "Desire for the Future: Radical Hope in Pleasure and Passion," pp. 401–410. See Amber Hollibaugh and Cherríe Moraga, "What We're Rollin Around in Bed with: Sexual Silences in Feminism," and Alice Echols, "The New Feminism of Yin and Yang," in *Powers of Desire: The Politics of Sexuality,* eds. Ann Snitow, Christine Stansell, and Sharon Thompson (London: Virago, 1984); *Heresies,* Vol. No. 12, 1981, the "sex issue"; Samois ed., *Coming to Power* (Berkeley: Samois, 1981); Dierdre English, Amber Hollibaugh, and Gayle Rubin, "Talking Sex: A Conversation on Sexuality and Feminism," *Socialist Review,* No. 58, July–August 1981; Barbara T. Kerr and Mirtha N. Quintanales, "The Complexity of Desire: Conversations on Sexuality and Difference," *Conditions,* #8; Vol. 3, No. 2, 1982, pp. 52–71.

54. Irigaray's perhaps most controversial claim has been that the structure of the vulva as "two lips touching" constitutes the nonunitary and auto-erotic pleasure of women prior to the "separation" of this doubleness through the pleasure-depriving act of penetration by the penis. See Irigaray, *Ce sexe qui n'en est pas un.* Along with Monique Plaza and Christine Delphy, Wittig has argued that Irigaray's valorization of that anatomical specificity is itself an uncritical replication of a reproductive discourse that marks and carves up the female body into artificial "parts" like "vagina," "clitoris," and "vulva." At a lecture at Vassar College, Wittig was asked whether she had a vagina, and she replied that she did not.

55. See a compelling argument for precisely this interpretation by Diana J. Fuss, *Essentially Speaking* (New York: Routledge, 1989).

56. If we were to apply Fredric Jameson's distinction between parody and pastiche, gay identities would be better understood as pastiche. Whereas parody, Jameson argues, sustains some sympathy with the original of which it is a copy, pastiche disputes the possibility of an "original" or, in the case of gender, reveals the "original" as a failed effort to "copy" a phantasmatic ideal that cannot be copied without failure. See Fredric Jameson,

"Postmodernism and Consumer Society," in *The Anti-Aesthetic: Essays on Postmodern Culture,* ed. Hal Foster (Port Townsend, WA: Bay Press, 1983).

2. PROHIBITION, PSYCHOANALYSIS, AND THE PRODUCTION OF THE HETEROSEXUAL MATRIX

1. During the semester in which I write this chapter, I am teaching Kafka's "In the Penal Colony," which describes an instrument of torture that provides an interesting analogy for the contemporary field of power and masculinist power in particular. The narrative repeatedly falters in its attempt to recount the history which would enshrine that instrument as a vital part of a tradition. The origins cannot be recovered, and the map that might lead to the origins has become unreadable through time. Those to whom it might be explained do not speak the same language and have no recourse to translation. Indeed, the machine itself cannot be fully imagined; its parts don't fit together in a conceivable whole, so the reader is forced to imagine its state of fragmentation without recourse to an ideal notion of its integrity. This appears to be a literary enactment of Foucault's notion that "power" has become so diffuse that it no longer exists as a systematic totality. Derrida interrogates the problematic authority of such a law in the context of Kafka's "Before the Law" (in Derrida's "Before the Law," in *Kafka and the Contemporary Critical Performance: Centenary Readings,* ed. Alan Udoff [Bloomington: Indiana University Press, 1987]). He underscores the radical unjustifiability of this repression through a narrative recapitulation of a time before the law. Significantly, it also remains impossible to articulate a critique of that law through recourse to a time before the law.

2. See Carol MacCormack and Marilyn Strathern, eds. *Nature, Culture and Gender* (New York: Cambridge University Press, 1980).

3. For a fuller discussion of these kinds of issues, see Donna Haraway's chapter, "Gender for a Marxist Dictionary: The Sexual Politics of a Word," in *Simians, Cyborgs, and Women: The Reinvention of Nature* (New York: Routledge, 1990).

4. Gayle Rubin considers this process at length in "The Traffic in Women: Notes on the 'Political Economy' of Sex," in *Toward an Anthropology of Women,* ed. Rayna R. Reiter (New York: Monthly Review Press, 1975). Her essay will become a focal point later in this chapter. She uses the

notion of the bride-as-gift from Mauss's *Essay on the Gift* to show how women as objects of exchange effectively consolidate and define the social bond between men.

5. See Claude Lévi-Strauss, "The Principles of Kinship," in *The Elementary Structures of Kinship* (Boston: Beacon Press, 1969), p. 496.

6. See Jacques Derrida, "Structure, Sign, and Play," in *The Structuralist Controversy,* eds. Richard Macksey and Eugene Donato (Baltimore: Johns Hopkins University Press, 1964); "Linguistics and Grammatology," in *Of Grammatology,* trans. Gayatri Chakravorty Spivak (Baltimore: Johns Hopkins University Press,1974); "Différance," in *Margins of Philosophy,* trans. Alan Bass (Chicago: University of Chicago Press, 1982).

7. See Lévi-Strauss, *The Elementary Structures of Kinship,* p. 480; "Exchange—and consequently the rule of exogamy which expresses it—has in itself a social value. It provides the means of binding men together."

8. Luce Irigaray, *Speculum of the Other Woman,* trans. Gillian C. Gill (Ithaca: Cornell University Press, 1985), pp. 101–103.

9. One might consider the literary analysis of Eve Sedgwick's *Between Men: English Literature and Homosocial Desire* (New York: Columbia University Press, 1985) in light of Lévi-Strauss's description of the structures of reciprocity within kinship. Sedgwick effectively argues that the flattering attentions paid to women in romantic poetry are both a deflection and an elaboration of male homosocial desire. Women are poetic "objects of exchange" in the sense that they mediate the relationship of unacknowledged desire between men as the explicit and ostensible object of discourse.

10. Luce Irigaray, *Sexes et parentés* (Paris: Éditions de Minuit, 1987), translated as *Sexes and Genealogies,* trans. Gillian C. Gill (New York: Columbia University Press, 1993).

11. Clearly, Lévi-Strauss misses an opportunity to analyze incest as both fantasy *and* social practice, the two being in no way mutually exclusive.

12. Lévi-Strauss, *The Elementary Structures of Kinship,* p. 491.

13. To be the Phallus is to "embody" the Phallus as the place to which it penetrates, but also to signify the promise of a return to the preindividuated *jouissance* that characterizes the undifferentiated relation to the mother.

14. I devote a chapter to Lacan's appropriation of Hegel's dialectic of master and slave, called "Lacan: The Opacity of Desire," in my *Subjects of Desire:*

Hegelian Reflections in Twentieth-Century France (New York: Columbia University Press, 1987; paperback edition, 1999).

15. Freud understood the achievement of femininity to require a double-wave of repression: "The girl" not only has to shift libidinal attachment from the mother to the father, but then displace the desire for the father onto some more acceptable object. For an account that gives an almost mythic cast to Lacan's theory, see Sarah Kofman, *The Enigma of Woman: Woman in Freud's Writings,* trans. Catherine Porter (Ithaca: Cornell University Press, 1985), pp. 143–148, originally published as *L'Enigme de la femme: La femme dans les textes de Freud* (Paris: Editions Galilée, 1980).

16. Jacques Lacan, "The Meaning of the Phallus," in *Feminine Sexuality: Jacques Lacan and the École Freudienne,* eds. Juliet Mitchell and Jacqueline Rose, trans. Jacqueline Rose (New York: Norton, 1985), pp. 83–85. Hereafter, page references to this work will appear in the text.

17. Luce Irigaray, *Ce sexe qui n'en est pas un* (Paris: Éditions de Minuit, 1977), p. 131.

18. The feminist literature on masquerade is wide-ranging; the attempt here is restricted to an analysis of masquerade in relation to the problematic of expression and performativity. In other words, the question here is whether masquerade conceals a femininity that might be understood as genuine or authentic, or whether masquerade is the means by which femininity and the contests over its "authenticity" are produced. For a fuller discussion of feminist appropriations of masquerade, see Mary Ann Doane, *The Desire to Desire: The Woman's Film of the 1940s* (Bloomington: Indiana University Press, 1987); "Film and Masquerade: Theorizing the Female Spectator," *Screen,* Vol. 23, Nos. 3–4, September–October 1982, pp. 74–87; "Woman's Stake: Filming the Female Body," *October,* Vol. 17, Summer 1981. Gayatri Spivak offers a provocative reading of woman-as-masquerade that draws on Nietzsche and Derrida in "Displacement and the Discourse of Woman," in *Displacement: Derrida and After,* ed. Mark Krupnick (Bloomington: Indiana University Press, 1983). See also Mary Russo's "Female Grotesques: Carnival and Theory" (Working Paper, Center for Twentieth-Century Studies, University of Wisconsin-Milwaukee, 1985).

19. In the following section of this chapter, "Freud and the Melancholia of Gender," I attempt to lay out the central meaning of melancholia as the

consequence of a disavowed grief as it applies to the incest taboo which founds sexual positions and gender through instituting certain forms of disavowed losses.

20. Significantly, Lacan's discussion of the lesbian is contiguous within the text to his discussion of frigidity, as if to suggest metonymically that lesbianism constitutes the denial of sexuality. A further reading of the operation of "denial" in this text is clearly in order.

21. Joan Riviere, "Womanliness as a Masquerade," in *Formations of Fantasy*, eds. Victor Burgin, James Donald, Cora Kaplan (London: Methuen, 1986), pp. 35–44. The article was first published in *The International Journal of Psychoanalysis*, Vol. 10, 1929. Hereafter, page references to this work will appear in the text. See also the fine essay by Stephen Heath that follows, "Joan Riviere and the Masquerade."

22. For a contemporary refutation of such plain inferences, see Esther Newton and Shirley Walton, "The Misunderstanding: Toward a More Precise Sexual Vocabulary," in *Pleasure and Danger*, ed. Carole Vance (Boston: Routledge, 1984), pp. 242–250. Newton and Walton distinguish among erotic identities, erotic roles, and erotic acts and show how radical discontinuities can exist between styles of desire and styles of gender such that erotic preferences cannot be directly inferred from the presentation of an erotic identity in social contexts. Although I find their analysis useful (and brave), I wonder whether such categories are themselves specific to discursive contexts and whether that kind of fragmentation of sexuality into component "parts" makes sense only as a counterstrategy to refute the reductive unification of these terms.

23. The notion of a sexual "orientation" has been deftly called into question by bell hooks in *Feminist Theory: From Margin to Center* (Boston: South End Press, 1984). She claims that it is a reification that falsely signals on openness to all members of the sex that is designated as the object of desire. Although she disputes the term because it puts into question the autonomy of the person described, I would emphasize that "orientations" themselves are rarely, if ever, fixed. Obviously, they can shift through time and are open to cultural reformulations that are in no sense univocal.

24. Heath, "Joan Riviere and the Masquerade," pp. 45–61.

25. Stephen Heath points out that the situation that Riviere faced as an intellectual woman in competition for recognition by the psychoanalytic

establishment suggests strong parallels, if not an ultimate identification, with the analysand that she describes in the article.

26. Jacqueline Rose, in *Feminine Sexuality,* eds. Mitchell and Rose, p. 85.

27. Jacqueline Rose, "Introduction-II" in *Feminine Sexuality,* eds. Mitchell and Rose, p. 44.

28. Ibid., p. 55.

29. Rose criticizes the work of Moustapha Safouan in particular for failing to understand the incommensurability of the symbolic and the real. See his *La sexualité féminine dans la doctrine freudienne* (Paris: Éditions de Seuil, 1976). I am indebted to Elizabeth Weed for discussing the anti-developmental impetus in Lacan with me.

30. See Friedrich Nietzsche, "First Essay," in *The Genealogy of Morals,* trans. Walter Kaufmann (New York: Vintage, 1969), for his analysis of slave-morality. Here as elsewhere in his writing, Nietzsche argues that God is created by the will-to-power as a self-debasing act and that the recovery of the will-to-power from this construct of self-subjection is possible through a reclaiming of the very creative powers that produced the thought of God and, paradoxically, of human powerlessness. Foucault's *Discipline and Punish* is clearly based on *On the Genealogy of Morals,* most clearly the "Second Essay" as well as Nietzsche's *Daybreak.* His distinction between productive and juridical power is also clearly rooted in Nietzsche's analysis of the self-subjection of the will. In Foucault's terms, the construction of the juridical law is the effect of productive power, but one in which productive power institutes its own concealment and subordination. Foucault's critique of Lacan (see *History of Sexuality, Volume I, An Introduction,* trans. Robert Hurley [New York: Vintage, 1980], p. 81) and the repressive hypothesis generally centers on the overdetermined status of the juridical law.

31. Irigaray, *Speculum of the Other Woman,* pp. 66–73.

32. See Julia Kristeva *Desire in Language: A Semiotic Approach to Literature and Art,* ed. Leon Roudiez, trans. Thomas Gora, Alice Jardine, and Leon S. Roudiez (New York: Columbia University Press, 1980); *Soleil noir: Dépression et mélancolie* (Paris: Gallimard, 1987), translated as *Black Sun: Depression and Melancholia,* trans. Leon Roudiez (New York: Columbia University Press, 1989). Kristeva's reading of melancholy in this latter text is based in part on the writings of Melanie Klein. Melancholy is the

matricidal impulse turned against the female subject and hence is linked with the problem of masochism. Kristeva appears to accept the notion of primary aggression in this text and to differentiate the sexes according to the primary object of aggression and the manner in which they refuse to commit the murders they most profoundly want to commit. The masculine position is thus understood as an externally directed sadism, whereas the feminine is an internally directed masochism. For Kristeva, melancholy is a "voluptuous sadness" that seems tied to the sublimated production of art. The highest form of that sublimation seems to center on the suffering that is its origin. As a result, Kristeva ends the book, abruptly and a bit polemically, extolling the great works of modernism that articulate the tragic structure of human action and condemning the postmodern effort to affirm, rather than to suffer, contemporary fragmentations of the psyche. For a discussion of the role of melancholy in "Motherhood According to Bellini," see chapter 3, section i, of this text, "The Body Politics of Julia Kristeva."

33. See Freud, "The Ego and the Super-Ego (Ego-Ideal)," *The Ego and the Id,* trans. Joan Riviere, ed. James Strachey (New York: Norton, 1960, originally published in 1923), for Freud's discussion of mourning and melancholia and their relation to ego and character formation as well as his discussion of alternative resolutions to the Oedipal conflict. I am grateful to Paul Schwaber for suggesting this chapter to me. Citations of "Mourning and Melancholia" refer to Sigmund Freud, *General Psychological Theory,* ed. Philip Rieff, (New York: MacMillan, 1976), and will appear hereafter in the text.

34. For an interesting discussion of "identification," see Richard Wollheim's "Identification and Imagination: The Inner Structure of a Psychic Mechanism," in *Freud: A Collection of Critical Essays,* ed. Richard Wollheim (Garden City: Anchor Press, 1974), pp. 172–195.

35. Nicolas Abraham and Maria Torok take exception to this conflation of mourning and melancholia. See note 39 below.

36. For a psychoanalytic theory that argues in favor of a distinction between the super-ego as a punishing mechanism and the ego-ideal (as an idealization that serves a narcissistic wish), a distinction that Freud clearly does not make in *The Ego and the Id,* one might want to consult Janine Chasseguet-Smirgell, *The Ego-Ideal, A Psychological Essay on the Malady of the Ideal,* trans. Paul Barrows, introduction by Christopher Lasch (New

York: Norton, 1985), originally published as *L'ideal du moi*. Her text engages a naïve developmental model of sexuality that degrades homosexuality and regularly engages a polemic against feminism and Lacan.

37. See Foucault, *The History of Sexuality,Volume I,* p. 81.

38. Roy Schafer, *A New Language for Psycho-Analysis,* (New Haven: Yale University Press, 1976), p. 162. Also of interest are Schafer's earlier distinctions among various sorts of internalizations—introjection, incorporation, identification—in Roy Schafer, *Aspects of Internalization* (NewYork: International Universities Press, 1968). For a psychoanalytic history of the terms *internalization* and *identification,* see W. W. Meissner, *Internalization in Psychoanalysis* (New York: International Universities Press, 1968).

39. This discussion of Abraham and Torok is based on "Deuil ou mélancholie, introjecter-incorporer, réalité métapsychologique et fantasme," in *L'Écorce et le noyau,* (Paris: Flammarion, 1987) translated as *The Shell and the Kernel: Renewals of Psychoanalysis,* ed., trans., and with intro. *by* Nicholas T. Rand (Chicago: University of Chicago Press, 1994). Part of this discussion is also to be found in English as Nicolas Abraham and Maria Torok, "Introjection-Incorporation: Mourning or Melancholia," in *Psychoanalysis in France,* eds. Serge Lebovici and Daniel Widlocher (New York: International University Press, 1980), pp. 3–16. See also by the same authors, "Notes on the Phantom: A Complement to Freud's Metapsychology," in *The Trial(s) of Psychoanalysis,* ed. Francoise Meltzer (Chicago: University of Chicago Press, 1987), pp. 75–80; and "A Poetics of Psychoanalysis: 'The Lost Object-Me,'" *Substance,* Vol. 43, 1984, pp. 3–18.

40. Irigaray, *Speculum of the OtherWoman,* p. 68.

41. See Schafer, *A New Language for Psychoanalysis,* p. 177. In this and in his earlier work, *Aspects of Internalization,* Schaefer makes clear that the tropes of internalized spaces are phantasmatic constructions, but not processes. This clearly coincides in an interesting way with the thesis put forward by Nicholas Abraham and Maria Torok that "Incorporation is merely a fantasy that reassures the ego" ("Introjection-Incorporation," p. 5).

42. Clearly, this is the theoretical foundation of Monique Wittig's *The Lesbian Body,* trans. Peter Owen (NewYork: Avon, 1976), which suggests that the heterosexualized female body is compartmentalized and rendered sexu-

ally unresponsive. The dismembering and remembering process of that body through lesbian love-making performs the "inversion" that reveals the so-called integrated body as fully disintegrated and deeroticized and the "literally" disintegrated body as capable of sexual pleasure throughout the surfaces of the body. Significantly, there are no stable surfaces on these bodies, for the political principle of compulsory heterosexuality is understood to determine what counts as a whole, completed, and anatomically discrete body. Wittig's narrative (which is at once an anti-narrative) brings those culturally constructed notions of bodily integrity into question.

43. This notion of the surface of the body as projected is partially addressed by Freud's own concept of "the bodily ego." Freud's claim that "the ego is first and foremost a bodily ego" (*The Ego and the Id,* p. 16) suggests that there is a concept of the body that determines ego-development. Freud continues the above sentence: "[the body] is not merely a surface entity, but is itself the projection of a surface." For an interesting discussion of Freud's view, see Richard Wollheim, "The bodily ego," in *Philosophical Essays on Freud,* eds. Richard Wollheim and James Hopkins (Cambridge: Cambridge University Press, 1982). For a provocative account of "the skin ego," which, unfortunately, does not consider the implications of its account for the sexed body, see Didier Anzieu, *Le moi-peau* (Paris: Bordas, 1985), published in English as *The Skin Ego: A Psychoanalytic Theory of the Self,* trans. Chris Turner (New Haven: Yale University Press, 1989).

44. See chapter 2, n. 4. Hereafter page references to this essay will appear in the text.

45. See Gayle Rubin, "Thinking Sex: Notes for a Radical Theory of the Politics of Sexuality," in *Pleasure and Danger,* pp. 267–319. Rubin's presentation on power and sexuality at the 1979 conference on Simone de Beauvoir's *The Second Sex* occasioned an important shift in my own thinking about the constructed status of lesbian sexuality.

46. See (or, rather, don't see) Joseph Shepher, ed., *Incest: A Biosocial View* (London: Acadaemic Press, 1985) for a deterministic account of incest.

47. See Michele Z. Rosaldo, "The Use and Abuse of Anthropology: Reflections on Feminism and Cross-Cultural Understanding," *Signs: Journal of Women in Culture and Society,* Vol. 5, No. 3, 1980.

48. Sigmund Freud, *Three Essays on the Theory of Sexuality,* trans. James Strachey (New York: Basic Books, 1962), p. 7.

49. Peter Dews suggests in *The Logics of Disintegration: Post-Structuralist Thought and the Claims of Critical Theory* (London: Verso, 1987) that Lacan's appropriation of the Symbolic from Lévi-Strauss involves a considerable narrowing of the concept: "In Lacan's adaptation of Lévi-Strauss, which transforms the latter's multiple 'symbolic systems' into a single symbolic order, [the] neglect of the possibilities of systems of meaning promoting or masking relations of force remains" (p. 105).

3. SUBVERSIVE BODILY ACTS

1. This section, "The Body Politics of Julia Kristeva," was originally published in *Hypatia,* in the special issue on French Feminist Philosophy, Vol. 3, No. 3, Winter 1989, pp. 104–118.

2. Julia Kristeva, *Revolution in Poetic Language,* trans. Margaret Walker, introduction by Leon Roudiez (New York: Columbia University Press, 1984), p. 132. The original text is *La Revolution du language poetique* (Paris: Editions du Seuil, 1974).

3. Ibid., p. 25.

4. Julia Kristeva, *Desire in Language, A Semiotic Approach to Literature and Art,* p. 135. See chapter 2, n. 32. This is a collection of essays compiled from two different sources: *Polylogue* (Paris: Editions du Seuil, 1977), and Σημειωτιχη: *Recherches pour une sémanalyse* (Paris: Editions du Seuil, 1969).

5. Ibid., p. 135.

6. Ibid., p. 134.

7. Ibid., p. 136.

8. Ibid.

9. Ibid., p. 239.

10. Ibid., pp. 239–240.

11. Ibid., p. 240. For an extremely interesting analysis of reproductive metaphors as descriptive of the process of poetic creativity, see Wendy Owen, "A Riddle in Nine Syllables: Female Creativity in the Poetry of Sylvia Plath," doctoral dissertation, Yale University, Department of English, 1985.

12. Kristeva, *Desire in Language,* p. 239.

13. Ibid., p. 239.

14. Gayle Rubin, "The Traffic in Women: Notes on the 'Political Economy' of Sex," p. 182. See chapter 2, n. 4.

15. See Plato's *Symposium,* 209a: Of the "procreancy ... of the spirit," he writes that it is the specific capacity of the poet. Hence, poetic creations are understood as sublimated reproductive desire.

16. Michel Foucault, *The History of Sexuality, Volume I: An Introduction,* trans. Robert Hurley (New York: Vintage, 1980), p. 154.

17. Michel Foucault, ed., *Herculine Barbin, Being the Recently Discovered Memoirs of a Nineteenth Century Hermaphrodite,* trans. Richard McDongall (New York: Colophon, 1980), originally published as *Herculine Barbin, dite Alexina B. presenté par Michel Foucault* (Paris: Gallimard, 1978). All references will be from the English and French versions of that text.

18. "The notion of 'sex' made it possible to group together, in an artificial unity, anatomical elements, biological functions, conducts, sensations, pleasures, and it enabled one to make use of this fictitious unity as a causal principle" Foucault, *The History of Sexuality, Volume I,* p. 154. See chapter 3, section i, where the passage is quoted.

19. "Sexual Choice, Sexual Act: Foucault and Homosexuality," trans. James O'Higgins, originally printed in *Salmagundi,* Vols. 58–59, Fall 1982–Winter 1983, pp. 10–24; reprinted in *Michel Foucault, Politics, Philosophy, Culture: Interviews and Other Writings, 1977–1984,* ed. Lawrence Kritzman (New York: Routledge, 1988), p. 291.

20. Michel Foucault, *The Order of Things: An Archaelogy of the Human Sciences* (New York: Vintage, 1973), p. xv.

21. Michel Foucault, ed., *I, Pierre Rivière, Having Slaughtered My Mother, My Sister, and My Brother: A Case of Parricide in the 19th Century,* trans. Frank Jellinek (Lincoln: University of Nebraska Press, 1975), originally published as *Moi, Pierre Rivière ayant égorgé ma mère, ma soeur et mon frère ...* (Paris: Editions Gallimard, 1973).

22. Jacques Derrida, "From Restricted to General Economy: A Hegelianism without Reserve," in *Writing and Difference,* trans. Alan Bass (Chicago: University of Chicago Press, 1978), originally published as *L'Ecriture et la différence* (Paris: Editions du Seuil, 1967).

23. See Hélène Cixous, "The Laugh of Medusa," in *New French Feminisms.*

24. Quoted in Anne Fausto-Sterling, "Life in the XY Corral," Women's

Studies International Forum, Vol. 12, No. 3, 1989, Special Issue on Feminism and Science: In Memory of Ruth Bleier, edited by Sue V. Rosser, p. 328. All the remaining citations in this section are from her article and from two articles she cites: David C. Page, et al., "The sex-determining region of the human Y chromosome encodes a finger protein," in *Cell,* No. 51, pp. 1091–1104, and Eva Eicher and Linda Washburn, "Genetic control of primary sex determination in mice," *Annual Review of Genetics,* No. 20, pp. 327–360.

25. Wittig notes that "English compared to French has the reputation of being almost genderless, while French passes for a very gendered language. It is true that strictly speaking, English does not apply the mark of gender to inanimate objects, to things or nonhuman beings. But as far as the categories of the person are concerned, both languages are bearers of gender to the same extent" ("The Mark of Gender," *Feminist Issues,* Vol. 5, No. 2, Fall 1985, p. 3. Also in *The Straight Mind and Other Essays,* pp. 76–89. See chapter 3, n. 49).

26. Although Wittig herself does not argue the point, her theory might account for the violence enacted against sexed subjects—women, lesbians, gay men, to name a few—as the violent enforcement of a category violently constructed. In other words, sexual crimes against these bodies effectively reduce them to their "sex," thereby reaffirming and enforcing the reduction of the category itself. Because discourse is not restricted to writing or speaking, but is also social action, even violent social action, we ought also to understand rape, sexual violence, "queer-bashing" as the category of sex in action.

27. Monique Wittig, "One is Not Born a Woman," *Feminist Issues,* Vol. 1, No. 2, Winter 1981, p. 48. Also in *The Straight Mind and Other Essays,* pp. 9–20, see chapter 3, n. 49.

28. Ibid., p. 17.

29. Wittig, "The Mark of Gender," p. 4.

30. Monique Wittig, "The Straight Mind," *Feminist Issues,* Vol. 1, No. 1, Summer 1980, p. 105. Also in *The Straight Mind and Other Essays,* pp. 21–32, see chapter 3, n. 49.

31. Ibid., p. 107.

32. Ibid., p. 106.

33. "The Mark of Gender," p. 4.

34. Ibid., p. 5.

35. Ibid., p. 6.

36. Ibid.

37. Ibid.

38. Ibid.

39. Monique Wittig, "Paradigm," in *Homosexualities and French Literature: Cultural Contexts/Critical Texts,* eds. Elaine Marks and George Stambolian (Ithaca: Cornell University Press, 1979), p. 119. Consider the radical difference, however, between Wittig's acceptance of the use of language that valorizes the speaking subject as autonomous and universal and Deleuze's Nietzschean effort to displace the speaking "I" as the center of linguistic power. Although both are critical of psychoanalysis, Deleuze's critique of the subject through recourse to the will-to-power sustains closer parallels to the displacement of the speaking subject by the semiotic/unconscious within Lacanian and post-Lacanian psychoanalytic discourse. For Wittig, it appears that sexuality and desire are self-determined articulations of the individual subject, whereas for both Deleuze and his psychoanalytic opponents, desire of necessity displaces and decenters the subject. "Far from presupposing a subject," Deleuze argues, "desire cannot be attained except at the point where someone is deprived of the power of saying 'I'," Gilles Deleuze and Claire Parnet, *Dialogues,* trans. Hugh Tomlinson and Barbara Habberjam [New York: Columbia University Press, 1987], p. 89.

40. She credits the work of Mikhail Bahktin on a number of occasions for this insight.

41. Monique Wittig, "The Trojan Horse," *Feminist Issues,* Fall 1984, p. 47. Also in *The Straight Mind and Other Essays,* pp. 68–75. See chapter 3, n. 49.

42. See "The Point of View: Universal or Particular?" *Feminist Issues,* Vol. 3, No. 2, Fall 1983. Also in *The Straight Mind and Other Essays,* pp. 59–67. See chapter 3, n. 49.

43. See Wittig, "The Trojan Horse."

44. See Monique Wittig, "The Site of Action," in *Three Decades of the French New Novel,* ed. Lois Oppenheimer (Urbana: University of Illinois Press, 1986). Also in *The Straight Mind and Other Essays,* pp. 90–100. See chapter 3, n. 49.

45. Wittig, "The Trojan Horse," p. 48.

46. "The Site of Action," p. 135. In this essay, Wittig distinguishes between a "first" and "second" contract within society: The first is one of radical reciprocity between speaking subjects who exchange words that "guarantee" the entire and exclusive disposition of language to everyone" (135); the second contract is one in which words operate to exert a force of domination over others, indeed, to deprive others of the right and social capacity for speech. In this "debased" form of reciprocity, Wittig argues, individuality itself is erased through being addressed in a language that precludes the hearer as a potential speaker. Wittig concludes the essay with the following: "the paradise of the social contract exists only in literature, where the tropisms, by their violence, are able to counter any reduction of the 'I' to a common denominator, to tear open the closely woven material of the commonplaces, and to continually prevent their organization into a system of compulsory meaning" (139).

47. Monique Wittig, *Les Guérillères,* trans. David LeVay (New York: Avon, 1973), originally published under the same title (Paris: Éditions du Minuit, 1969).

48. Wittig, "The Mark of Gender," p. 9.

49. In "On the Social Contract," a paper presented at Columbia University in 1987 (in *The Straight Mind and Other Essays* [Boston: Beacon Press, 1992], pp. 33–45), Wittig places her own theory of a primary linguistic contract in terms of Rousseau's theory of the social contract. Although she is not explicit in this regard, it appears that she understands the presocial (preheterosexual) contract as a unity of the will—that is, as a general will in Rousseau's romantic sense. For an interesting use of her theory, see Teresa de Lauretis, "Sexual Indifference and Lesbian Representation" in *Theatre Journal,* Vol. 40, No. 2 (May 1988) and "The Female Body and Heterosexual Presumption," in *Semiotica,* Vol. 3–4, No. 67, 1987, pp. 259–279.

50. Wittig, "On the Social Contract."

51. See Wittig, "The Straight Mind," and "One is Not Born a Woman."

52. Wittig, "On the Social Contract," pp. 40–41.

53. Wittig, "The Straight Mind," and "On the Social Contract."

54. Michel Foucault, "Nietzsche, Genealogy, History," in *Language, Counter-Memory, Practice: Selected Essays and Interviews by Michel Foucault,* trans. Donald F. Bouchard and Sherry Simon, ed. Donald F. Bouchard (Ithaca:

Cornell University Press, 1977), p. 148. References in the text are to this essay.

55. Mary Douglas, *Purity and Danger* (London, Boston, and Henley: Routledge and Kegan Paul, 1969), p. 4.

56. Ibid., p. 113.

57. Simon Watney, *Policing Desire: AIDS, Pornography, and the Media* (Minneapolis: University of Minnesota Press, 1988).

58. Douglas, *Purity and Danger,* p. 115.

59. Ibid., p. 121.

60. Ibid., p. 140.

61. Foucault's essay "A Preface to Transgression" (in *Language, Counter-Memory, Practice*) does provide an interesting juxtaposition with Douglas' notion of body boundaries constituted by incest taboos. Originally written in honor of Georges Bataille, this essay explores in part the metaphorical "dirt" of transgressive pleasures and the association of the forbidden orifice with the dirt-covered tomb. See pp. 46–48.

62. Kristeva discusses Mary Douglas's work in a short section of *Powers of Horror: An Essay on Abjection,* trans. Leon Roudiez (New York: Columbia University Press, 1982), originally published as *Pouvoirs de l'horreur* (Paris: Éditions de Seuil, 1980). Assimilating Douglas' insights to her own reformulation of Lacan, Kristeva writes, "Defilement is what is jettisoned from the *symbolic system*. It is what escapes that social rationality, that logical order on which a social aggregate is based, which then becomes differentiated from a temporary agglomeration of individuals and, in short, constitutes a *classification system* or a *structure*" (p. 65).

63. Ibid., p. 3.

64. Iris Marion Young, "Abjection and Oppression: Dynamics of Unconscious Racism, Sexism, and Homophobia," paper presented at the Society of Phenomenology and Existential Philosophy Meetings, Northwestern University, 1988. In *Crises in Continental Philosophy*, eds. Arleen B. Dallery and Charles E. Scott with Holley Roberts (Albany: SUNY Press, 1990), pp. 201–214.

65. Parts of the following discussion were published in two different contexts, in my "Gender Trouble, Feminist Theory, and Psychoanalytic Discourse," in *Feminism/Postmodernism,* ed. Linda J. Nicholson (New York: Routledge, 1989) and "Performative Acts and Gender Constitution: An

Essay in Phenomenology and Feminist Theory," *Theatre Journal,* Vol. 20, No. 3, Winter 1988.

66. Michel Foucault, *Discipline and Punish: the Birth of the Prison,* trans. Alan Sheridan (New York: Vintage, 1979), p. 29.

67. Ibid., p. 30.

68. See the chapter "Role Models" in Esther Newton, *Mother Camp: Female Impersonators in America* (Chicago: University of Chicago Press, 1972).

69. Ibid., p. 103.

70. Fredric Jameson, "Postmodernism and Consumer Society," in *The Anti-Aesthetic: Essays on Postmodern Culture,* ed. Hal Foster (Port Townsend, WA.: Bay Press, 1983), p. 114.

71. See Victor Turner, *Dramas, Fields and Metaphors* (Ithaca: Cornell University Press, 1974). See also Clifford Geertz, "Blurred Genres: The Refiguration of Thought," in *Local Knowledge, Further Essays in Interpretive Anthropology* (New York: Basic Books, 1983).

Index

217